PHRENOLOGY
A Practical Guide to Your Head

PHRENOLOGY
A Practical Guide to Your Head

by O. S. and L. N. Fowler

Introduction by Andrew E. Norman

CHELSEA HOUSE PUBLISHERS

Orson Fowler's Phrenology

To the ancient Egyptians, to the Hebrews of biblical times, and to other ancient peoples, it was obvious that the brain had little or nothing to do with thinking and the control of behavior. Aristotle, for example, wondered what the brain was for and decided that its function was to cool the blood. Other classical writers, however, including Plato and Pythagoras, and most medieval authorities, had views closer to the modern, and the brain was generally accepted as the main residence of the mind by the time that scientific anatomy gathered momentum in the Renaissance. When the various parts of the brain began to be differentiated, men naturally began to question which parts performed which mental functions, a line of inquiry that still generates a large volume of research.

Meanwhile, there seems never to have been a time when men did not think they could learn something about each other by skillful looking, nor a time when systematic thinkers refrained from exercising their talents on the subject. If the character of every other object could be understood by study of its form, the relationship between the human character and the human form should be no exception. Resemblances to other animals, for example, have always been considered significant. Aristotle thought that the appearance of a person's nose gave a useful insight into his character: one's beak or snout might reveal the magnanimity of the lion or the insensitivity of the pig, the irascibility of the dog or the impudence of the crow — these being the special characteristics that these creatures personified in his view.

If this classical physiognomy now seems a little too arbitrary and whimsical, it can at least be credited with more wit and less wackiness than the persistent practice of reading both character and fate from the daily shifting angular relationships between the earth and stars whose (apparent)

v

constellations have been thought to suggest a crab, a goat, a virgin, a centaur, a scale, and a school of fish.

In the 18th century, many of the greatest contributions to science took the form of classification. Classification required system, and the quest for system stimulated both the search for new data and the radical revision of ways of looking at data, both old and new. The methods which thus revolutionized zoology, botany, and chemistry were bound, sooner or later, to be applied to human psychology, but the dominance of the moralistic, theological approach to thought and behavior made for slow progress. When Dr. Franz Josef Gall, a German physician living in Austria, began in the 1790's to classify the mental faculties and to identify, by empirical research, the specific portion of the brain that governed each faculty, popular interest in his work gave quick rise to ecclesiastical repression. In 1802, four years after his first writings on the subject were published, Gall was forbidden to continue his public lectures in Austria. He moved to Paris, where he and his pupil Dr. Johannes C. Spurzheim continued to develop and teach the science that came to be known as phrenology — the science of the mind. And it was Spurzheim and his great English disciple (and later, naturally, his rival) George Combe who brought phrenology to America.

For a time the new science was greeted in the United States with limited enthusiasm. Its greatest appeal, of course, derived from the fact that it was the first system that permitted detailed analysis of the human brain without the inconvenience of autopsy. The relative development of the various "organs" of the mind could be observed and measured without removing the brain from the skull. But perhaps the two factors that impeded phrenology's popularity were the hostility that so often confronts a radical new science and the pompous academicism of the early phrenological societies. It was the latter, certainly, that caused the first American journal, the quarterly *Annals of Phrenology*, sponsored with high expectations by the Boston Phrenological Society in 1833, to die after two years of publication with a circulation of 300.

During the same two years, however, American phrenology produced one of the most extraordinary intellectual figures of the Jacksonian era, Orson Squire Fowler of Cohocton, New York. In 1833, Fowler's Amherst College class-

mate, and lifelong friend, Henry Ward Beecher, was assigned the negative side in a college debate on the merits
of phrenology as a science. The thoroughness of his research, combined with his brilliance as a speaker, led to
victory in the debate. But as soon as the decision was an-
nounced, Beecher declared to the audience that he had
been completely converted to the theories he had just argued against. Beecher and Fowler, both at the time planning to become Protestant ministers, attended phrenology
lectures in Boston, started lecturing on the subject themselves, and soon began to "read" people's heads for the
modest fee of two cents. They were, in effect, the founders
of a new profession: practical phrenology. Upon gradua-
tion, Beecher reverted to theological studies, though he
maintained an active interest in phrenology for many years.
He and his brother Lyman became two of the most famous
and (up to a point) respected preachers of their time, and
their sister Harriet, with her *Uncle Tom's Cabin*, one of
the most politically influential novelists of any time.

For Fowler, on the other hand, phrenology was to become both passion and profession, and to involve his whole
family in joint enterprise with the sole exception of his
own wife, the young widow Martha Chevalier, neé Brev-
oort, of New York City, whom he married in 1835. He
instructed his younger brother Lorenzo Niles Fowler in
the science, and with him opened an office at 135 Nassau
Street in New York City in 1835, where they read heads,
wrote and published books, arranged lecture tours for
themselves, trained and managed a rapidly growing fleet of
practical phrenologists, and assembled an impressive
museum of skulls, busts, and pictorial materials. The
museum was free, but the charge for individual readings
rose to $1 for filling in a standard chart or $3 for a full-
scale handwritten analysis.

Orson and Lorenzo soon recruited their younger sister
Charlotte into the firm, and when Lorenzo married Lydia
Folger of Nantucket in 1844, she became one of the
strongest members of the team. Without ceasing her lifelong commitment to phrenology, Lydia was graduated in
1850 from the Central Medical College in Syracuse, N. Y.
as the second woman Doctor of Medicine in America. Her
appointment to the Central Medical College faculty made
her America's first woman medical instructor. Charlotte

was also married in 1844 — to a medical student, Samuel R. Wells, who had been working for the Fowlers for the previous year. The firm's name was subsequently changed to Fowlers and Wells.

It would be absurd to put Orson Fowler on an equal level with Benjamin Franklin (a grandson, incidentally, of Peter Folger, one of the leaders among the original score of white settlers of Nantucket and the ancestor not only of Lydia but of a number of notable bearers of the Folger name), but there is hardly anyone else to compare him to. Like Franklin, Fowler had broad and ever-expanding interests. Like Franklin, his morality was basically conventional, but he applied it with enthusiasm and daring and often reached unconventional conclusions. What perhaps most unites him with Franklin as archetypes of the American genius is their avid belief that better ways of doing almost everything can and must be found. Above all they shared a strong faith that the practically superior way is the morally superior way. In the Puritan theological climate that still prevailed through the 19th century, it could not be positively asserted that a practice was moral simply because it worked — the pragmatism of the early 20th century. Morality was still a theocentric concept and had to be demonstrated independently of practicality. Part of the genius of both Franklin and Fowler was their ability to prove that it always could be.

Fowler was, of course, far less of an originator than Franklin, but he had a similar instinct for grasping what was in the wind and making it concrete. In place of the myriad useful objects and social institutions that Franklin invented or redesigned, Fowler's energy and versatility propelled him into most of the controversial and far-reaching reform movements of which his period was so startlingly productive. A quintessential product of the Jacksonian era, with its equalitarian enthusiasm, anticlassicism, and religious revivalism, Fowler dedicated himself to bringing the better things and better ways of life to all. While phrenology and its adjuncts remained his chief focus of interest (and source of income), he also advocated in person and in print, and published and befriended the leading advocates of, temperance, vegetarianism, *avant garde* architecture (wherein he made perhaps his most original and lasting mark), shorthand, hydropathy (the uses of water to cure a variety of ills), the abolition of slavery, and the liberation of women.

In an era of tireless orators and prolific writers, Orson Fowler was a standout. *Phrenology Proved, Illustrated and Applied* was so successful that it required constant revision and expansion as edition after edition clattered off the presses. Fowler took on the task of editing, publishing, and often almost single-handedly writing the *American Phrenological Journal*. He was the head of an aggressively expansive publishing enterprise. He maintained a heavy teaching schedule at the school for practical phrenologists that he and Lorenzo ran at their "Phrenological Cabinet." He embarked on long, frequent lecture tours. In the midst of this frantic activity, Fowler developed in the 1840's a secondary career as marriage expert and pioneer in the forbidden area of public sex education. His *Love and Parentage* was an enormous success, and he followed it with the even more popular *Amativeness, or Evils and Remedies of Excessive and Perverted Sensuality*. Behind the loud Puritanism of the latter title, Fowler advocated ample, healthy, equalitarian —and, needless to say, exclusively marital—sex. His lectures on sex and sexual hygiene were so bold that he had to give them to completely segregated audiences—only women for the first sitting, only men for the second. Working in this area, as in phrenology, as a high-powered team, Orson, Lorenzo, and Lydia allied themselves as friends, platform colleagues, publishers, or all three, with such radical reformers of women's rights and dress as Amelia Bloomer, Lucy Stone, Susan B. Anthony, Reverend Antoinette Brown, Thomas L. and Mary Gove Nichols (who were later deeply immersed in hydropathy), and a pioneer in birth control theory and advocacy, R. T. Trall. Among these fearless individualists, Orson Fowler demonstrated his fertile originality by launching a campaign against the painful, unhealthy, deceptive, and demeaning practice of compressing the female torso into tightly laced corsets. The title of his major treatise on the subject, *Intemperance and Tight Lacing Considered in Relation to the Laws of Life*, is a perfect example of the way Fowler saw all reforms and scientific advances: as interpenetrating and interdependent.

It was this breadth and magnanimity of vision that made Fowler the valued intimate of so many of his most distinguished contemporaries. Horace Greeley, Horace Mann, William Cullen Bryant, Charles A. Dana, and Charles Sumner were only a few of the devoted admirers of phrenology and Fowler whose names are still remembered a century and more later. Greeley was so convinced of the usefulness of phrenology that he argued in an 1852 editorial that railroad accidents could be reduced if trainmen were selected *"by the aid of phrenology, and not otherwise."*

The relationship between the Fowlers and Walt Whitman was an outstanding case of mutual admiration. Whitman's capacious head was read by Lorenzo in 1849. The reading was so much to Whitman's liking that he included it in two editions of his *Leaves of Grass*: "Leading traits of character appear to be Friendship, Sympathy, Sublimity and Self-Esteem, and markedly among his combinations the dangerous faults of Indolence, a tendency to the pleasure of Voluptuousness and Alimentativeness, and a certain swing of animal will, too unmindful, probably, of the conviction of others." Fowlers and Wells not only put the first edition of *Leaves of Grass* on sale in 1855 but continued to promote and sell it for three more years, long after its controversial reception had caused other booksellers to remove it from their shelves. For a brief period in the late 1850's Whitman was employed as a staff writer for *Life Illustrated*, a Fowlers and Wells periodical.

But Fowler's most original contribution to American life, the one of which he was most proud, and the one that indirectly blasted his career, was the Octagon House. Through the years of soaring success Fowler dreamed of building himself a magnificent home overlooking the incomparably beautiful Hudson River. Like Thomas Jefferson, Fowler studied architecture and construction wherever his travels took him. Characteristically, however, Fowler's radical turn of mind was not satisfied with superficial innovations of style and decoration. With the same unfettered clarity of insight that was to lead R. Buckminster Fuller to similar conclusions nearly a century later, Fowler realized that the rectangle had little more than custom to recommend it as the basic plan for home-building.

A rectangular structure with forty feet of wall can enclose a maximum of one hundred square feet. A circular structure with forty feet of wall encloses approximately 127 square feet, but a regular octagon does almost as efficient a job—some 120 square feet, or 20 per cent more space than a square with the same amount of outer wall. The octagon plan also brings more windows nearer the inner parts of the house yet reduces loss of heat, shortens distances between rooms, and allows infinite variety of room sizes and arrangements. Odd corners provide opportunities for an ample supply of closets. All these major advantages and many minor ones were passionately urged upon the American public by Orson Fowler in *A Home for All* in 1848. In his preface, Fowler wrote of himself: "Let no one suppose that he has forsaken, or even turned aside from, Phrenology—that first and only occupation of his enthusiastic youth, and the idol of his matured and declining years [Fowler was thirty-nine at the time.] He has turned aside only to build him a good home, and in doing so, has made and learned improvements to adopt which will greatly increase *home comforts*; and this work is written to propagate them. . . ."

Directly and indirectly, *A Home for All* did propagate octagonal houses by the score from coast to coast, in all sizes, materials, and decorative styles. Architectural books and builder's manuals, which were profusely published in the 1850's, helped spread the concept, as did the steady sales of Fowler's own book. The June 1946 *Art Bulletin* listed 115 surviving examples in eighteen states, not including a number in the southern states, Pennsylvania, New Jersey, and Kansas. Perhaps the most notable survivor is the baroquely ornate Philip Armour house in Irvington-on-Hudson, New York, capped with both a dome and a cupola, which has been for many years the home of Carl Carmer. (Carmer wrote a *New Yorker* article on "The Fowlers, Practical Phrenologists" in 1937, and included a charming chapter entitled "Eight Sides to a Home" in his 1939 classic *The Hudson*.)

But Fowler was not quite ready "to build him a good home" until an 1850 lecture tour took him to Janesville, Wisconsin. There Joseph Goodrich had recently devised a new building material composed of sand, lime, and small stones, a forerunner of modern concrete. Goodrich offered to let Fowler hammer his parlor walls with a sledge at six cents a blow, a sum he promised would cover any possible damage. Fowler "found his walls as hard as stone itself, and harder than brick walls." He started to build his own mansion of Goodrich-style gravel-wall grout in Fishkill, New York, and in 1854 published a revised edition of *A Home for All*, now subtitled *The Gravel Wall and Octagon Mode of Building*.

Fowler's five-storey octagonal tower was both his triumph and, in conformity with Aristotle's definition of tragedy, his downfall. The tragic flaw was not its eighty-foot height; nor its proud complement of sixty-five rooms, including a "gymnastic room for females" and a "dancing room"; nor the vast glass cupola crowning the stairwell, inspired by the revolutionary use of glass in the comtemporaneous London Crystal Palace; nor the inclusion of such radical and not yet accepted innovations as illuminating-gas piping, hot-and-cold running water kept at constant pressure by a roof tank, a sand-and-charcoal water filter and speaking tubes. The central heating system, with the furnace in the basement, was not yet a widely accepted arrangement, but it fully lived up to Fowler's hopes, as did the location of the entrance in the basement to contain winter drafts and the design of the central stairwell as a ventilating chimney for summer heat. The most modern house of its time was, in fact, an almost complete success. Neighbors flocked to lectures in the auditorium that Fowler created by folding back the partitions of the first storey. Distinguished reformers and intellectuals provided the Fowlers with a steady stream of guests. In 1855 Orson and Lorenzo sold their interests in the flourishing publishing business to their brother-in-law Samuel Wells, and Fowler devoted himself to writing in his beloved top-floor studio, with its commanding view of the Hudson Valley.

Fowler had the courage to put toilets inside his own house and to recommend them in *A Home for All*. Yet his advocacy of the indoor water closet hardly lived up to his usual standards of audacity and whole-heartedness. "To squeamish maidens and fastidious beaus this point is not submitted, but matrons, the aged and feeble, are asked, is not such a closet a real household necessity and luxury? Yet it need be used only in cases of *special* need, the one generally used being outside, as usual." Perhaps it was this squeamishness which prevented Fowler from investigating the cesspool question with his characteristic thoroughness and avidity for the most advanced theories and technology. Whatever the reason, in 1859, a bare two years after completion of the mansion, a plague laid low many of its distinguished residents, and several died. Typhoid was the eventual diagnosis; investigation proved that a gravel-wall bulkhead had permitted seepage from the cesspool into the well.

Fowler was crushed. He and his wife moved to Manchester, Massachusetts, renting the octagonal tower to a military academy for Spanish and Cuban boys. When its director absconded in 1865, Fowler leased the tower to a Mrs. Cunningham, who operated it as a boarding house. Not long after, the poor lady was wrongly identified by local rumor as the Mrs. Cunningham who had been tried eight years earlier for a particularly brutal knife murder in New York City, and her business was ruined beyond recovery. Fowler sold the house for a reported $150,000, but it changed ownership an average of once a year, at declining prices, for the next thirty-two years. At last, in 1897, having been completely neglected for some seventeen years, the structure was considered too dangerous to leave standing as an attraction for neighborhood children, tourists, and roving students of architecture and cultural history. The Town of Fishkill ordered it destroyed—a task that required no small quantity of dynamite.

Fowler continued to write and lecture on phrenology for the rest of his life, but with declining success in the post-Civil War years. His first wife died, and his second. At the age of seventy-three he married again and had three children. He died in 1887 on a farm in Sharon, Connecticut, where he had spent the last seven years of his life.

Meanwhile Lorenzo and Lydia went to England in 1860 for a lecture tour, and it proved so profitable that they spent the rest of their lives there. Their daughter Jessie joined her father in the business of phrenology and social reform after Lydia's death in 1879. She became editor of the *Phrenological Magazine* of London ten years later and, returning to America after her father's death in 1896, took over the editorship of the *Phrenological Journal*. In the great Fowler tradition, Jessie studied brain dissection at London's School of Medicine for Women, wrote several books on phrenology, and received a law degree from New York University in 1901. Carmer closed his *New Yorker* article, "So far as I know, she was the last of the phrenological Fowlers."

In fact, the 20th century has seen few phrenological non-Fowlers either. While old phrenology busts, with their now mysterious outlines, numbers and abbreviations glazed or incised on bald, white pates, have had a decorative revival, the science that spawned them has been eclipsed by psychoanalytical and behavioral psychologies, undermined by anatomical research, and overshadowed by DNA, RNA, LSD, Dianetics, Scientology, group analysis, confrontation therapy, and a torrent of popular movements, fads, mysteries, pseudo-sciences, and concrete scientific discoveries.

For all the rush of progress, the Fowlers' phrenology retains a timeless appeal along with the period quaintness of its lush vocabulary. To the Fowlers and their contemporaries, it was exciting news that the scientific approach could reveal one's strengths and weaknesses and that one could, with skill, enthusiasm, and persistent application, make oneself better.

Andrew E. Norman

Palisades, New York
November 2, 1969

CONTENTS

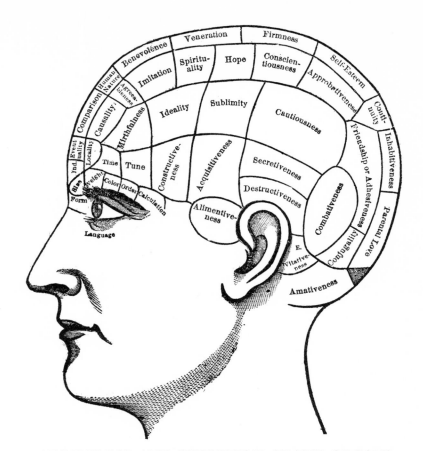

NUMBERING AND DEFINITION OF THE ORGANS.

AMATIVENESS, Love between the sexes.
CONJUGALITY, Matrimony—love of one. [etc.
PARENTAL LOVE, Regard for offspring, pets,
FRIENDSHIP, Adhesiveness—sociability.
INHABITIVENESS, Love of home.
CONTINUITY, One thing at a time.
VITATIVENESS, Love of life.
COMBATIVENESS, Resistance—defense.
DESTRUCTIVENESS, Executiveness—force.
ALIMENTIVENESS, Appetite—hunger.
ACQUISITIVENESS, Accumulation.
SECRETIVENESS, Policy—management.
CAUTIOUSNESS, Prudence—provision.
APPROBATIVENESS, Ambition—display.
SELF-ESTEEM, Self-respect—dignity.
FIRMNESS, Decision—perseverance.
CONSCIENTIOUSNESS, Justice, equity.
HOPE, EXPECTATION—enterprise.
SPIRITUALITY, Intuition—faith—credulity.
VENERATION, Devotion—respect.
BENEVOLENCE, Kindness—goodness.

20. CONSTRUCTIVENESS, Mechanical ingenuity
21. IDEALITY, Refinement—taste—purity.
21b. SUBLIMITY, Love of grandeur—infinitude.
22. IMITATION, Copying—patterning.
23. MIRTHFULNESS, Jocoseness—wit—fun.
24. INDIVIDUALITY, Observation.
25. FORM, Recollection of shape.
26. SIZE, Measuring by the eye.
27. WEIGHT, Balancing—climbing.
28. COLOR, Judgment of colors.
29. ORDER, Method—system—arrangement.
30. CALCULATION, Mental arithmetic.
31. LOCALITY, Recollection of places.
32. EVENTUALITY, Memory of facts.
33. TIME, Cognizance of duration.
34. TUNE, Sense of harmony and melody.
35. LANGUAGE, Expression of ideas.
36. CAUSALITY, Applying causes to effect. [tion.
37. COMPARISON, Inductive reasoning—illustra.
37b. HUMAN NATURE, Perception of motives.
37c. AGREEABLENESS, Pleasantness—suavity.

PREFACE

To teach learners those organic conditions which indicate character is the first object of this manual. And to render it accessible to all, it condenses facts and conditions, rather than elaborates arguments — because to expound Phrenology is its highest proof — states laws and results, and leaves them upon their naked merits; embodies recent discoveries, and crowds into the fewest words and pages just what learners need to know, and hence requires to be Studied rather than merely read. "Short, yet clear," is its motto. Its analysis of the faculties and numerous engravings embody the results of the very extensive observation and experience of the Authors.

To record character is its second object. In doing this, it describes those organic conditions which affect and indicate character in Seven degrees of power — very large, large, full, average, moderate, small, and very small — indicated by the seven numerals 7, 6, 5, 4, 3, 2, and 1 — and refers those who have their physiological and phrenological conditions correctly marked in the accompanying table, to those paragraphs which both describe themselves, and also contain specific directions how to *perfect* their characters and improve children. Its plan for recording character is seen at a glance in the following

EXPLANATION OF THE TABLES.

The examiner will mark the power, absolute and relative, of each function and faculty, by placing a figure, dot, or dash on a line with the name of the organ marked, and in the column headed "large," or "small," according to the size of the organ marked, while the printed figure in the square thus marked refers to those pages in this book where, under the head "large," "small," etc., will be found a description of the character of the one examined in respect to that organ, and at the end of this description, in the book, another figure will be found, which refers to "Fowler's Phrenology," a standard work, in which will be found an extended description of those shadings of character caused by various combinations of faculties, while in the two right-hand columns, in the tables marked "cultivate" and "restrain," are figures referring to pages in this work where directions for cultivating and restraining may be found; and at the close of these sentences are figures which refer the reader to the *numbered paragraphs* in three books, entitled "Physiology," "Self-Culture," and "Memory," or called, when bound together, "Education Complete." These works give extended directions for self-improvement and the management of children.

When an organ is half way between two sizes, it is represented by two figures, as 5 to 6, or 3 to 4, etc., which is equivalent to $5\frac{1}{2}$ or $3\frac{1}{2}$. In these cases both sentences referred to may be read, and a medium between the two will be appropriate.

The sign +, *plus*, signifies about one third of a degree more, and —, *minus*, one third of a degree less, than the marks indicate, thus giving virtually a scale of twenty-one degrees.

Several persons can be marked on one table by using a dot for one, and dashes, horizontal, perpendicular, slanting to the right, left, etc., for each of the others.

Those organs and conditions marked 7, or very large, are sovereign in their influence over character and conduct, and, combining with those marked large, direct and control feeling and action. Those marked 6, or large, have a powerful and almost controlling influence, both singly, and especially in combination, and press the smaller ones into their service. Those marked 5, or full, play subordinate parts, yet their influence is considerable, though more potential than apparent. Those marked 4, or average, have only a medium influence, and mainly in combination with larger ones. Those marked 3, or moderate, are below par in fact, and still more so in appearance; exert but a subordinate influence, and leave character defective in these respects. Those marked 2, or small, are deficient, so much so as easily to be perceived; leave their possessor weak and faulty in these respects, and should be assiduously cultivated; while those marked 1 are very small, and render their possessor almost idiotic in these respects.

Orson Fowler

SECTION I

ORGANIC CONDITIONS AFFECTING LIFE

PHYSIOLOGICAL CONDITIONS AFFECTING LIFE

1. LIFE—ITS OBJECT, ORGANS, AND FUNCTIONS.

A *problem* how wonderful! an entity, an embodiment how complicated, yet how perfect! How worthy even a GOD to create, and man to possess, improve, and study! These it is the object of this volume to expound.

What, then, *is* life? In what does it consist? In its vast variety of *functions*, so embodied as to act together.

But its *end* alone can expound its entity. That end is *happiness*. This is the one, single, only ultimate of both life in the aggregate, and of each of its individual functions. And the more there is of life, the more there is of happiness, and *vice versa*. Hence, to promote or impair either, thereby promotes or impairs the other. And the conditions of either are equally those of the other—a base line of incalculable value in deciphering our problem of life, its functions and improvement. And the fact is both coincident and important, that the happy exercise of every faculty improves, while its painful exercise impairs, both it and its organ. That is, present enjoyment increases our capacities for future happiness. Hence the happier we are, the higher and truer our life. And the better. For all goodness consists in obeying, and all badness in violating, the laws of our being. All happiness also consists in this same obedience, as all misery is occasioned by this same violation, of these very same laws. Therefore he who is the happiest is so because the best; that is, because he obeys the most law. But he suffers the most who is the most sinful; that is, who has broken the most law. Therefore Happiness, Goodness, and Obedience to the laws of our being are all one and the same, while Suffering, Sinfulness, and Death are synonymous—are cause and effect. Then what is the *first* law and condition of health and happiness?

2. ORGANISM IS AS FUNCTION

Nature operates always and everywhere by means of *organs*, or instrumentalities—never without them. What one function ever is, has been, or *can* be, carried forward without them? None, ever, anywhere.

And what is more, the organism is in perfect *correspondence* with the function. Thus, whenever Nature would put

1

forth *power* of function, she does so by means of power in the *organ* which puts it forth. And so of quickness, and all other functional conditions. Thus the office of wood is to rear aloft that stupendous tree-top, and hold it there in spite of all the surgings of powerful winds upon its vast canvas of trunk, limbs, leaves, and fruit. Now this requires an immense amount of power, especially considering the great mechanical disadvantage involved. This power Nature supplies, not by bulk, because this, by consuming her material and space, would prevent her making many trees, whereas her entire policy is to form all the trees she can; but by rendering the organic *texture* of wood as solid and powerful as its function is potential. And the more solid its structure, the more powerful its function, as seen in comparing oak with pine, and lignum vitae with poplar. But, letting this single example suffice to illustrate this law, which obtains throughout the entire vegetable kingdom, let us apply it to the animal.

The elephant, one of the very strongest of beasts, is so powerfully knitted together, in dermis, muscle, and bone, that bullet after bullet shot at him, flatten and fall harmless at his feet. The lion, too, is as strong in texture as in function. Only those who know from observation can form any adequate idea of the wiry toughness of those muscles and tendons which bind his head to his body, or of the solidity of his bones — corresponding with the fact that, seizing bullock in his monster jaw, he dashes with him through jungle and over ravine, as a cat would handle a squirrel. And when he roars, a city trembles. The structures of the white and grizzly bear, of the tiger, hyena, and all powerful animals, and, indeed, of all weak ones, in like manner correspond equally with their functions. All quickness of function is put forth by quick-acting organs, all slowness by the slow; and thus of all organs and functions throughout every phase and department of universal life and nature. Indeed, in and by the very nature of things this correspondence *must* exist. For how *could* weak organs possibly put forth powerful functions, or slow organs quick functions? In short, this correspondence between organic conditions and functions is fixed and absolute — is necessary, not incidental — is universal, not partial — is a relation of cause and effect, and governs every organ and function throughout universal life and nature.

Governs, reader, you and I. And in all our functions. How can weak muscles put forth strength, or a sluggish brain manifest mental activity? Hence, to become great, one must first become *strong*—and in the special *organs* in whose functions he would excel. Would you become great mentally, then first become strong cerebrally. Or, would you render that darling boy a great man, first make him a *powerful animal..* Not that all powerful animals are great men, but that all great men are, and must needs be, powerful animals. Our animal nature is the basis of all mental and moral function. It so is in the very constitution of things, that mind can be put forth *only* in and by its material organism, and is strong or weak, quick or sluggish, as its organism is either. If, in the plenitude of Divine Wisdom, man had been created a purely mental being, he would have needed no body, and could not have used one; whereas, instead, he has been created a compound being, composed of both body and mind. Nor are those seemingly opposite entities strangers to each other. Instead, they are inter-related by ties of the most perfect reciprocity—so perfect that every conceivable condition of either reciprocally affects the other.

HEREDITARY ORGANISM AS AFFECTING MENTALITY.

Hereditary organic quality is the first, basilar, and all-potent condition of all power of function, all happiness, all everything. This is congenital—is imparted by the parentage along with life itself, of which it is the paramount condition and instrumentality. It depends mainly on the original nature of the parents, yet partly also on their existing states of body, mind, and health, their mutual love or want of it, and on other like *primal* life-conditions and causes. It lies behind and below, and is infinitely more potential than, education, and all associations and surrounding circumstances—is, in short, what renders the grain cereal, the oak oaken, fish fishy, fox foxy, swine swinish, tiger tigerish, and man human.

Each creature much resembles a galvanic battery, and its life-force depends mainly on how that battery is "got up," and this on those congenital conditions which *establish* the life-conditions—a subject infinitely important, and generally overlooked, but treated elsewhere. This condition can

3

NO. 1.—F. B. CARPENTER.

not well be described, hardly engraved, but is easily perceived by a practiced eye. It is quite analogous to Temperament, on which little has yet been written, but lies behind and below all temperaments — is, indeed, their determining cause. Some of its signs are coarseness and fineness of hair, skin, color, form, motion, general tone of action and mental operation, etc. A comparison of the following engravings of the artist Carpenter with the idiot Emerson will give some outline idea of this point. A still better is found in comparing man with animal. In fact, the main differences between vegetables and animals, as compared among one another, and all as compared with man, and different men as compared with each other, as well as the entire style and cast of character and sentiment, everything, is consequent on this condition — in short, is what we call "bottom" in the horse, "the breed" in full-blooded animals, and "blood" in those high and nobly born. Those marked

7. Are pre-eminently fine-grained, pure-minded, ethereal, sentimental, refined, high-toned, intense in emotion, full of human nature, most exquisitely susceptible to impressions of all kinds, most poetic in temperament, lofty in aspiration, and endowed with wonderful intuition as to truth, what is right, best, etc., are unusually developed in the interior or spirit life, and far above most of those with whom they come in contact, and hence find few congenial spirits, and are neither understood nor appreciated; when sick, suffer inexpressibly, and if children, are precocious — too smart, too good to live, and absolutely must be treated physiologically, or die early.

6. Are like 7, only less so; are finely organized, delicate, susceptible, emotional, pure-minded, intellectual, particular, and aspiring after a high state of excellence; full of human nature, and true to its intuitions and instincts; have a decided predominance of the mental over the physical; are able and inclined to lead excellent human lives, and capable of manifesting a high order of the human virtues.

5. Are more preinclined to the good than bad, to ascend than descend in the human scale; can, by culture, make excellent men and women, but require it; and should avoid those habits which clog or deprave the mental manifestations, and, to attain superiority, must "strive to enter in."

4

4. Are simply fair in organic tone; are good under good surroundings, but can be misled; must avoid all deteriorating habits and causes, spirits and tobacco, bad associates, etc.; assiduously cultivate the pure and good, and study to discipline intellect, as well as purify the passions, and rely the more on culture and a right physiological life, because the hereditary endowment is simply respectable.

3. Are rather lacking in organic quality, and better adapted to labor than study; rather sluggish mentally, and given to this world's pleasures; had but a commonplace parentage; need to be strictly temperate in all things, and avoid all forms of temptation, vulgar associates in particular, and make up by the more assiduous cultivation what has been withheld by nature.

2. Are coarse-grained in structure and sentiment, and both vulgar and non-intellectual; had poor parental conditions; are low, groveling, and carnal, as well as obtuse in feeling and intellect; are poorly organized, and incapable of high attainments; hence restrain the passions, and cultivate intellect and the virtues as much as possible, and especially avoid alcoholic liquors, tobacco, and low associates.

1. Are really dotish, and *non compos mentis*.

To Cultivate: First, guard against all perversion of the faculties, all forms of intemperance, over-eating, pork, rich pastry, especially late suppers; be much of the time in the open air; work and exercise abundantly; bathe daily, and keep the body in just as good condition as possible; mingle with the high and good; exercise all the faculties assiduously, in the best possible manner, and in strict accordance with their natural functions; cultivate a love of nature, art, beauties, and perfections — in short, encourage the good, true, and right, and avoid the bad.

To Restrain: Cultivate a love of the terrestrial — of this world, its pleasures and luxuries — for you require animalizing. You live too much in the ideal; live more with the actual and tangible. Callous yourself against much that now abraids your finer sentiments, and shrink not from contact with those not quite up to your standard. You are adapted to a more advanced state of humanity, but should come down to the present and material. Above all, do not be too fastidious, qualmish, or whimmy, but make the best of what is; cling to life; and enamor yourself of its objects and pleasures.

NO. 2.—EMERSON, AN IDIOT.

5

3. HEALTH—ITS VALUE, CONDITIONS, AND RESTORATION

Health consists in the normal and vigorous exercise of all the physical functions, and disease in their abnormal action. Health is pleasurable, disease painful. Health is life, for life consists in the normal action of those same functions in which health consists. And to improve health is to increase life itself, and all its pleasures. Some writer has appropriately defined health thus:

Planting your foot upon the green sod, looking around, and yielding yourself to whatever feelings naturally arise, health is proportionate to that buoyant, jubilant, exhilarating, ecstatic feeling which supervenes. It is to all our functions what motive power is to machinery—sets them off with a rush and a bound. It both makes us happy, and causes everything else to increase that happiness. But disease renders us miserable, and turns everything around us into occasion of misery. It both weakens and perverts the interior being. Indeed, health is the quintessence of every earthly good—disease, of every terrestrial evil. Poor indeed is he, however rich in money, in honors, in office, in everything else whatsoever, whose *health* is poor; for how can he enjoy his dollars and honors? But rich indeed is he who is healthy, however poor in money, for he *enjoys* whatsoever he has or is. A rich man may, indeed, purchase a luxuriant dinner, but without health does not, can not *relish* it; whereas a poor man, with health, enjoys even a dry crust.

The rich need health to enjoy their riches; the poor doubly, in order to prevent becoming poorer. But to be poor *and* sickly is the uttermost of human evil. Nor can the poor afford to be sick; for their health is their *all*, to themselves and families. Nor should they allow *any*thing whatsoever to impair it, but make *health paramount.*

Even the very talents of men depend mainly on health. Is not the brain confessedly the organ of the mind? Now, what means it, that the eye is the organ of vision, but that *all its existing states* reciprocate with its physical conditions? That the stomach is the organ of digestion, but that the nutritive function is vigorous or impaired, in exact correspondence with its existing states? That the brain is the organ of the mind, but that all *its* conditions similarly affect the mentality? And since all the states of the body

NO. 3.—HEALTH.

6

and brain act reciprocally — consequent on that vast network of nerves which ramify throughout every part and parcel of the body, and terminate in the brain — of course all existing conditions of the body similarly affect these nerves, and thereby the brain, and therefore the mind, rendering all the states of either body or mind reciprocal with those of the other. Is the body sick, or weak, or exhausted, or inflamed, or sleepy, or exhilarated, is not the mind equally so? Then to originate great thoughts, or to conceive pure and exalted sentiments, must not the *brain* be in a vigorous state? And in order to acquire cerebral vigor, must not all the bodily functions be equally vigorous? And to this end, must not those health-laws which cause this vigor be observed? Of what avail the learning of the sickly scholar, the talents of the invalid, or the goodness of the pious dyspeptic? They can *do* nothing, can *enjoy* nothing — are but a burden to themselves and friends. Can we think, or remember, or study without that energy furnished by the body? No more than move machinery without motive power. How, then, can that boy become a great or learned man without possessing physical vigor? Or that delicate and beautiful girl a capable or good woman, wife, or mother without possessing animal vigor? Let it be forever and everywhere remembered, that both judgment *and* memory, reason and poetry, eloquence and philosophy, even morality and religion, all the virtues and all the vices — in short, one and all of the human functions, are carried forward by animal power. Even the very sensual pleasures of the debauchee are exercised by this very animal force, and weaken when and because it declines. And as physical power depends on the observance of certain physical laws, the violation of which weakens both body and mind, of course the first duty of every human being to himself and Creator — of parents to their children — of ministers to people — writer to reader, and one to all, is to

LEARN AND OBEY THE HEALTH-LAWS.

And on this point is just where our whole educational system — collegiate especially — is radically defective. It eclipses more genius by weakening the body than it eliminates by study. Children are always smarter and better relatively than adults, because injured by that false educational

7

system which impairs mind, memory, and morals by breaking down a good physical constitution. The Romans appropriately named their schools "gymnasia," from those muscular *exercises* which both formed their leading feature, and secured a strong mind by strengthening the body. Our schools and colleges are, and will continue to be, fundamentally defective, till remodeled upon the basis of *health*, and *as a means* of scholarship and talents.

Nor intellect merely, but our very *morals* and piety, depend on health. Can we even pray or worship without vitality? And what is more, the very vices of mankind are consequent mainly on the infringement of the *physical* laws.

Hereditary conditions in parents cause depravity in their children; yet even they do it by deranging the body. It is what men eat and drink, it is how they live, sleep, etc., it is their *physiological* conditions and habits, that cause nine tenths of human depravity. Are not both children and adults depraved when cross, and cross because sick; that is, rendered sinful by being unwell? Who does not know that drinking engenders depravity — makes the best of men bad? *But why, and how?* By disordering the body. And since by alcohol, why not by tobacco, gluttony, or any other wrong physical state? Are not drunkenness and debauchery concomitants? Are not dyspeptics always irritable? The truth is, that all abnormal physical action causes abnormal mental action, which is sin. To become good, and answer the end of their being, men must *live* right — must learn to eat right, and sleep, exercise, bathe, breathe, etc., in accordance with nature's requisitions. And nine tenths of the evil in men have this purely physical origin, and can be cured by physical means.

Health is the natural state of man, animal, vegetable, all that lives — is the ultimate of life. Like all else in nature, it has its *laws*; and these laws obeyed, will render it perfect from birth to death. It even requires immense violation of these laws seriously to impair it. Bird and beast are rarely unhealthy, except when rendered sickly by man. Has our benevolent Creator granted this greatest of boons to beasts, but denied it to man? He has not. None need ever be sick, for there are health-laws, which, if obeyed, *guarantee* the very perfection of health. To become sickly is foolish; for it cuts off every pleasure, and induces every ill — is even wicked, for it is consequent only on a violation of the laws of our being, and all violation of law is sin. And the health-laws are as much laws of God—written by his finger on our very constitution—as the Decalogue. In short, none have any business to be sick. It is alike the privilege, as it is the sacred duty of one and all to be and keep well; that is, to observe the health laws. And of parents to keep their children well.

"But, you forget that sickness and death are God's chastising messengers, his special providences." Are they, indeed? Then in all conscience *submit* patiently, passively to them. Take no medicines. Do nothing whatever to restore health, for in so doing you *resist Providence*—you disobedient child. If sickness is providential, every attempt at restoration is open, direct rebellion against God—is practically saying to Him: "I know you sent this sickness as a providential messenger of good to me; but I am not going to be sick; I am going to get well if I can, in spite of Providence." The fact is, nobody believes *practically* that sickness is providential; for if so, their every restorative effort, nursing, medicine, all, is downright rebellion.

This ascribing sickness and premature death to Providence has killed millions. Long enough has it thrown on our heavenly Father the effects of our own sinful violation of his health-laws. Health is either governed by law, or it is not. If thus governed, it is *cause and effect*, not providential, except as the rising of the sun and all else in nature is providential. Therefore, oh, man, know that health is both your first privilege and bounden duty, and both learn and fulfill its conditions.

EXISTING STATES OF HEALTH, AND ITS IMPROVEMENT.

While this condition has a most important influence on both the quantity and quality of all the mental manifestations, yet to mark it correctly, without aid from those examined, is exceedingly difficult. It may seem good, when actually poor, because its functions may be exhilarated by inflammation, which both perverts and weakens; or it may seem much poorer than it really is, because of merely temporary debility, while the heart's core remains sound. But its serious impairment leaves all the functions, phrenological included, proportionally less vigorous than the sizes of their organs indicate. Those who have health—

7. Are full to overflowing of life, buoyancy, light-heartedness, and ecstasy; are strong and lively; enjoy food, sleep, action, nature, all the physical functions, to the highest degree; rarely ever have a pain or ache, or become tired; can do and endure almost any and everything; withstand miasma and disease remarkably; recuperate readily; experience a certain gush, glow, vivacity, and briskness in the action of all the faculties; as well as the highest and most perfect flow and exercise of each of the life-functions.

6. Are healthy and happy; exercise all the organs with vigor and power; turn everything into pleasure, and dash off trouble as if a mere trifle, and yet can endure any amount of pain and exposure; feel jubilant and joyous year in and year out; and do everything easily, all the functions being condensed and hearty, and the whole being full of snap and life.

5. Have a good, full share of life-force, vigor, and vivacity — of health, happiness, desire and ability to perform, enjoy, and accomplish; can stand a good deal, but must not go too far, and have sufficient stamina for all practical purposes, but none to spare or waste foolishly.

4. Have fair, average health, if it is well cared for, yet are sometimes subject to ailments; are in the main healthy and happy, but must live regularly; experience rather a tame, mechanical action of all the faculties, instead of that zest and rapture imparted by perfect health; can accomplish and enjoy much, but must take things leisurely; if careful, can live on and wear a good while yet, but if careless, are liable to break down suddenly and finally; and become irritable, dissatisfied, dull, forgetful, and easily fatigued, and must cherish what health remains.

3. Are deficient in animation and recuperative power, and feel tired and good for nothing most of the time; with activity 6 or 7 are constantly overdoing, and working up in mental or physical action those energies which ought to go to the restoration of health, not to labor; need abundance of rest and recreation, and give out at once if deprived of sleep; must stop all unnecessary vital drains, such as chewing, smoking, drinking, late hours, and all forms of dissipation, and should eliminate all the vitality possible, but expend the least.

2. Are weakly, sickly, and inert; feeble in desire and effort; capable of enduring and enjoying but little; live a

monotonous, listless, care-for-nothing, half-dead-and-alive life, and must either restore health or give up, and enjoy comparatively nothing.

1. Having barely life enough to keep soul and body together; are just alive, and have almost lost life's pleasures, powers, desires, and aspirations.

To Cultivate: First ascertain what causes your disease or debility; if heart, lungs, muscles, stomach, etc., are marked low, apply special culture to the weak organs — see the cultivation of each — and assiduously study the health-laws, and conscientiously fulfill them, making everything else subservient thereto. Especially take extra pains to *supply vitality*, but waste none in any form of excess.

Restrain You Need Not: Health can not be too good. When, however, you find a surplus of animal vigor, work it up in one or another of life's ends and efforts.

4. THE TEMPERAMENTS.

This term has long been employed to designate certain physical constitutions as indicative of certain mental characteristics. The idea expressed in our definition of "hereditary organism" is very like that of the temperaments. They were formerly classified thus: The nervous, indicated by light complexion, large brain, and smaller stature, and indicating superior talents, refinement, and scholarship; the billious, indicated by dark complexion, large bones, powerful muscles, prominent features, and a large and spare form, and indicating by a supposed surplus of bile, irritability, violence of passion, and melancholy, along with strength of character; the sanguine, indicated by a florid complexion, sandy hair, blue eyes, fullness of person, and abundance of blood, and indicating warmth, ardor, impulsiveness, and liability to passional excesses; and the lymphatic, indicated by full, plethoric habit, distended abdomen, excessive adipose deposit, and indicating a good, cosy, lax, enjoying disposition, with a stronger proclivity to sensuous pleasures, rather than intellect or action of any kind. But this classification is practically discarded, without its place having been supplied. The doctrine of the temperaments in full remains unwritten. Meanwhile we propound the following

Man is composed physically of three great classes of organs, the predominance or deficiency of each of which is called a predominant or deficient temperament, both giving a particular form to the body — shape being its index — and likewise a particular set of phrenological developments, and consequent traits of character. That is, given forms of body indicate and accompany special talents, dispositions, and mental proclivities; and the art in delineating phrenological character depends in a great degree on reading correctly the temperament and organic conditions, and their controlling influence on character; for they exert, as it were, the ground-swell as to the direction and action of the phrenological manifestations. Thus Causality, with the vital temperament predominant, takes on the phase of planning, of common sense, of reasoning on matter, of adapting ways and means to ends, etc. But with the nervous or mental predominant, the same sized Causality manifests itself in logic, metaphysics, investigation, the origination of ideas, in intellectual clearness and power, etc. And it requires the sharpest eye and clearest head in the examiner to discern the bearings and influences of these temperaments and organic conditions on the intellectual and moral manifestations. And the mistakes of amateurs, of connoisseurs even, are more temperamental than phrenological. Still they are sometimes consequent on health conditions. Thus the same person in one state of health is irritable, violent, passional, perhaps even sensual and wicked, who in another physical condition is amiable, even-tempered, moral, and good. A given amount of Ideality is much more idea, of Language much more expressive, of the affections more affectional, and moral tone more lofty, in combination with the mental temperament than vital. But our proposed limits do not allow us to extend our observations. Still, the following descriptions give the outline, and put inquirers on the track of further observations.

5. THE VITAL TEMPERAMENT.

This embraces the heart, lungs, stomach, liver, bowels, and that entire system of internal organs which creates life-force. It is very large in Hall, and small in Rev. J. N. Walter.

The large end of a good egg is warmer than its other parts, because its vitality resides there; but, this cold, life is extinct. Incubate it a short time, and break the shell at this end, and you will find the heart palpitating and blood-vessels formed—the yolk furnishing the required nutrition. The vital apparatus forms first, and deposits the material for forming the other portions; is more active during juvenility than the other parts; sustains the whole animal economy; is the source of all power and energy; creates animal heat; resists cold and heat, disease and death; and re-supplies muscle, brain, and nerve with that life-power expended by their every exertion. It is to the man what fire, fuel, water, and steam are to machinery—the *vis animoe*, the *primum mobile*—the first great pre-requisite of life itself and all its functions.

Its decided predominance is accompanied by a round head, well developed at the base, large Amativeness, Acquisitiveness, Alimentiveness, Benevolence, and Language; large organs of the animal propensities generally; a rapid widening of the head from the corners of the eyes to the tips of the ears; side-head spherical and well filled out; forehead generally full or square, and broad rather than high; perceptive organs large, and all the organs short and broad rather than long or pointed.*

7. Are fleshy; short and broad built; stocky; deep and large-chested; broad and round-shouldered; impetuous; impulsive; enthusiastic; hearty; good livers; fond of meats, condiments, stimulants, and animal pleasures; have a strong, steady pulse; large lungs and nostrils; a full habit; florid complexion; flushed face; light or sandy hair and whiskers; sound and well-set teeth; great endurance of fatigue, privation, and exposure; great love of fresh air, out-of-door exercise, and physical action, but not of *hard* work; a restlessness which can not endure in-door confinement, but must be abroad, and constantly doing something with great zeal, ardor of desire, and more practical common sense than book learning, and of general knowledge of men and things than accurate scientific attainments; more shrewdness and off-hand talent than depth; more availability than profundity; and love of pleasure than power of thought.

6. Are like 7, though not in as great extremes; generally fleshy and of good size and height, if not large; well-proportioned; broad-shouldered; muscular; prominent and

*The raised figures, called superiors, refer the reader to the numbered sections found throughout this work, and are employed to save repetition.

NO. 4—WM. G. HALL

NO. 5—REV. I. N. WALTER

13

strongly-marked in features; coarse and homely; stern and harsh; strong, but often awkward, and seldom polished; best adapted to some laborious occupation, and enjoy hard work more than books or literary pursuits; have great power of feeling, and thus require much self-government; possess more talent than can exhibit to others; manifest mind more in business, in creating resources and managing matters, than in literary pursuits, or mind as such; prefer some light, stirring, active business, but dislike drudgery; turn everything, especially bargains, to good account; look out for self; get a full share of what is to be had; feel and act out, "every man for himself," and are selfish enough, yet abound in good feeling; incline to become agents, overseers, captains, hotel-keepers, butchers, traders, speculators, politicians, public officers, aldermen, contractors, etc., rather than anything requiring steady or hard work; and are usually healthy, yet very sick when attacked, brought at once to the crisis, and predisposed to gout, fevers, apoplexy, congestion of the brain, etc.

5. Have a good share of life-force, yet none to spare; withstand a good deal, yet must not waste vitality, and should live in a way to improve it.

4. Have sufficient vitality to sustain life, and impart a fair share of energy to the functions, but by no means sufficient to put forth their full power, and should make its increase a first life-object.

3. Are rather weakly and feeble; often half prostrated by a feeling of languor and lassitude; can keep doing about all the time if slow, and careful not to overdo, the liability to which is great when Activity is 6 or 7; need much rest; can not half work, or enjoy either body or mind; suffer much from fatigue and exhaustion, and would be glad to do, but hardly feel able.

2. Are too weak and low to be able either to do, enjoy, or accomplish much; should both give the vital organs every possible facility for action, and also husband every item of vitality; be extremely careful not to overwork, and spend much time in listless, luxuriating ease, while nature restores the wanting vitality.

1. Are almost dead from sheer inanition.

To Cultivate: Ascertain which of the vital organs is deficient, and take all possible pains to improve its action; see directions for increasing the action of heart, lungs, stomach, etc.; alternate with rest and exercise; "away with melancholy," banish sadness, trouble, and all gloomy associations, and cultivate buoyancy and light-heartedness; enjoy the present, and make life a glorious holiday instead of a weary drudgery; if engaged in any confining business, break up this monotony by taking a long leave of absence — a trip to Europe or Lake Superior, a long journey, by horticulture, or parties, or frolicking with children; by going into young and lively society, and exercising the affections; bringing about as great a change as possible in all your habits and associations. Especially cultivate a love of everything beautiful and lovely in nature, as well as study her philosophies; bear patiently what you must, but enjoy all you can; keep doing all you are able, but other things than formerly, and what interests you. You should watch and follow your intuitions or instincts, and if you feel a special craving for any kind of food or pleasure, indulge it; especially be regular in sleep, exercise, eating, and all the vital functions, as well as be temperate in all things; and above all, keep your *mind* toned up to sustain the body; aid your weak organs by will-power — that is, bring a strong *will* to aid digestion, breathing, etc., and keep yourself up thereby. Determine that you *won't* give up to weakness or death, but will live on and keep doing in *spite* of debility and disease. Fight life's battles like a true hero, and keep the head cool by temperance; the feet warm by exercise; the pores and evacuations open by ablution and laxative food; and heart warm by cherishing a love of life and its pleasures. And don't fail to keep up a gentle pounding and frequent brisk rubbing of chest, abdomen, and feet, so as to start the mechanical action of the visceral organs. Nothing equals this for revivifying dormant or exhausted vitality, and none are too poor or too much occupied to avail themselves of it.

To Restrain: Those who manufacture vitality faster than they expend it, are large in the abdomen; too corpulent; even obese; often oppressed for breath; surcharged with organic material; too sluggish to expend vitality as fast as it accumulates, and hence should work, work, work, early and late, and with all their might, and as much as possible with their muscles, and out of doors; should eat sparingly, and of simple food; avoid rich gravies, butter,

15

sweets, fat, and pastry, but live much on fruits; sleep little; keep all the excretory organs free and open by an aperient diet, and especially the skin by frequent ablutions, the hot bath, etc.; breathe abundantly, so as to burn up the surplus carbon; sit little, but walk much; never yield to indolence; work up energy by hands and head, business and pleasure, any way, every way, but keep consuming vitality as fast as possible. Some fleshy persons, especially females, give up to indolence and inanity; get "the blues," and lounge on rocking-chair and bed. What is wanted is to *do*, not to loiter around. *Inertia* is your bane, and *action* your cure. If flushed, feverish, nervous, etc., be careful not to overdo, and rely on *air*, warm bath, and gentle but continued exercise, active or passive, but not on medicines.

6a. THE LUNGS—BREATHING.

All that live, down even to vegetables and trees, breathe—*must* breathe in order to live—live in proportion as breathe—begin life's first function with breathing, and end its last in their last breath. And breathing is the *most important* function of life from first to last, because the grand stimulator and sustainer of all. Would you get and keep warm when cold, breathe copiously, for this renews that carbonic consumption all through the system which creates all animal warmth. Would you cool off and keep cool in hot weather, deep, copious breathing will burst open all those myriads of pores, each of which, by converting the water in the system into insensible perspiration, casts out heat, and refreshes mind and body. Would you labor long and hard, with intellect or muscle, without exhaustion or injury, breathe abundantly; for breath is the great re-invigorator of life and all its functions. Would you keep well, breath is your great preventive of fevers, of consumption, of "all the ills that flesh is heir to." Would you break up fevers, or colds, or unload the system of morbid matter, or save both your constitution and doctor's fee, cover up warm, drink soft water—cold, if you have a robust constitution sufficient to produce a reaction; if not, hot water should be used—then let in the fresh air, and breathe, breathe, breathe, just as fast and much as possible, and in a few hours you can "forestall and prevent" the worst attack of disease you ever will have; for this will both unload disease at every pore of skin and lungs, and infuse into the system that *vis animoe* which will both grapple in with and expel disease in all its forms, and restore health, strength, and life. Nature has no panacea like it. *Try the experiment*, and it will revolutionize your condition. And the longer you try, the more will it regenerate your body and your mind. Even if you have the blues, deep breathing will soon dispel them, especially if you add vigorous exercise. Would you even put forth your greatest mental exertions in speaking or writing, keep your lungs clear up to their fullest, liveliest action. Would you even breathe forth your highest, holiest orisons of thanksgiving and worship—deepening your inspiration of fresh air will likewise deepen and quicken your *divine* inspiration. Nor can even bodily pleasures be fully enjoyed except in and by copious breathing. In short, proper breathing is the alpha and omega of all physical, and thereby of all mental and moral function and enjoyment.

7 and 6. Have either a full, broad, round chest, or a deep one, or both; breathe freely, but rather slowly; fill the lungs clear up full at every inspiration, and empty them well out at every expiration; are warm, even to the extremities; red-faced; elastic; buoyant; rarely ever subject to colds, and cast them off readily; feel buoyant and animated, and are thus qualified to be vigorous in all the functions, physical and mental.

5 and 4. Are neither pale nor flushed, neither ardent nor cold, but a little above medium in these respects, and somewhat liable to colds.

3. Breathe little, and mainly with the top of the lungs; move the chest but little in breathing, and the abdomen less, perhaps none at all; are often pale, yet sometimes flushed because feverish; frequently do and should draw in long breaths; are quite liable to colds and coughs, which should be broken up at once, or they may induce consumption; often have blue veins and goose-flesh, and are frequently tired, listless, and sleepy, and should take particular pains to increase lung action.

2. Are strongly predisposed to lung diseases; have blue veins and sallow complexion, and are very subject to coughs and colds; are often dull, and always tired; frequently catch a long breath, which should be encouraged by making all the breaths long and frequent; are predis-

posed to consumptive diseases, but can stave them off, provided proper means are adopted; break up colds as soon as they appear, and take particularly good care of health.

1. Have barely lung action enough to live, and every function of body or mind is poorly performed.

To Cultivate: First and mainly *breathe* deeply and rapidly; that is, draw long and full breaths; fill your lungs clear up full at every inspiration, and empty them out completely at every expiration; not only heave the chest in breathing, but work the abdomen. To do this, dress loosely and sit erect, so that the diaphragm can have full play; begin and keep up any extra exertion with extra lung action; often try how many deep and full breaths you can take; ventilate your rooms, especially sleeping apartments, well, and be much of the time in the open air; take walks in brisk weather, with special reference to copious respiration; and everywhere try to cultivate full and frequent lung inflation, by breathing clear out, clear in, and low down — that is, make all your breathing as when taking a long breath.

THE CIRCULATION.

"For the blood thereof is the life thereof." The blood is the great porter of the system; carries all the material with which to build up and repair every part, and hurries off all the waste material, which it expels through lungs and skin.

And the heart is this circulatory instrumentality. Without heart, even lungs would be of no account, nor heart without lungs. They are twin brothers, are co-workers at the very fountain-head of life and all its energies. Even diseased organs are unloaded of morbid matter, reanimated, and rebuilt mainly by blood. Blood good or poor, the whole system, brain and mind included, is in a good or poor condition; but blood wanting, all is wanting; heart poor, all is poor; heart improved, all improved.

7 and 6. Have an excellent and uniform circulation, and warm hands, feet, and skin; never feel chilly; withstand cold and heat well; perspire freely; have a slow, strong, steady pulse, and are not liable to sickness.

5 and 4. Have a fair, yet not remarkably good, circulation, and generally, though not always, warm hands and feet; are not much pinched by cold; perspire tolerably freely, yet better if more; and need to promote circulation, at least not impede it.

3. Have but poor circulation, along with uneasiness and palpitation of the heart; are subject to cold hands and feet, headache, and a dry or clammy skin; find the heart to beat quicker and stronger when drawing than expiring breath; are chilled by cold, and overcome by hot, weather; are subject to palpitation of the heart on any extra exertion, walking fast or up stairs, or a sudden startle, etc., and very much need to *equalize* and *promote* the circulation.

2. Have weak circulatory functions, and either a fluttering pulse, very fast and very irregular, or it is weak and feeble; suffer from chilliness, even in summer; are very much affected by changes in the weather; very cold in the extremities, and suffer much from headache and heat and pressure on the brain; are subject to brain fever, and often a wild, incoherent action of the brain, because the blood which should go to the extremities is confined mainly to the head and vital organs; feel a sudden pain in the head when startled or beginning to put forth any special exertion, and suffer very much mentally and physically from heart affections and their consequences.

1. Have scarcely any pulse, and that little is all on a flutter; are cold, and "more dead than alive."

To Cultivate: Immerse hands and feet daily in water as hot as can be borne, ten minutes, then dash on or dip in cold water, and rub briskly, and heat by the fire till warm, and follow with active exercise, breathing at the same time according to directions just given; if there is heat or pain about the heart, lay on a cloth, wrung out of cold water at night; rub and pat or strike the chest on its upper and left side, and restrain appetite if it is craving, and cultivate calmness and quiet. If sufficient vitality remains to secure reaction, putting the feet in ice-cold water will be of great service.

To Restrain is not necessary, except when excessive circulation is consequent on disease, in which case remove the cause. A healthy circulation can not be too great.

ALIMENTATION.

By that truly wonderful process, digestion, food and drink are made to subserve intellect and moral sentiment—converted into thought and emotion. Then, must not different *kinds* of food produce different mental and moral traits? A vast variety of facts answer affirmatively.

19

Rollin says that pugilists, while training for the bloody arena, were fed exclusively on raw meat. Does not the *food* of lion, tiger, shark, eagle, etc., re-increase their ferocity, and that of deer, dove, and sheep redouble their docility? Does not this principle explain the ferocity of the Indian, force of the Anglo-Saxon, and subserviency of the Hindoo? Since alcoholic drinks excite the animal passions more than the intellectual and moral faculties, why not also meat, condiments, and all stimulating food as well? And why not vegetables and the cereals, by keeping the system cool, promote mental quiet, intellectual clearness, and moral elevation? At all events, less meats and more vegetables, grains, and fruits would render men less sensual, and more talented and good. And those who would become either, *must mind what and how they eat.*

Stomach: 7. Can eat anything with impunity, and digest it perfectly; can live on little, or eat much, and need not be very particular as to diet.

6. Have excellent digestion; both relish and dispose of food to perfection; are not liable to dyspepsia; have good blood, and plenty of it, and a natural, hearty appetite, but prefer the substantials to knicknacks; hate a scanty meal, and have plenty of energy and good flesh.

5. Have good, but not first-rate digestion, and it will continue good till bad eating impairs it, still must not invite dyspepsia by bad living.

4. Have only fair digestive vigor—too little to be abused—and need to promote it.

3. Have a weak digestive apparatus, and variable appetite—very good, or else very poor; are a good deal pre-inclined to dyspepsia; often feel a goneness and sinking at the stomach, and a general lassitude and inertia; sleep poorly, and feel tired and qualmish in the morning; have either a longing, hankering, pining, hungry feeling, or a loathing, dainty, dormant appetite; are displeased and dissatisfied with everything; irritable and peevish, dispirited, discouraged, gloomy, and miserable; feel as if forsaken and neglected; are easily agitated, and oppressed with an indefinable sense of dread, as if some impending calamity awaited; and should make the improvement of digestion the first business of life.

2 and 1. Are like 3, only more so. Everything eaten gives pain, and life is but a burden.

To Cultivate: Eat simple, plain, dry food, of which un-bolted wheaten bread, and especially crackers made of the same, are best; and but little at that, especially if the appetite is ravenous; and masticate and salivate thoroughly; eat in a cheerful, lively, pleasant spirit, talking and laughing at meals; consult appetite, or eat sparingly and leisurely that which relishes; boiled wheat, or puddings made of wheaten flour, or grits, or oatmeal, or rye-flour, eaten with cream and sugar, being the best staple article — say a tea-cupful of wheat or Graham flour per day, thoroughly boiled; should eat little after 5 P.M., and if hurried in business, before or after, but not during business hours, nor in a hurried, anxious state of mind, but as if determined to enjoy it; above all, should cast off care, grief, business anxieties, troubles, and all painful remembrances and fore-bodings, and just luxuriate in the passing moment.

Dyspepsia, now so alarmingly prevalent, is more a mental than corporeal disease — is consequent more on a worried, feverish, unhappy state of mind, than stomachic disorder merely. It is usually brought on by eating very fast right after working very hard, and then working very hard right after eating too fast and too much, which allows so little energy to go to the stomach, so that its contents ferment instead of being digested, which inflames the whole system, and causes the morbid action of both the mental and physical functions. This inflammation creates a morbid, craving, hankering appetite, as well as a general irritable state of mind. But the more food is eaten the more it re-inflames the stomach, and thereby re-increases these morbid hankerings; while denying appetite diminishes this inflammation and consequent hungering and irritability. Sometimes eating gives temporary relief right at first, before what has just been eaten ferments, but only re-increases the pain soon afterward. Starvation is the cure in all cases of a craving appetite, but a poor appetite needs pampering, by proving any dainties that may relish. Or, perhaps the system is pining for want of some *special* aliment. If so, the appetite will hanker after it, and should be gratified, how-ever seemingly unnatural, provided it be an alimentary article. See Alimentiveness. Above all, avoid alcohol and tobacco in all their forms, and also tea and coffee, using, instead, a coffee made by browning wheat, rye, peas, corn, sweet potatoes, bread, etc., and prepare the same as Java.

Next, rub and pat, or lightly pound the stomach, liver, and bowels. While in college, a graduate came around advertising a specific panacea for dyspepsia, but requiring secrecy. It consisted simply in rubbing and kneading the abdomen. This supplies that *mechanical* action which restores them to normal action. Those manual exercises, which call the abdominal muscles into special action, are pre-eminently useful, such as rowing, chopping wood, hoeing, and various gymnastic exercises.

If the stomach is sore or painful, lay on at night a wet cloth, with a dry one over it, folded several thicknesses. If the bowels are torpid, induce an action of them at a given hour daily, and live much on boiled wheat, unbolted wheaten bread, and puddings, figs, and fruits, if the stomach will bear them. Observe all the health laws with scrupulous fidelity, relying more on nature, but little on medicines, and remit no efforts and spare no exertions to restore digestion; for, till you do, you can only half think, study, remember, feel, transact business, or do or enjoy anything.

To Restrain it, make less a god of the appetite, direct, or work up in other respects those energies now consumed by the stomach, and "be temperate in all things."

The Abdominal Viscera complete the digestive functions. The stomach may solve its food, yet dormant liver, intestines, and mesentery glands fail to appropriate it. Or the latter may be good, and former poor.

7 and 6. Are very fleshy, round favored, and fat, and eliminate food material faster than is consumed, besides sleeping well, and enjoying ease and comfort, and do only what must be done.

5 and 4. Have a good, fair share of flesh and abdominal fullness, and appropriate about as much food as their systems require.

3. Are rather slim, poor in flesh, and gaunt; may digest food well, but sluggish bowels and mesenteries fail to take up and empty into the circulation enough to fully sustain the life-functions, and have hence strong tendencies to constipation.

2. Are very slim, poor, dormant, weak, and dyspeptic.

To Cultivate: Eat aperient food, and keep the whole system open and free as possible.

To Restrain: Breathe deeply, work hard, sleep little, and eat lightly.

6b. THE MOTIVE OR MUSCULAR TEMPERAMENT.

Motion is a necessary, an integral part and parcel of life itself. What could man do, what be, without it? How walk, work, or move? How even breathe, digest, or circulate blood? — for what are these, indeed all the physical functions, but *action* in its various phases?

And this action is effected by means of bones and muscles or fibers, the fleshy portions of the system. These bones constitute the foundation on which the muscular superstructure is built, are articulated at their ends by the joints, and firmly bound together by ligaments, yet allowed free motion. Toward the middle of these bones the muscles are firmly attached, so that when they contract they give motion to the *end* of the bone *opposite* the belly of the muscle. These muscles, of which there are some 527 in the human body, constitute the lean meat or red flesh of all animals, and are rendered red by the immense number of minute blood-vessels which are ramified upon every fiber of every muscle, in order to re-supply that vital power which is expended by its exercise. The contractile power of these muscles is truly astonishing, as is evident from the wonderful feats of strength and agility of which man is capable; and that, too, though these muscles act under a great mechanical disadvantage.

These bones and muscles collectively constitute the framework of the system — give it its build and form — are to the man what the timbers, ropes, and pulleys are to the ship, and constitute the Motive Temperament. Its predominance confers *power* of constitution, and strength of character, and feeling.

7. Are lean, spare; of good size and height, and athletic; have strongly marked features; a large, Roman nose; high and large cheek-bones; large and broad front teeth — all the bones of the body projecting; a deep, grum, bass voice; distinctly marked muscles and blood-vessels; large joints; hard flesh; great muscular power or physical strength; ease of action, and love of physical labor, of lifting, working, etc.; dark, and often coarse, stiff, abundant, and perhaps bushy hair; a black and heavy beard; dark skin and eyes; a harsh, expressive visage; strong, but coarse and

NO. 6—ALEXANDER CAMPBELL

harsh feelings — the movements like those of the draught-horse, slow, but powerful and efficient; tough; thorough-going; forcible; strongly marked, if not idiosyncratic; determined, and impressive both physically and mentally; and stamp their character on all they touch, of whom Alexander Campbell furnishes a good example.

The motive, 7, mental, 6, and vital, 5, are capable of powerful and *sustained* mental effort, and great *power* in any department, especially that of mind as mind, of swaying a commanding influence over mankind, taking the lead in a large business, etc.

This temperament is always accompanied by prodigious coronal and perceptive regions, Firmness, and Combativeness, and large Destructiveness — its natural accompaniment — the very organs required to re-increase its force and efficiency, and indispensable to its exercise.

6. Are like 7, except less in degree; are tough, hardy, and strong constitutioned; evince power, efficiency, and force in whatever they undertake; use strong expressions; are stout, limber-jointed, and both need and can endure a world of action and fatigue; are like a fire made of hard wood, or anthracite coal, making a slow but powerful and continuous heat, and will make a decided mark in the business world, or in whatever other department these energies may be exercised. With the vital 6 or 7, and the mental 3 or 4, are broad and prominent in form; large, tall, well proportioned, broadshouldered, and muscular; usually coarse-featured, homely, stern, and awkward; enjoy hard work more than books or literary pursuits; have great power of feeling, and thus require much self-government; are endowed with good sense, but have a poor way of showing it; are strong minded, but possess more talents than power to exhibit them; manifest talents more in managing machinery, creating resources, and directing large operations than in mind as such; improve with age, growing better and more intellectual as they grow older; accomplish wonders; are hard to beat, indomitable, and usually useful citizens, but endowed with strong passions when once roused; and capable of being deeply depraved, especially if given to drink.

5. Have a good share of the hearty, enduring, efficient, and potential; move right forward, with determination and vigor, irrespective of hindrances, and bring a

good deal to pass; and are like 6, only less so.

4. Are not deficient in motive power, yet more would be better; wrought up by special circumstances, can put forth unwonted strength, but it will be spasmodic, and liable to overstrain; can work hard, but are loth to; prefer the sedentary to the active, and business to labor; with the vital 6 or 7 are indolent physically, and do only what they must, and need to cultivate muscular power.

3. Dislike work; prefer sitting to moving, and riding to labor; may be quick and flashy, but are not powerful; lack strength and weight of character; *need* much more exercise than they love to take; and first of all should cultivate both muscular action and strength of character. With the vital 6, and mental 6 or 7, are rather smallboned, but plump, well formed, light complexioned, and often handsome; have usually auburn or brown hair; are most exquisitely organized, most pathetic and sympathetic, sentimental, exalted, and spiritual; have redoubled glow and fervor of feeling, derived from both the vital and mental, which they are hardly able to contain; easily receive and communicate impressions; are quite too much influenced by first impressions, and intuitive likes and dislikes; have hobbies; are most enthusiastic; throw a great amount of feeling into everything; use strong and hyperbolical expressions; are fond of company, if not forward in it; have a quick, clear, sharp, keen, active mind, and good business talents; a ready flow of ideas and a talent for communicating them, either on paper or in social conversation; show taste, refinement, and delicacy in everything; have an under-current of pure virtuous feeling, which will prevent the grosser manifestation of animal passion, and give the intellectual and moral the ascendency; sin only under some sudden and powerful excitement; are passionately fond of poetry, novels, tales, light and sentimental reading, belles-lettres, newspapers, etc., and inclined to attempt this kind of composition; have a retentive memory, shrewdness, smartness, and enough of selfishness to take good care of self, yet not sufficient momentum or power to become great, but are rather effeminate. This temperament is found much oftener and more perfect in the female than male, and is admirably illustrated by Fanny Forrester. Children thus organized are precocious, and liable to die prematurely, and their physical culture would save to their parents and the

VITAL MOTIVE.

NO. 7.—PHINEAS STEVENS.

25

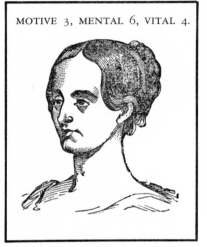

MOTIVE 3, MENTAL 6, VITAL 4.

NO. 8.—FANNY FORRESTER.

world those brightest stars, which now generally set while rising, to shine no more on earth.

Mental 7, vital 5, and motive 3, may be smart, but can not be great; may be brilliant, but are flashy, meteoric, vapid, too emotional, imaginative, and impulsive, and like a fire made of pine wood or shavings—intense, but momentary.

2 and 1. Work, walk, move, and use muscles only when obliged to; run much more to the emotional and vapid than potential, and should cultivate the muscles assiduously.

Muscular exercise is indispensable to greatness and happiness. By a law of things, all parts must be exercised in about equal proportions. When the brain is worked more than the muscles, it becomes partially congested, loses its snap, leaves the mind dull, memory indefinite, and thought obtuse, which exercise remedies. None need ever think of becoming great intellectually, however splendid their heads or temperaments, without a world of vigorous *exercise*—of *real* hard work, even. All eminent men have laid the foundations of their superiority by working hard during their minority, and continuing to exercise daily through life; while those students brought up without labor rarely take a high intellectual stand, except in parrot-like scholarship. They always lack vim and pith, and close, hard thought. And this deficiency grows on them. J. Q. Adams always rose before the sun to take his exercise, and as he became old took much of it in swimming, which he said gave the required exercise without heating his blood. Benton took a great amount of exercise. Jefferson always worked "like a Trojan." Polk rose before the sun to take his morning walk. Webster would have his seasons of hunting, fishing, and rowing, besides taking a daily walk. Washington was a robust, hard-working farmer and soldier. *Physical exercise* is as indispensable to greatness as the intellectual organs themselves. And one principal reason why so many men, having all the phrenological indications of greatness, do not distinguish themselves, is *a want of physical exercise.*

To Cultivate: Take all the muscular exercise you can any way endure, but only gentle; make yourself comfortably tired every day; choose those kinds of exercise most agreeable, but practice *some* kind assiduously; dance more and sit less; if a child, should be allowed to run and play, to skate and slide down hill, romp and race, climb and tear around all it likes, and furnished with playmates to encourage this out-of-door life. Fear neither exposure nor dirt, clothes or shoes, bad associates, or anything else that furnishes this *great* desideratum, *exercise*.

To Restrain: Use your muscles less and brain more.

7. THE MENTAL TEMPERAMENT.

This embraces the brain and nerves, or that portion of the system called into exercise in the production of mind as such—thought, feeling, sensation, memory, etc.

The brain consists at first of a mere ganglion of nervous matter, formed at the top of the spinal column. To this additions are made upward and forward, forming, successively, the brains of various animals, from that of the fish and toad, through that of the dog and monkey, up to the perfectly developed brain of the human adult. Let it be observed that the base of the brain, or the animal organs, which alone can be exercised by infants, are developed first, while Benevolence, Amativeness, Veneration, Constructiveness, and some others which cannot be exercised by them, are not developed till some years after birth.

The construction of the brain is most interesting. Its internal portion is fibrous, while its outer is soft and gelatinous. It is folded up into layers or furrows, called convolutions, which are expanded, by dropsy of the brain, into a nervous sheet or web. These convolutions allow a great amount of nervous matter to be packed up in a small compass, and their depth and size are proportionate to the amount of mind and talent. Thus in animals and idiots they are small and shallow; in men of ordinary talents, much deeper; while the dissectors of the brains of Cuvier, Lord Byron, and other great men, remark with astonishment upon their size and depth.

Some writers say five times as much blood is sent to the brain in proportion to its volume as is sent to any other portion of the system, some say eight times, others fifteen, and one twenty; but *all* agree as to the general fact. The difference between them is doubtless owing to the

MENTAL TEMPERAMENT.

NO. 9.—EDGAR ALLAN POE.

27

difference in the talents of those operated upon, intellectual subjects having the most. The distinctness and protrusion of the veins in the heads of great men, as also the immediate filling up of these veins when one laughs or becomes excited, have the same cause.

Through the medium of the spinal column, and by means of the nerves that go off from the spinal marrow through the joints of the back-bone, the brain holds intercourse with every part of the body, the nerves being ramified upon every portion of its surface, so that not even the point of a needle can penetrate any portion of it without lacerating them, and thus producing pain. This spinal marrow is composed of four principal columns, the two anterior ones exercising voluntary motion, the two posterior ones sensation. Let the nerves that go off from the two posterior columns be severed at their root, and the parts on which they are ramified will be destitute of sensation, not feeling anything, though able to move; but on severing the nerves that go off from the two anterior columns, though the patient will feel the prick of the needle, he will be unable to move the limb to which the nerve goes. Now, observe that these two *anterior* or *motor* columns are in direct connection with the *frontal* portion of the brain, in which the *intellectual* organs are located, so that each can communicate freely with the other, while the two *posterior* columns, or those of *sensation*, are in connection with the *back* part of the brain, in which the organs of the *feelings* are located. They are most abundant on the outer surface of the body, and accordingly the skin and adjacent flesh is the seat of much more intense pain from wounds than the internal portions.

7. Have a small stature; light build; small bones and muscles; a slim, tall, spare, sprightly person; quickness of motion; great physical activity—too much for strength; sharp features and phrenological organs; thin lips; small, pointed nose; and sharp teeth, liable to premature decay. They are characterized mentally by a predominance of mind over body, so that its states affect the body more than the body mind; are in the highest degree susceptible to the influence of stimuli, and of all exciting causes; are refined and delicate in feeling and expression, and easily disgusted with anything coarse, vulgar, or out of taste;

28

enjoy and suffer in the highest degree; are subject to extremes of feeling; have their disgusts, sympathies, and prepossessions easily excited; experience a vividness and intensity of emotion, and a clearness, pointedness, and rapidity of thought, perception, and conception, and a love of mental exercise imparted by no other temperament; have a deep flow of pure and virtuous feeling, which will effectually resist vicious inclinations; intense desires, and put forth correspondingly vigorous efforts to gratify them; are eager in pursuits, and feel that their ends are of the *utmost* importance, and must be answered *now*; are thus liable to overdo, and prematurely exhaust the physical powers, which at best are none too good; are very fond of reading and study; of thinking and reasoning; of books and literary pursuits; of conversation, and all kinds of information, and apt to lie awake at night, thinking, or feeling, or reading; incline to some profession, or light mental occupation, such as a clerk, merchant, teacher, or, if a mechanic, should be a goldsmith, or something requiring light action, but not hard lifting — more head work than hand work; should avoid close application; take much pleasurable recreation and exercise; avoid all kinds of stimulants, wines, tobacco, tea and coffee included; use vegetable food mostly; endeavor to enjoy existence; and avoid being worried.

6. Are like 7 in character, only less in *degree*; more given to intellectual and moral than animal pleasures, and action than rest; can not endure slow or stupid employees; with the motive 6, are of good size; rather tall, slim, lean, and raw-boned, if not homely and awkward; have prominent bones and features, particularly front teeth and nose; a firm and distinct muscle; a tough, wiry, excellent physical organization; a firm, straightforward, rapid, energetic walk; great ease and efficiency of action, with little fatigue; a keen, penetrating eye; large joints, hands, feet, etc.; a long face and head, and a high head and forehead; a brain developed more from the nose over to the occiput than around the ears; large intellectual and moral organs; strong desires, and great power of will and energy of character; vigorous passions; a natural love of hard work, and capacity for carrying forward and managing great undertakings; that thorough-going spirit which takes right hold of great projects with both hands, and drive into and through thick

and thin, in spite of obstacles and opposition, however great, and thus accomplish wonders; superior business talents; unusual strength and vigor of intellect; strong common sense; good general judgment; with a large intellectual lobe, and a cool, clear, long, calculating head; a reflective, planning, discriminating cast of mind, and talents more solid than brilliant; are more fond of the natural sciences than literature; of philosophy than history; of the deep, solid branches than belles-lettres; of a professional and mental than laborious vocation; of mental than bodily action; and the moral than sensual.

5. Have good, fair muscles; are quite prominent-featured, easy of motion, enduring, tough, hardy, clear-headed, and fond of intellectual pursuits; have good ideas, and excellent native sense and judgment; talk, speak, and write to the purpose, if at all; love action and exercise, and walk and work easily; are efficient, and capable of doing up a good life labor, but not a genius. With the vital 6, are sprightly, lively, vivacious, and happy; and with the motive 3, are not adapted to a life of labor, but should choose some office business, yet exercise a great deal — no matter how much.

4. Have fair mental action, if circumstances fully call it forth; if not, are commonplace; must depend for talents more on culture and plodding studiousness than natural genius; with culture, can do well, without it little; with the motive and vital 6 or 7, are by far best adapted to farming or manual pursuits than literary, and should cultivate intellect and memory.

3. Have little love of literary pursuits; are rather dull, and fall asleep over books and sermons; and can not marshal ideas for speaking or writing.

2. Are exceedingly dull of comprehension; slow of perception; poor in judgment and memory; hate books; must be told what and how to do; and should seek the direction of superior minds.

1. Are almost senseless and idiotic.

8. A WELL-BALANCED TEMPERAMENT

Is by far the best. That most favorable to true greatness and general genius, to strength of character, along with perfection, and to harmony and consistency throughout, is one in which each is strongly marked, and all about equally developed.

Excessive motive with deficient mental gives power with sluggishness, so that the talents lie dormant. Excessive vital gives physical power and enjoyment, but too little of the mental and moral, along with coarseness and animality. Excessive mental confers too much mind for body, too much sentimentalism and exquisiteness, along with greenhouse precocity. Whereas their equal balance gives an abundant supply of vital energy, physical stamina, and mental power and susceptibility. They may be compared to the several parts of a steamboat and its appurtenances. The vital is the steam-power; the motive, the hulk or framwork; the mental, the freight and passengers. The vital predominating, generates more animal energy than can well be worked off, and causes restlesssness, excessive passion, and a pressure which endangers outbursts and overt actions; predominant motive gives too much frame or hulk; moves slowly, and with weak mental, is too light freighted to secure the great ends of life; predominant mental overloads, and endangers sinking; but all equally balanced and powerful, carry great loads rapidly and well, and accomplish wonders. Such persons unite cool judgment with intense and well-governed feelings; great force of character and intellect with perfect consistency; scholarship with sound common sense; far-seeing sagacity with brilliancy; and have the highest order of both physiology and mentality. Such a temperament had the immortal Washington, and his character corresponded.

Most diseases, too, are consequent on this predominance or deficiency of one or another of these temperaments, and when either fail, all fail. Hence the infinite importance of cultivating those that are weak. A well-balanced phrenology is equally important, and its absence unfavorable.

7 or 6. Are uniform, consistent, harmonious in character, eventempered, popular, and generally liked; not remarkable for any specialties of talents or character, nor for any deficiencies, and "maintain the even tenor of their way" among men.

5 or 4. Are in the main consistent, and in harmony with themselves, but more or less affected by circum-

A WELL-BALANCED TEMPERAMENT

NO. 10.—WASHINGTON.

stances; show general uniformity of life and doctrine, but different circumstances change their characters.

3. Have uneven heads and characters; are singular in expression, looks, and doctrine, and variable in conduct; often inconsistent, and with excitability 6 or 7, the creatures of circumstances; take one-sided views of things; are poor counselors; need and should take advice; are easily warped in judgment; propound strange ideas, and run after novelties; and need to cultivate unity and homogeneousness of opinion and conduct.

2. Are like 3, only more so; are nondescripts; idiosyncratic in everything; just like themselves, but unlike anybody else; and neither like, nor are liked by, others.

To Cultivate: Exercise the weaker and restrain the stronger faculties and temperaments according to directions in this work.

9. SIZE OF BRAIN.

That size, other conditions being equal, is a measure of power, is a universal law. In general, the larger a piece of iron, wood, anything, the stronger; and large men and animals are stronger than those that are small. This is a natural law. Still, sometimes smaller men, horses, etc., are stronger, can lift, draw, and endure more than others that are larger, because they are different in organic quality, health, etc.[2345] But where the *quality* is the same, whatever is largest is proportionally the most powerful. And this undisputed law of things is equally true of the brain, and that mental power put forth thereby. All really *great* men have great heads — merely smart ones, or those great only in certain faculties or specialties of character, not always. The brains of Cuvier, Byron, and Spurzheim were among the very heaviest ever weighed. True, Byron's *hat* was small, doubtless because his brain was conical, and most developed in the base; but its great *weight* establishes its great size. So does that of Bonaparte. Besides, he wore a very large hat — one that passed clear over the head of Col. Lehmenouski, one of his body-guard, whose head measured $23\frac{1}{2}$ inches, so that Bonaparte's head must have measured nearly or quite 24 inches. Webster's head was massive, measuring over 24 inches, and Clay's $23\frac{1}{2}$; and this is about Van Buren's size; Chief Justice Gibson's, the greatest jurist in Pennsylvania, $24\frac{1}{4}$; and Hamilton's hat passed over the head of a man whose head measured $23\frac{1}{2}$. Burke's head was immense, so was Jefferson's, while Franklin's hat passed over the ears of a 24-inch head. Judge McLean's head exceeds $23\frac{1}{2}$ inches. The heads of Washington, Adams, and a thousand other celebrities, were also very large. Bright, apt, smart, literary, knowing, even eloquent men, etc., often have only average, even moderate-sized heads, because endowed with the very highest organic *quality*, yet such are more admired than commanding; more brilliant than powerful; more acute than profound; though they may show off well in an ordinary sphere, yet are not the men for *great* occasions; nor have they that giant *force* of intellect which molds and sways nations and ages. The phrenological law is, that size, *other things being equal*, is a measure of power; yet these other conditions, such as activity, power of motive, health, physiological habits, etc., increase or diminish the mentality, even more than size. Quality is *more* important than quantity, but true greatness requires both cerebral quantity and quality.

Still, those again who have very large heads, are sometimes dull, almost foolish, because their organic quality is low[2]. As far, then, as concerns Phrenology itself, this doctrine of size appertains to the different organs in the *same head*, rather than to different heads. Still this doctrine, that size is the measure of power, is no more a special doctrine of Phrenology than of every other department of nature. And those who object to this science on this ground are objecting to a known law of things. If size were the *only* condition of power, their cavils might be worthy of notice; as it is, they are not.

Though tape measurements, taken around the head, from Individuality to Philoprogenitiveness or Parental Love, give some idea of the size of the brain, the fact that some heads are round, others long, some low, and others high, so modifies these measurements that they do not convey any very correct idea of the actual quantity of brain. Yet these measurements range somewhat as follows in adults:

7 or Very Large, $23\frac{3}{4}$ inches and upward; 6 or Large, from $22\frac{3}{4}$ to $23\frac{3}{4}$; 5 or Full, from 22 to $22\frac{3}{4}$; 4 or Average, from $21\frac{1}{2}$ to 22; 3 or Moderate, from $20\frac{3}{4}$ to $21\frac{1}{2}$;

2 or Small, from 20 to 20¾; 1 Below, 20. Female heads are half an inch to an inch below these measurements.

Very Large. With quality good, are naturally great; with quality and activity 6 or 7, and the intellectual organs 6 or 7, are a natural genius, a mental giant; even without education, will surmount all disadvantages, learn with wonderful facility, sway mind, and become pre-eminent; with the organs of practical intellect and the propelling powers 6 or 7, will possess the first order of natural abilities; manifest a clearness and force of intellect which will astonish the world, and a power of feeling which will carry all before them; and, with proper cultivation, become bright stars in the firmament of intellectual greatness, upon which coming ages will gaze with delight and astonishment. With quality and activity 5 or 4, are great on great occasions, and, when thoroughly roused, manifest splendid talents, and naturally take the lead among men, otherwise not; with activity or quality deficient, must cultivate much in order to become much.

Large. With activity and quality 6 or 7, combine great *power* of mind with great activity; exercise a commanding influence over other minds to sway and persuade; and enjoy and suffer in the extreme; with perceptives 6, can conduct a large business or undertaking successfully; rise to eminence, if not pre-eminence; and evince great originality and power of intellect, strong native sense, superior judgment, great force of character and feeling, and make a conspicuous and enduring mark on the intellectual or business world, or in whatever direction these superior capacities are put forth. With activity and quality 5, are endowed with superior natural talents, yet require strong incentives to call them out; undeveloped by circumstances, may pass through life without accomplishing much, or attracting notice, or evincing more than ordinary parts; but with the perceptive and forcible organs also 6, and talents disciplined and called out, manifest a vigor and energy far above mediocrity; are adequate to carry forward great undertakings, demanding originality and force of mind and character yet are rather indolent. With activity only *average*, possess considerable energy of intellect and feeling, yet seldom manifest it, unless brought out by some powerful stimulus, and are rather too indolent to exert, especially *intellect*.

Full. With quality or activity 6 or 7, and the organs of practical intellect and of the propelling powers large, or very large, although not really *great* in intellect, or deep, are very clever; have considerable talent, and that so distributed that it shows to be even more or better than it really is; are capable of being a good scholar, doing a fine business, and, with advantages and application, of becoming distinguished somewhat, yet inadequate to great undertakings; can not sway an extensive influence, nor become really great, yet have excellent natural capacities; with activity 4 or 5, will do tolerably well, and manifest a common share of talent; with activity only 3, will neither be nor do much worthy of notice.

Average. With activity 6, manifest a quick, clear, sprightly mind, and off-hand talents; and are capable of doing a fair business, especially if the stamina is good; with activity 7, and the organs of the propelling powers and of practical intellect 6 or 7, are capable of doing a good business, and possess fair talent, yet are not original or profound; are quick of perception; have a good practical understanding; will do well in an ordinary business or sphere, yet never manifest greatness, and out of this sphere are commonplace; with activity only 4, discover only an ordinary amount of intellect; are indisposed and inadequate to any important undertaking; yet, in a common sphere, or one that requires only a mechanical routine of business, can do well; with *moderate* or *small* activity, will hardly accomplish or enjoy anything worthy of note.

Moderate. With quality, activity, and the propelling and perceptive faculties 6 or 7, possess an excellent intellect, yet are more showy than sound; with others to plan and direct, can execute to advantage, yet are unable to do much alone; have a very active mind, and are quick of perception, yet, after all, have a contracted intellect; possess only a fair mental caliber, and lack momentum, both of mind and character; with activity only 4, have but a moderate amount of intellect, and even this too sluggish for action, so as neither to suffer nor enjoy much; with activity 3 or 2, are dull, and hardly *compos mentis.*

2 or 1. Are weak in character and inferior in intellect—indeed, simple or idiotic.

This doctrine, that "size is a measure of power," is equally true of different *groups* of organs, and *regions* of the brain. Those who have a large forehead, with a deficient back and side-head, if of good temperament, will be a deep, original *thinker*, but lack force and energy of character; while those who have heavy base and back-head, with a smaller forehead, will possess energy, courage, passion, sociability, and vim, but lack intellectual capacity. But this point will be eliminated hereafter.

10. FORM AS CORRESPONDING WITH CHARACTER.

Nature classifies all her works into orders, genera, and species. Form constitutes her great base of this classification. She always does up similar characteristics in like configurations — apple character in apple shape, fish character in fish configuration, bear nature in bear form, human nature in human shape, and so on throughout all her works. And things alike in character are so in form — all oaks and pines like all. All kernels of wheat, corn, rye, etc., are formed like all others of the same character. All tigers are like all others, and all canines resemble each other in shape and character. All human beings resemble all others in looks and mentality, and monkeys approximate toward man in both shape and character. Therefore, since outline shape indicates outline character, of course all the minute details of shape indicate like peculiarities of character, so that every wrinkle and shade of configuration indicates a like diversity in their mentality. And since the brain is confessedly the organ of the mind, its special form must of course correspond with the special traits of character. Or thus: since universal shape corresponds with universal character, of course the form of the head is as the special characteristics of the mind. And this involves the doctrines of Phrenology. In short, the correspondence between form and character is absolute and universal — on a scale at once the broadest and most minute possible. Then, what *special* forms indicate what *particular* characteristics?

11. HOMOGENEOUSNESS, OR ONENESS OF STRUCTURE.

Every part of everything bears an exact correspondence to that thing AS A WHOLE. Thus, tall-bodied trees have long branches and leaves; short-bodied trees, short branches and roots; and creeping vines, as the grape, honeysuckle, etc., long, slim roots, that run under ground as extensively as their tops do above. The Rhode Island Greening, a large, well-proportioned apple, grows on a tree large in trunk, limb, leaf, and root, and symmetrical, while the gillifleur is conical, and its tree long-limbed, and runs up high to a peak at the top, while flat and broad-topped trees bear wide, flat, sunken-eyed apples. Very thrifty growing trees,

37

as the Baldwin, Fall Pippin, Bartlett, Black Tartarian, etc., generally bear large fruit, while small fruit, as the Seckel Pear, Lady Apple, Bell de Choisy Cherry, etc., grow slowly and have many small twigs and branches. Trees that bear red fruit, as the Baldwin, etc., have red inner bark; while yellow and green-colored fruits grow on trees the inner rind of whose limbs is yellow or green. Peach-trees that bear early peaches have deeply-notched leaves, and the converse of late ones; so that, by these and other physiognomical signs, experienced nurserymen can tell what a given tree bears at first sight.

Correspondingly, long-handed persons have long fingers, toes, arms, legs, bodies, heads, and phrenological organs; while short and broad shouldered persons are short and broad-handed, fingered, faced, nosed, and limbed, and wide and low bodied. When the bones on the hand are prominent, all the bones, nose included, are equally so, and thus of all other characteristics of the hand, and every other portion of all bodies. Hence, a hand thrust through a hole proclaims the general character of its owner, because if it is large or small, hard or soft, strong or weak, firm or flabby, coarse-grained or fine-textured, even or prominent, rough or smooth, small-boned or large-boned, or whatever else, the whole body is built upon the same principle, with which the brain and mentality also correspond. Hence, also, small-nosed persons have little soul, and large-nosed a great deal of character of some kind.

Bonaparte chose large-nosed men for his generals, and the opinion prevails that large noses indicate long heads and strong minds. Not that great noses cause great minds, but that the motive or powerful temperament cause both[6]. Flat noses indicate flatness of mind and character, by indicating a poor, low organic structure[2]. Broad noses indicate large passage-ways to the lungs, and this, large lungs and vital organs, and this, great strength of constitution, and hearty animal passions, along with selfishness; for broad noses, broad shoulders, broad heads, and large animal organs go together. But when the nose is narrow at the base, the nostrils are small, because the lungs are small, and need but small avenues for air; and this indicates a predisposition to consumptive complaints, along with an active brain and nervous system, and a passionate fondness for literary pursuits. Sharp noses indicate a quick, clear, penetrating, searching, knowing, sagacious mind[15], and also a scold; indicate warmth of love, hate, generosity, moral sentiment — indeed, positiveness in everything, while blunt noses indicate and accompany obtuse intellects and perceptions, sluggish feelings, and a soulless character. The Roman nose indicates a martial spirit, love of debate, resistance, and strong passions, while hollow, pug noses indicate a tame, easy, inert, sly character, and straight, finely-formed Grecian noses harmonious characters. Seek their acquaintance. We have chosen our illustrations from the nose, because it is easily seen and described, and renders observation on the character easy and correct. But the *principle* here exemplified applies to all the other organs and portions of the face and body.

And the general forms of the head correspond with those of the body and nose. Where the nose is sharp, all the bones and phrenological organs, and of course mental characteristics, are equally sharp — the whole person being built on the sharp principle, and of breadth, prominence, length, etc.

Tall persons have high heads, and are aspiring, aim high, and seek conspicuosity, while short ones have flat heads, and seek the lower forms of worldly pleasures. Tall persons are rarely mean, though often grasping; but very penurious persons are often broad built. Small persons generally have exquisite mentalities, yet less power — the more precious the article the smaller the package in which it is done up — while great men are rarely dwarfs, though great size often co-exists with sluggishness. To particularize — there are four leading forms which indicate generic characteristics, all existing in every one, yet in different DEGREES. They are.

12. BREADTH AS INDICATING ANIMALITY.

Spherical forms are naturally self-protecting. Roundness protects its possessor. So all round-built animals, as Indian pony, bull-dog, elephant, etc., are round favored and strong-constitutioned, tough, enduring, and very hardy, but less active and sprightly in body and mind. And this applies equally to human beings. Broad-built persons may

"LONG OR ACTIVE"

NO. 11.—CAPTAIN E. KNIGHT.

be industrious, plodding, good feeling, and the like, but love their ease, are not brilliant, and take good care of self. Yet they wear like iron, and unless health has been abused, can live to a great age. This form corresponds with the vital temperament[5].

13. PROMINENCE INDICATES POWER.

"A lean horse for a long pull" is an observation as true as trite. This corresponds with the motive temperament, which it indicates[6].

14. ACTIVITY INDICATED BY LENGTH.

In and by the nature of things length of form facilitates ease of action. Thus, deer, gazelle, grayhound, giraffe, tiger, weasel, eel, and all long and slim animals, are quick-motioned, lively, sprightly, nimble, and agile. The same principle applies equally to persons. Thus, those very long-favored, or in whom this form is:

7. Are as quick as a flash to perceive and do; agile; light-motioned; limber-jointed; nimble; always in motion; restless as the wind; talk too rapidly to be emphatic; have no lazy bones in their bodies; are always moving head, hands, feet, something; are natural scholars; quick to learn and understand; remarkably smart and knowing, and love action—to keep doing—for its own sake; wide awake; eager; uncommonly quick to think and feel; sprightly in conversation; versatile in talent; flexible; suggestive; abounding in idea; apt at most things; exposed to consumption, because action exceeds strength; early ripe; brilliant; liable to premature exhaustion and disease, because the mentality predominates over the vitality, of which the late Captain Knight, who had a world-wide reputation for activity, enterprise, daring, impetuousness, promptness, judgment, earnestness, executiveness, affability, and sprightliness, furnishes a good example.

6. Are active, restless, brisk, stirring, lively, anything but lazy, with a good organism; are quick-spoken; clear-headed; understand matters and things at the first glance; see right into and through business, and all they touch readily; are real workers with head or hands, but prefer

40

head-work; positive; the one thing or the other; and are strongly pre-inclined to the intellectual and moral. Their characters, unless perverted, like their persons, *ascend* instead of descending; and they are better adapted to law, merchandise, banking, or business than to farming, or heavy mechanical work. Yet, if mechanics, should choose those kinds requiring more sprightliness than strength, and mind than muscle.

5 or 4. Have a fair, but only fair, share of natural activity and sprightliness; do what they well can, and with tolerable ease, but do not love action for its own sake.

3. Are rather inactive; do only what they must, and that grudgingly; love to be waited on, but not to wait; and get along with the fewest steps possible; seek a sedentary life, and are as loth to exercise mind as body.

2 and 1. Are downright slothful, lazy, and good for nothing to themselves or others.

To Cultivate: Keep doing, doing, doing all the time, and in as lively and sprightly a manner as possible; and live more on foot than seated.

To Restrain: Sit down and rest when tired, and let the world jog on while you enjoy it. Do only half you think you must, and be content to let the rest go undone. Do for once just see if you can't be lazy. Work as few hours as possible, and take all the advantage you can to get along with the least outlay of strength possible. Do sit down, and enjoy what you have already got, instead of trying to get so much more. Live on your laurels. Don't tear and fret so, if all is not exactly to your liking, but cultivate contentment.

15. EXCITABILITY INDICATED BY SHARPNESS.

All sharp things are, in and by the very nature of their form, penetrating, of which the needle furnishes an example. And this law applies equally to human beings. From time immemorial a sharp nose has been considered indicative of a scolding disposition; yet it is equally so of intensity in the other feelings, as well as those which scold.

7. Are extremely susceptible to impressions of all kinds; intensely excited by trifles; apt to magnify good, bad, everything, far beyond the reality; a creature of impulse and mere feeling; subject to extreme ups and downs of emotion; one hour in the garret, the next in the cellar;

extremely liable to neuralgia and nervous affections; with quality and activity 6 or 7, have ardent desires; intense feelings; keen susceptibilities; enjoy and suffer in the extreme; are wholesouled; sensitive; positive in likes and dislikes; cordial; enthusiastic; impulsive; have hobbies; abound in good feeling, yet are quick-tempered; excitable; liable to extremes; have a great deal of soul or passion, and warmth of feeling; are brilliant writers or speakers, but too refined and sensitive for the mass of mankind; gleam in the career of genius, but burn out the vital powers on the altar of nervous excitability, and like Pollok, H. K. White, McDonald Clarke, and Leggett, fall victims to premature death, and should keep clear from all false excitements and stimulants, mental and physical — tea, coffee, tobacco, drugs, and alcoholic drinks, and cool off and keep cool.

6. Are like 7, only less so; warm-hearted, impetuous, impulsive, full of soul, and too susceptible to external influences; swayed too much by feeling; and need much self-government and coolness.

5. Are sufficiently sensitive and susceptible to exciting causes, yet not passional, nor impulsive; and easily roused, yet not easily carried away by excitements. With activity 6 or 7, are very quick, but perfectly cool; decide and act instantly, yet knowingly; do nothing without thinking, but think and do instantaneously; are never flustered, but combine great rapidity with perfect self-possession.

4. Are like the placid lake — no waves, no noise, and evince the same quiet spirit under all circumstances.

3. Are rather phlegmatic; slow to perceive and feel; rather cold and passionless; rarely ever elated or depressed; neither love nor hate, enjoy nor suffer, with much spirit; are enthusiastic in nothing, and throw little life or soul into expression or action.

2. Are torpid, soulless, listless, spiritless, half asleep about everything, and monotonous and mechanical in everything.

1. Are really stupid, and about as dead and hard as sole-leather — having the texture of humanity, but lacking its life and glow, and enjoy and suffer very little.

To Cultivate: Yield yourself up to the effects or influences, persons and things, naturally operating on you;

seek amusements and excitements; and try to *feel more* than comes natural to you.

To Restrain: First, fulfill all the *health* conditions, so as thereby to allay all false excitement, and secure a quiet state of the body. Eat freely of lettuce, but avoid spices and condiments. Air, exercise, water, and sleep, and avoiding stimulants, constitute your great physical opiates. Second, avoid all unpleasant mental excitements, and by mere force of will cultivate a calm, quiet, luxurious, to-day-enjoying frame of mind. If in trouble, banish it, and make yourself as happy as possible.

These primary forms and characteristics usually combine in different degrees, producing, of course, corresponding differences in the talents and characteristics. Thus, eloquence accompanies breadth combined with sharpness. They create that gushing sympathy, that spontaneous overflowing of soul, that high-wrought, impassioned ecstacy and intensity of emotion in which true eloquence consists, and transmit it less by words than look, gesture, and those touching, melting, soul-stirring, thrilling intonations which storm the citadel of the soul. Hence it can never be written, but must be seen, heard, and felt. This sharpness and breadth produce it first by giving great lungs to exhilarate the speaker, and send the blood frothing and foaming to the brain, and secondly, by conferring the utmost excitability and intensity of emotion, and it is in this exhilaration that real eloquence mainly consists. This sharp and broad form predominates in Bascom, whom Clay pronounced the greatest natural orator he ever heard; in Chapin and Beecher, to-day confessedly our finest speakers in the pulpit or the rostrum; in Everett; in "the old man eloquent," indeed, both the Adamses; in Dr. Bethune, and a host of others. Still, in Patrick Henry, Pitt, and John B. Gough, each unequaled in his day and sphere, the *sharp* combine with the *long*. This gives activity united with excitability. Yet this form gives also the poetic more than the oratorical — gives the *impassioned* which is the soul of both.

Authorship, again, is usually accompanied by the long, prominent, and sharp. Reference is not now had to flippant scribblers of exciting newspaper squibs, or even of dashing editorials, or highfalutin productions, nor to mere compilers, but to the authors of deep, sound, original, philosophical, clear-headed, labored productions. It predominates in Revs. Jonathan Edwards, Wilbur Fiske, N. Taylor, E. A. Parke, Leonard Bacon, Albert Barnes, Oberlin, Pres. Day, Drs. Parish and Rush, Hitchcock, B. F. Butler, Hugh L. White, Dr. Caldwell, Elias Hicks, Franklin, Alexander Hamilton, Chief-Justice Marshall, Calhoun, John Q. Adams, Percival, Noah Webster, George Combe, Lucretia Mott, Catherine Waterman, Mrs. Sigourney, and nearly every distinguished author and scholar.

THE POETIC, OR LONG AND SHARP FORM.

Poetry inheres in various forms. Some distinguished poets are broad and sharp, others long and sharp, but all sharp. Those who evolve the highest, finest, and most fervid style and cast of sentiment, have more of the long, yet less of the prominent, yet with the long a predominance of the sharp, and are often quite tall. Wm. C. Bryant furnishes an excellent illustration of this shape, as his character does of its accompanying mentality. Those who poetize the passions are, like orators, broad and sharp, of whom Byron furnishes an example in poetry and configuration. The best combination of forms for writers and scholars is the sharp predominant, long next, prominent next and all conspicuous. The best form for contractors, builders, managers of men and large mechanical operations, is the broad and prominent combined. But they should *not* be slim. A farmer may have any form but a spindling one, yet a horticulturist or nurseryman may be slim.

16. RESEMBLANCE BETWEEN MEN AND ANIMALS.

That certain men "look like" one or another species of animals is an ancient observation. And when in looks, also in character. That is, some have both the lion, or bull-dog, or eagle, or squirrel expression of face, and likewise traits of character. Thus, Daniel Webster was called the "Lion of the North," from his general resemblance in form, having shoulders, hair, and general expression to that king of beasts; and a lion he indeed was, in his sluggishness when at his ease, but power when roused; in his magnanimity to opponents, and the power of his passions.

He had a distinguished contemporary, whose color,

THE MENTAL-MOTIVE TEMPERAMENT.

NO. 12.—WILLIAM CULLEN BRYANT.

NO. 13.—DANIEL WEBSTER.—THE LION FACE.

44

expression of countenance, manners, everything, resembled those of the fox, and foxy indeed he was, in character as well as looks, and introduced into the political machinery of our country that wire-working, double-game policy and chicanery, which has done more to corrupt our ever-glorious institutions than everything else combined, even endangering their very existence. Freemen, hunt it down.

Those who resemble the bull-dog are broad-built, round favored, square-faced, round-headed, having a forehead square, and perhaps prominent, but low; mouth rendered square by the projection of the eye or canine teeth, and smallness of those in front; corners of the mouth drawn down; and voice deep, guttural, growling, and snarling. Such, if fed, will bark and bite *for* you, but, if provoked, will lay right hold of you, and hold on till you or they perish in the struggle. And when this form is found on female shoulders. "the Lord deliver you."

Tristam Burges, called in Congress the "Bald Eagle," from his having the aquiline or eagle-bill nose, a projection in the upper lip, falling into an indentation in the lower, his eagle-shaped eyes and eyebrows, as seen in the accompanying engraving, was eagle-like in character, and the most sarcastic, tearing, and soaring man of his day, John Randolph excepted. And whoever has a long, hooked, hawkbill, or Roman nose, wide mouth, spare form, prominence at the lower and middle part of the forehead, is very fierce when assailed, high tempered, vindictive, efficient, and aspiring, and will fly higher and farther than others.

Tigers are always spare, muscular, long, full over the eyes, largemouthed, and have eyes slanting downward from their outer to inner angles; and human beings thus physiognomically characterized, are fierce, domineering, revengeful, most enterprising, not over humane, a terror to enemies, and conspicuous somewhere.

Swine — fat, loggy, lazy, good-dispositioned, flat and hollow-nosed — have their cousins in large-abdomened, pug-nosed, double-chinned, talkative, story-enjoying, beer-loving, good-feeling and feeding, yes-yes humans, who love some easy business, but hate hard work.

Horse, oxen, sheep, owls, doves, snakes, and even frogs, etc., also have their men and women cousins, with their accompanying characters.

These resemblances are plain, but more difficult to de-

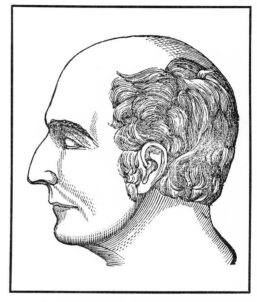

NO. 14. — TRISTAM BURGES. — THE EAGLE FACE.

45

scribe; but the voice, forms of mouth, nose, and chin are the best bases of observation.

17. BEAUTIFUL, HOMELY, AND OTHER FORMS.

In accordance with this general law, that shape is as character, well-proportioned persons have harmony of features and well-balanced minds; whereas those, some of whose features stand right out, and others fall far in, have uneven, ill-balanced characters, so that homely, disjointed exteriors indicate corresponding interiors, while evenly-balanced and exquisitely formed men and women have well-balanced and susceptible mentalities. Hence, woman, more beautiful than man, has finer feelings and greater perfection of character, yet is less powerful—and the more beautifully formed the more exquisite and perfect the mentality. Nature never deceives—never clothes that in a beautiful, attractive exterior which is intrinsically bad or repellant. True, the handsomest women sometimes make the greatest scolds, just as the sweetest things, when soured, become correspondingly sour. The finest things, when perverted, become the worst. These two extremes are the worst tempered—those naturally beautiful and exquisitely organized, that when perverted they become proportionally bad, and those naturally ugly-formed are naturally bad-dispositioned.

Yet homely persons are often excellent tempered, benevolent, talented, etc., because they have a few powerful traits, and also features—the very thing we are explaining—that is, they have extremes alike of face and character. Thus it is that every diversity of character has its correspondence in both the physiognomical form and organic texture.

18. WALK AS INDICATING CHARACTER.

As already shown, texture corresponds with character[2], and motion with texture, and therefore character. Those whose motions are awakward yet easy, possess much efficiency and positiveness of character yet lack polish; and just in proportion as they become refined in mind will their movements be correspondingly improved. A short and quick step indicates a brisk and active but rather con-

46

tracted mind, whereas those who take long steps generally
have long heads; yet if the step is slow, they will make
comparatively little progress, while those whose step is
long and quick will accomplish proportionately much,
and pass most of their competitors on the highway of
life. Their heads and plans, too, will partake of the same
far-reaching character evinced in their carriage. Those who
sluff or drag their heels, drag and drawl in everything;
while those who walk with a springing, bounding step,
abound in mental snap and spring. Those whose walk is
mincing, affected, and artificial, rarely, if ever, accomplish
much; whereas those who walk carelessly, that is, naturally,
are just what they appear to be, and put on nothing for
outside show. Those who in walking roll from side to side,
lack directness of character, and side every way, according
to circumstances; whereas those who take a bee line — that
is, whose body moves neither to the right nor left, but
straight forward — have a corresponding directness of purpose, and oneness of character. Those, also, who tetter up
and down when they walk, rising an inch or two every
step, will have many corresponding ups and downs in life,
because of their irregularity of character and feeling.
Those, too, who make a great ado in walking, will make
much needless parade in everything else, and hence spend a
great amount of useless steam in accomplishing nothing;
whereas those who walk easily, or expend little strength in
walking, will accomplish great results with but little outlay of strength, both mental and physical. In short, every
individual has his own peculiar mode of moving, which
exactly accords with his mental character; so that, as far as
you can see such modes, you can decipher such outlines of
character.

To dancing these principles apply equally. A small, deli-
cately molded, fine skinned, pocket-Venus, whose motions
are light, easy, waving, and rather characterless, who puts
forth but little strength in dancing, is very exquisite in
feelings, but rather light in the upper story, lacking sense,
thought, and strength of mind; but a large, raw-boned,
bouncing Betty, who throws herself far up, and comes
down good and solid, when she dances, is a strong, powerful, determined character, well suited to do up rough work,
but destitute of polish, though possessed of great force.
Some dance all dandy, others all business, yet few all intellect.

19. LAUGH AS CORRESPONDING WITH CHARACTER.

Laughter is very expressive of character. Those who laugh very heartily have much cordiality and whole-souledness of character, except that those who laugh heartily at trifles have much feeling, yet little sense. Those whose giggles are rapid, but light, have much intensity of feeling, yet lack power; whereas those who combine rapidity with force in laughing, combine them in character. One of the greatest workers I ever employed, I hired just because he laughed heartily, his giggles being rapid *and* loud. But a colored domestic who laughed very rapidly, but lightly, took a great many steps to do almost nothing, and though she worked fast, accomplished little. Vulgar persons always laugh vulgarly, and refined persons show refinement in their laugh. Those who ha, ha right out, unreservedly, have no cunning, and are open-hearted in everything; while those who suppress laughter, and try to control their countenances in it, are more or less secretive. Those who laugh with their mouths closed are non-committal; while those who throw it wide open are unguarded and unequivocal in character. Those who, suppressing laughter for a while, burst forth volcano-like, have strong characteristics, but are well governed, yet violent when they give way to their feelings. Then there is the intellectual laugh, the love laugh, the horse laugh, the philoprogenitive laugh, the friendly laugh, and many other kinds of laugh, each indicative of corresponding mental developments.

20. THE MODE OF SHAKING HANDS.

Also expresses character. Thus, those who give a tame and loose hand, and shake slightly, have a cold, if not heartless and selfish disposition, rarely sacrificing much for others, are probably conservatives, and lack warmth and soul. But those who grasp firmly, and shake heartily, have a corresponding whole-souledness of character, are hospitable, and will sacrifice business to friends; while those who bow low when they shake hands, add deference to friendship, and are easily led, for good or bad, by friends.

21. MOUTH AND EYES PECULIARLY EXPRESSIVE OF CHARACTER.

Every mouth differs from ever other, and indicates a coincident character. Large mouths express a corresponding quantity of mentality, while small ones indicate a lesser amount. A coarsely formed mouth indicates power, while one finely formed indicates exquisite susceptibilities. Hence small, delicately-formed mouths indicate only common minds, with very fine feelings and much perfection of character. Whenever the muscles about the mouth are distinct, the character is correspondingly positive, and the reverse. Those who open their mouths wide and frequently, thereby evince an open soul, while closed mouths, unless to hide deformed teeth, are proportionately secretive.

And thus of the eyes. In traveling west, in 1837, we examined a man who made great pretension to religion, but was destitute of Conscience, whom we afterward ascertained to be an impostor. While attending the Farmer's Club, in New York, this scamp came in, and besides keeping his eyes half closed half the time, frequently shut them so as to peep out upon those present, but opened them barely enough to allow vision. Those who keep their eyes half shut are peekaboos and eavesdroppers.

Those, too, who keep their coats buttoned up, fancy high-necked and closed dresses, etc., are equally non-communicative, but those who like open, free, flowing garments, are equally open-hearted and communicative.

22. INTONATIONS AS EXPRESSING CHARACTER.

Whatever makes a noise, from the deafening roar of sea, cataract, and whirlwind's mighty crash, through all forms of animal life, to the sweet and gentle voice of woman, makes a sound which agrees perfectly with the maker's character. Thus the terrific roar of the lion, and the soft cooing of the dove, correspond exactly with their respective dispositions; while the rough and powerful bellow of the bull, the fierce yell of the tiger, the coarse, guttural moan of the hyena, the swinish grunt, the sweet warblings of birds, in contrast with the raven's croak and owl's hoot, each corresponds perfectly with their respective characteristics. And this law holds equally true of man. Hence human intonations are as superior to brutal as human character exceeds animal. Accordingly, the peculiarities of all human beings are expressed in their voices and mode of speaking. Coarse-grained and powerful animal organizations have a coarse, harsh, and grating voice, while in exact proportion as persons become refined and elevated mentally, will their tones of voice become correspondingly refined and perfected. We little realize how much of character we infer from this source. Thus, some female friends are visiting me transiently. A male friend, staying with me, enters the room, is seen by my female company, and his walks, dress, manners, etc., closely scrutinized, yet he says nothing, and retires, leaving a comparatively indistinct impression as to his character upon my female visitors, whereas, if he simply said yes or no, the mere sound of his voice communicates to their minds much of his character, and serves to fix distinctly upon their minds clear and correct general ideas of his mentality.

The barbarous races use the guttural sounds more than the civilized. Thus Indians talk more down the throat than white men, and thus of all, whether lower or higher in the human scale. Those whose voices are clear and distinct have clear minds, while those who only half form their words, or are heard indistinctly, say by deaf persons, are mentally obtuse. Those who have sharp, shrill intonations have correspondingly intense feelings, and equal sharpness both of anger and kindness, as is exemplified by every scold in the world; whereas those with smooth or sweet voices have corresponding evenness and goodness of character. Yet, contradictory as it may seem, these same persons not unfrequently combine both sharpness and softness of voice, and such always combine them in character. There are also the intellectual, the moral, the animal, the selfish, the benignant, the mirthful, the devout, the love, and many other intonations, each accompanying corresponding peculiarities of characters. In short, every individual is compelled, by every word uttered, to manifest something of the true character — a sign of character as diversified as correct.

23. COLOR AND TEXTURE OF HAIR, SKIN, BEARD, ETC.

Everything in nature is colored, inside and out; and the color always corresponds with the character. Nature paints her coarse productions in coarse drab, but adorns all her finer, more exquisite productions with her most beautiful colors. Thus, highly-colored fruits are always highly-flavored; the birds of the highest quality are arrayed in the most gorgeous tints and hues.

So, also, *particular* colors signify particular qualities. Thus, throughout all nature black signifies power, or a great amount of character; red, the ardent, loving, intense, concentrated, positive; green, immaturity; yellow, ripeness, richness, etc. Hence all black animals are powerful, of which bear, Morgan horse, black snake, etc., furnish examples. So black fruits, as blackberry, black raspberry, whortle berry, black Tartarian, cherry, etc., are highly-flavored and full of rich juices. So, also, the dark races, as Indian and African, are strong, muscular, and very tough. All red fruits are acid, as the strawberry; but the darker they are the sweeter, as the Balwin, gillifleur, etc.; while striped apples blend the sweet with the sour. But whatever is growing, that is, still immature, is green; but all grasses, grains, fruits, etc., pass, while ripening, from the green to the yellow, and sometimes through the red. The red and yellow fruits are always delicious. Other primary colors signify other characteristics.

Now, since coarseness and fineness of texture indicate coarse and fine-grained feelings and characters[2], and since black signifies power, and red ardor, therefore coarse black hair and skin signify great power of character of some kind, along with considerable tendency to the sensual; yet fine black hair and skin indicate strength of character, along with purity and goodness. Dark-skinned nations are always behind the light-skinned in all the improvements of the age, as well as in the higher and finer manifestations of humanity. So, too, dark-haired persons, like Webster, sometimes called "Black Dan," possess great power of intellect and propensity, yet lack the finer and more delicate shadings of sensibility and purity. Coarse black hair and skin, and coarse red hair and whiskers, indicate powerful animal passions, together with corresponding strength of character; while fine, or light, or auburn hair indicates quick susceptibilities, together with refinement and good taste. Fine dark or brown hair indicates the combination of exquisite susceptibilities with great strength of character, while auburn hair, with a florid countenance, indicates the highest order of sentiment and intensity of feeling, along with corresponding purity of character, combined with the highest capacities for enjoyment and suffering. And the intermediate colors and textures indicate intermediate mentalities. Curly hair or beard indicate a crisp, excitable, and variable disposition, and much diversity of character — now blowing hot, now cold — along with intense love and hate, gushing, glowing emotions, brilliancy, and variety of talent. So look out for ringlets; they betoken April weather — treat them gently, lovingly, and you will have the brightest, clearest sunshine, and the sweetest, balmiest breezes; but ruffle them, and you raise — oh, what a storm! a very hurricane, changeable, now so very hot, now so cold — that you had better not ruffle them. And this is doubly true of auburn curls; though auburn ringlets need but a little right, kind, fond treatment to render them all as fair and delightful as the brightest spring morning.

Straight, even, smooth, and glossy hair indicates strength, harmony, and evenness of character, and hearty, whole-souled affections, as well as a clear head and superior talents; while stiff, straight, black hair and beard indicate a coarse, strong, rigid, straightforward character. Abundance of hair and beard signifies virility and a great amount of character; while a thin beard signifies sterility and a thinly settled upper story, with rooms to let; so that the beard is very significant of character. And we shall soon see a reason why it should not be shorn.

Coarse-haired persons should never turn dentists or clerks, but seek some out-door employment; and would be better contented with rough, hard work than a light or sedentary occupation, although mental and sprightly occupations would serve to refine and improve them; while dark and fine-haired persons may choose purely intellectual occupations, and become lecturers or writers with fair prospects of success. Red-haired persons should seek out-door employment, for they require a great amount of air and exercise; while those who have light, fine hair should choose occupations involving taste and mental acumen, yet take bodily exercise enough to tone up and invigorate their system.

Generally, whenever skin, hair, or features are fine or coarse, the others are equally so[11]. Yet some inherit fineness from one parent, and coarseness from the other, while the color of the eye generally corresponds with that of the skin, and expresses character. Light eyes indicate warmth of feeling, and dark eyes power.

The mere expression of the eye conveys precise ideas of the existing and predominant states of the mentality and physiology. As long as the constitution remains unimpaired, the eye is clear and bright, but becomes languid and soulless in proportion as the brain has been enfeebled. Wild, erratic persons have a half-crazed expression of eye, while calmness, benignancy, intelligence, purity, sweetness, love, lasciviousness, anger, and all the other mental affections, express themselves quite as distinctly by the eye as voice, or any other mode.

24. REDNESS AND PALENESS OF FACE.

Thus far our remarks have appertained to the constant colors of the face, yet those colors are often diversified or changed for the time being.

Thus, at one time the whole countenance will be pale, at another very red; each of which indicates the existing states of body and mind. Or thus: when the system is in a perfectly healthy state, the whole face will be suffused with the glow of health and beauty, and have a red, but never an inflamed aspect; yet any permanent injury of health, which prostrates the bodily energies, will change this florid complexion into dullness of countenance, indicating that but little blood comes to the surface or flows to the head, and a corresponding stagnation of the physical and mental powers. Yet, after a time, this dullness frequently gives way to a fiery redness; not the floridness of health, but the redness of inflammation and false excitement, which indicates a corresponding depreciation of the mental faculties. Very red-faced persons, so far from being the most healthy, are frequently the most diseased, and are correspondingly more animal and sensual in character; because physiological inflammation irritates the propensities more, relatively, than the moral and intellectual faculties, though it may, for the time being, increase the latter also. When the moral and intellectual faculties greatly predominate over the animal, redness may not cause coarse animality, because, while it heightens the animal nature, it also increases the intellectual and moral, which, being the larger,

53

hold them in check; but when the animal about equals or exceeds the moral and intellectual, this inflammation evinces a greater increase of animality than intellectuality and morality. Gross sensualists and depraved sinners generally have a fiery red countenance. Stand aloof from them, for their passions are all on fire, ready to ignite and explode on provocations so slight that a healthy physiology would scarcely notice them. This point can hardly be more fully intelligible; but let readers note the difference between a healthy floridness of face and the fiery redness of drunkards, debauchees, meat-eaters, etc. Nor does an inflamed physiology merely increase the animal nature, but gives it a far more *depraved* and sensual cast, thereby doubly increasing the depraved tendencies.

25. PHYSIOGNOMY A TRUE SCIENCE.

That nature has instituted a science of Physiognomy as a *facial* expression of mind and character is proclaimed by the very instincts of man and animals. Can not the very dog tell whether his master is pleased or displeased, and the very slave, who will make a good, and who a cruel master—and all by the expressions of the countenance? The fact is, that nature compels all her productions to proclaim their interior virtues—their own shame, even—and hoists a true flag of character at their masthead, so that he who runs may read.

Thus, all apples both tell that they possess apple character by their apple shape[10], but what *kind* of apple—whether good, bad, or indifferent—by their special forms, colors, etc.; all fish, not only that they are fish, but whether trout or sturgeon; and all humans that they are human by their outline aspect. And thus of all things.

Moreover, though all human beings have the general human form and features—though all have eyes, nose, mouth, skin, etc., yet every one has a *different* face and look from every other. And more yet, the *same* person has a very different facial look at different times, according as he is angry or friendly, etc. And always the *same* look when in the same mood. Of course, then, something *causes* this expression—especially, since *all* who are angry, friendly, etc., have one general or *similar* expression; that is, one look expresses anger, another affection, another devotion,

54

another kindness, etc. And since nature always works by means, she must needs have her *physiognomical* tools. Nor are they under the control of will, for they act *spontaneously*. We can not *help*, whether we will or no, laughing when merry, even though in church, pouting when provoked, and expressing all our mental operations, down even to the very innermost recesses of our souls, in and by our countenances. And with more minuteness and completeness than by words, especially when the expressions are intense or peculiar. Spirits are said to converse mainly by their expressions of countenance — to *look* their thoughts and emotions, instead of talking them.

PHYSIOGNOMY.

Certain it is that the countenance expresses a greater amount of thought and feeling, together with their nicer shades and phases, than words can possibly communicate. By what means, then, is this effected? By magnetic centers, called poles. Every physical and mental organ has its pole stationed in a given part of the face, so that, when such organ acts, it influences such poles, and contracts those facial muscles which express this action. That there exists an intimate relation between the stomach and one part of the face, the lungs and another, etc., is proved by the fact that consumptive patients always have a hectic flush on the cheek, just externally from the lower portion of the nose, while inactive lungs cause paleness, and healthy ones give the rosy cheek; and that dyspeptic patients are always lank and thin opposite the double teeth, while those whose digestion is good are full between the corners of the mouth and lower portion of the ears. Since, therefore, some of the states of some of the internal organs express themselves in the face, of course every organ of the body must do the same. The magnetic pole of the heart is in the chin. Hence, those whose circulation is vigorous, have broad and rather prominent chins; while those who are small and narrow-chinned have feeble hearts; and thus all the other internal organs have their magnetic poles in various parts of the face. Now, since the beard covers these facial poles of the internal organs, of course it helps to guard heart, viscera, etc., from atmospheric changes. Obviously, it was not created for naught, and can not be amputated with impunity.

It also protects the throat and chest, especially of elderly men. And why shave off this natural sign of masculinity? Shaving is, to say the least of it, rather *barbarous*.

So all the phrenological organs have likewise their facial poles, some of which are as follows: That of Acquisitiveness is on each side of the middle portion of the nose, at its junction with the cheek, causing breadth of nose in proprtion to the money-grasping instincts, as in Jews, while a narrow nose indicates a want of the speculative turn. Firmness is indicated by length, prominence, and a compression of the upper lip. Hence, when we would exhort to determined perseverance, we say, "Keep a stiff upper lip." Self-Esteem has its pole externally from that of Firmness, and between the outer portion of the nose and the mouth, causing a fullness, as if a quid were under the upper lip. The affections have their poles in the edges of the lips; hence the philosophy of kissing. The pole of Mirthfulness is located outward and upward from the outer corners of the mouth; hence the drawing up of these corners in laughter. Approbativeness has its pole directly outward from these corners, and hence the approbative laugh does not turn the corners of the mouth upward, but draws them straight back, or outwardly. Like locations are assigned to all the other organs. That physiognomy has its science — that fixed and absolute relations exist between the phrenological organs and given portions of the face — is an unquestionable truth. By these and other means the inherent character of every living being and thing gushes out through every organ of the body, every avenue of the soul; and both brute and man have a character-reading faculty, to take intuitive cognizance of the mental operations. Nor will she let any one lie, any more than lie herself, but compels all to carry their hearts in their hands, so that all acquainted with these signs may read them through. If we attempt deception, the very effort convicts us. And if all nature's signs of character were fully understood, all could read, not only all the main characters of all they see, but even most of the thoughts and feelings passing in the mind for the time being — a gift worth more than Astor's millions. And the great rule for reading one and all, is, "Notice all one says and does, ask *why*, what faculty did or said this, or that, and, especially, yield yourself up to drink in or be affected by these manifestations."

26. DEFINITION AND PROOF.

Phrenology points out those relations established by nature between given developments and conditions of Brain and corresponding manifestations of Mind. Its simple yet comprehensive definition is this: every faculty of the mind is manifested by means of a particular portion of the Brain, called its organ, the size of which, other things being equal, is proportionate to its power of function. For example: it teaches that parental love is manifested by one organ, or portion of the brain; appetite by another, reason by a third, etc., which are the larger in proportion as these corresponding mental powers are stronger.

Are, then, particular portions of the brain larger or smaller in proportion as particular mental characteristics are stronger or weaker? Our short-hand mode of proof is illustrated by the following anecdote. A Mr. Juror once summoned to attend court, died before its sitting. It therefore developed upon Mr. Simple to state to the court the reason of his non-appearance. Accordingly, when Mr. Juror's name was called, Mr. Simple responded, "May it please the court, I have twenty-one reasons to offer why Mr. Juror is not in attendance. The first is, he is Dead. The second is—" "That One will answer," replied the judge. "One *such* reason is amply sufficient." But few of the many proofs that Phrenology is true will here be stated, yet those few are Decisive.

Firstly. The Brain is the Organ of the Mind. This is assumed, because too universally admitted to require proof.

Secondly. Is the brain, then, a Single organ, or is it a bundle of organs? Does the Whole brain think, remember, love, hate, etc., or does *one portion* reason, another worship, another love money, etc.? This is the determining point. To decide it affirmatively, establishes Phrenology; negatively, overthrows it. It is proved by the following facts.

The Exercise of Different Functions Simultaneously: We can walk, think, talk, remember, love, and many other things, all Together—the mind being, in this respect, like a stringed instrument, with several strings vibrating at a time, instead of like a flute, which stops the preceding sound when it commences a succeeding one; whereas, if it were a single organ, it must stop thinking the instant it began to talk, could not love a friend and

57

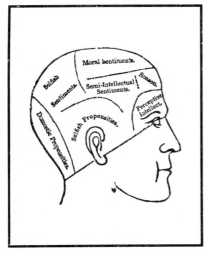

NO. 15.—GROUPING OF ORGANS.

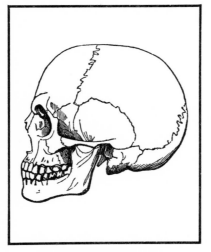

NO. 16.—HUMAN SKULL.

express that love at the same time, and could do *but one* thing at once.

Monomania: Since mental derangement is caused only by cerebral disorder, if the brain were a single organ, the Whole mind must be sane or insane together; whereas most insane persons are deranged only on one or two points, a conclusive proof of the plurality of the organs of the brain and of the mental faculties.

Diversity of Talent, or the fact that some are remarkable for sense, but poor in memory, or the reverse; some forgetting names, but remembering faces; some great mechanics, but poor speakers, or the reverse; others splendid natural singers, but no mechanics, etc., conducts us to the same conclusion.

Injuries of the Brain furnish still more demonstrative proof. If Phrenology is true, to inflame Tune, for example, would create a singing disposition; Veneration, a praying desire; Cautiousness, groundless fears; and so of all the other organs. And thus it Is. Nor can this class of facts be evaded. They abound in all phrenological works, especially periodicals, and drive and clench the nail of proof.

Comparative Phrenology, or the perfect coincidence existing between the developments and the characters of animals, constitutes the highest proof of all. Since man and brute are fashioned upon one great model—since the same great optical laws govern the vision of both, the same principle of muscular contraction which enables the eagle to soar aloft beyond our vision, and the whale to furrow and foam the mighty deep, also enables man to walk forth in the conscious pride of his strength, and thus of all their other common functions—of course, if man is created in accordance with certain phrenological laws, brutes must also be, and the reverse. If, then, this science is true of either, it must be true of both—must pervade all forms of organization. What, then, are the facts?

Phrenology locates the animal propensities at the Sides of the head, between and around the ears; the social affections in its Back and lower portion; the aspiring faculties in its Crown; the moral on its Top, and the intellectual on the Forehead; the perceptives, which relate us to matter, Over the Eyes; and the reflectives, in the Upper part of the forehead. (See cut No. 15.)

Now, since brutes possess at least only weak moral and reflective faculties, they should, if Phrenology were true, have little top-head, and thus it is. Not one of all the following drawings of animals have much brain in either the reflective or moral region. Almost all their mentality consists of the Animal Propensities, and nearly all their brain is found Between and Around Their Ears, just where, according to Phrenology, it should be. Yet the skulls of all human beings rise high above the eyes and ears, and are long on top, that is, have full intellectual and moral Organs, as we know they possess these mental Elements. Compare the accompanying human skull with those of brutes Those of snakes, frogs, turtles, alligators, etc., slope straight back from the nose; that is, have almost no moral or intellectual organs; tigers, dogs, lions, etc., have a little more, yet how insignificant compared with man, while monkeys are between them in these organs and their faculties. Here, then, is Inductive proof of Phrenology as extensive as the whole brute creation on the one hand, contrasted with the entire human family on the other.

Again, Destructiveness is located by Phrenology over the ears, so as to render the head wide in proportion as this organ is developed. Accordingly, all carnivorous animals should be wide-headed at the ears; all herbivorous, narrow. And thus they are, as seen in tigers, hyenas, bears, cats, foxes, ichneumons, etc., compared with rabbits, sheep, etc. (Cuts 19, 20, 21, 22, 23, 24, 25, 26, 27, 28, 29, and 30.)

To large Destructiveness, cats, foxes, ichneumons, etc., add large Secretiveness, both in character and head.

Fowls, in like manner, correspond perfectly in head and character with the phrenological requisitions. Thus, owls, hawks, eagles, etc., have very wide heads, and ferocious dispositions; while hens, turkeys, etc., have narrow heads, and little Destructiveness in character. (Cuts 31, 32, 33, and 34.)

The crow (cut 34) has very large Secretiveness and Cautiousness in the head, as it is known to have in character.

Monkeys, too, bear additional testimony to the truth of phrenological science. They possess, in character, strong perceptive powers, but weak reflectives, powerful propensities, and feeble moral elements. Accordingly, they are full over the eyes, but slope straight back at the reasoning and moral faculties, while the propensities engross most of their brain.

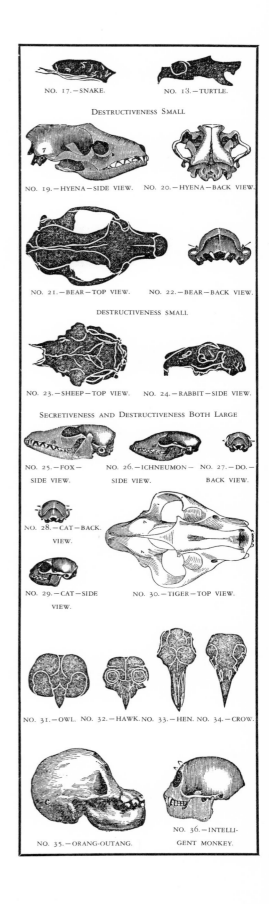

NO. 17.—SNAKE.　　NO. 18.—TURTLE.

DESTRUCTIVENESS SMALL

NO. 19.—HYENA—SIDE VIEW.　　NO. 20.—HYENA—BACK VIEW.

NO. 21.—BEAR—TOP VIEW.　　NO. 22.—BEAR—BACK VIEW.

DESTRUCTIVENESS SMALL

NO. 23.—SHEEP—TOP VIEW.　　NO. 24.—RABBIT—SIDE VIEW.

SECRETIVENESS AND DESTRUCTIVENESS BOTH LARGE

NO. 25.—FOX—　　NO. 26.—ICHNEUMON—　NO. 27.—DO.—
SIDE VIEW.　　　　SIDE VIEW.　　　　BACK VIEW.

NO. 28.—CAT—BACK.
VIEW.

NO. 29.—CAT—SIDE
VIEW.　　　　NO. 30.—TIGER—TOP VIEW.

NO. 31.—OWL. NO. 32.—HAWK. NO. 33.—HEN. NO. 34.—CROW.

NO. 35.—ORANG-OUTANG.　　NO. 36.—INTELLI-
GENT MONKEY.

The Orang-outang has more forehead — larger intellectual organs, both perceptive and reflective — than any other animal, with some of the moral sentiments, and accordingly is called the "half-reasoning man," its phrenology corresponding perfectly with its character.

PERCEPTIVES LARGER THAN REFLECTIVES.

The various races also accord with phrenological science. Thus, Africans generally have full perceptives, and large Tune and Language, but retiring Causality, and accordingly are deficient in reasoning capacity, yet have excellent memories and lingual and musical powers.

Indians possess extraordinary strength of the propensities and perceptives, yet have no great moral or inventive power; and, hence, have very wide, round, conical, and rather low heads, but are large over the eyes.

Indian skulls can always be selected from Caucasian, just by these developments; while the Caucasian race is superior in reasoning power and moral elevation to all the other races, and, accordingly, has a higher and bolder forehead, and more elevated and elongated top head.

Finally, contrast the massive foreheads of all giant-minded men — Bacons, Franklins, Miltons, etc., with the low, retiring foreheads of idiots. In short, every human, ever brutal head, is constructed throughout strictly on phrenological principles. Ransack air, earth, and water, and not one palapable exception ever has been, ever can be, adduced. This Wholesale view of this science precludes the possibility of mistake. Phrenology is therefore a Part and Parcel of Nature — A Universal Fact.

THE PHILOSOPHY OF PHRENOLOGY.

All truth bears upon its front unmistakable evidence of its divine origin, in its philosophical consistency, fitness, and beauty, whereas all untruth is grossly and palpably deformed. All truth, also, harmonizes with all other truth, and conflicts with all error, so that, to ascertain what is true, and detect what is false, is perfectly easy. Apply this test, intellectual reader, to one after another of the doctrines taught by Phrenology. But enough on this point of proofs. Let us proceed to its illustration.

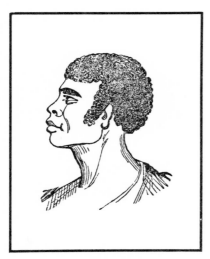

NO. 37. — AFRICAN.

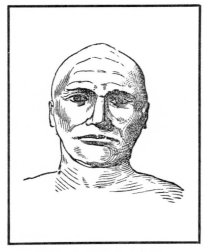

NO. 38. — INDIAN CHIEF.

The brain is not only the organ of the mind, the dome of thought, the palace of the soul, but is equally the organ of the *body*, over which it exerts an all-potent influence for good or ill, to weaken or stimulate, to kill or make alive. In short, the brain is the organ of the body in general, and of all its organs in particular. It sends forth those nerves which keep muscles, liver, bowels, and all the other bodily organs, in a high or low state of action; and, more than all other causes, invites or repels disease, prolongs or shortens life, and treats the body as its galley-slave. Hence, healthy cerebral action is indispensable to bodily health, while a longing, pining, dissatisfied, fretful, or troubled state of mind is most destructive of health, and productive of disease; so is violence in any and all the passions; indeed, the state of the mind has mainly to do with that of the health. Even dyspepsia is more a mental than physical condition, and to be cured first and mainly by banishing that agitated, flashy, eager, craving state of mind, and securing instead a calm, quiet, let-the-world-slide state; nor will any physical applicances avail much without this mental restorative. Hence, too, we walk or work so much more easily and efficiently when we take an *interest* in what we do. Therefore, those who would be happy or talented must first and mainly keep their Brain vigorous and healthy[3].

The brain is subdivided into two hemispheres, the right and left, by the falciform process of the dura mater—a membrane which dips down one to two inches into the brain, and runs from the root of the nose over to the nape of the neck. This arrangement renders all the phrenological organs Double. Thus, as there are two eyes, ears, etc., so that when one is diseased, the other can carry forward the functions, so there are two lobes to each phrenological organ, one on each side. The brain is divided thus: the feelings occupy that portion commonly covered by the hair, while the forehead is occupied by the intellectual organs. These greater divisions are subdivided into the animal brain, located between and around the ears; the aspiring faculties, which occupy the crown of the head; the moral and religious sentiments, which occupy its top; the physico-perceptives, located over the eyes; and the reflec-

LARGE AND SMALL

NO. 39.—BACON.

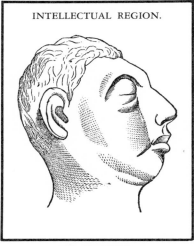

INTELLECTUAL REGION.

NO. 40.—IDIOT.

tives, in the upper portion of the forehead. The predominance of these respective groups produces both particular shape of head and corresponding traits of character. Thus, the head projecting far back behind the ears, and hanging over and downward in the occipital region, indicates very strong domestic ties and social affections, a love of home, its relations and endearments, and a corresponding capacity of being happy in the family, and making family happy. Very wide and round heads, on the contrary, indicate strong animal and selfish propensities, while thin, narrow heads indicate a corresponding want of selfishness and animality. A head projecting far up at the crown indicates an aspiring, self-elevating disposition, proudness of character, and a desire to be and to do something great; while the flattened crown indicates a want of ambition, energy, and aspiration. A head high, long, and wide upon the top, but narrow between the ears, indicates Causality, moral virtue, much practical goodness, and a corresponding elevation of character; while a low and narrow top-head indicates a corresponding deficiency of these humane and religious susceptibilities. A head wide at the upper part of the temples indicates a corresponding desire for personal perfection, together with a love of the beautiful and refined, while narrowness in this region evinces a want of taste, with much coarseness of feeling. Fullness over the eyes indicates excellent practical judgment of matters and things appertaining to property, science, and nature in general; while narrow, straight eyebrows indicate poor practical judgment of matter, things, their qualities, relations, and uses. Fullness from the root of the nose upward indicates great practical talent, love of knowledge, desire to see, and ability to do the right thing at the right time, and in the best way, together with sprightliness of mind; while a hollow in the middle of the forehead indicates want of memory, and inability to show off to advantage. A bold, high forehead indicates strong reasoning capabilities, while a retiring forehead indicates less soundness, but more availability of talent. And thus of other cerebral forms.

62

28. THE NATURAL LANGUAGE OF THE FACULTIES.

Phrenology teaches that every faculty, when active, throws head and body in the direction of the acting organ. Thus, intellect, in the fore part of the head, throws it directly forward, and produces a forward hanging motion of the head. Hence, intellectual men never carry their heads backward and upward, but always forward; and logical speakers move their heads in a straight line, usually forward, toward their audience; while vain speakers carry their heads backward. Hence it is not a good sign to stand so straight as to lean backward, for it shows that the brain is in the *wrong place*—more in the animal than intellectual region. Perceptive intellect, when active, throws out the chin and lower portions of the face; while reflective intellect causes the upper portion of the forehead to hang forward, and draws in the chin, as in the engravings of Franklin, Webster, and other great thinkers. Benevolence throws the head and body slightly forward, leaning toward the object which excites its sympathy; while Veneration causes a low bow, which, the world over, is a token of respect; yet, when Veneration is exercised toward the Deity, as in devout prayer, it throws the head upward; and, as we use intellect at the same time, the head is generally directed forward.

He who meets you with a long, low bow thinks more of you than of himself; but he who greets you with a short, quick bow—who makes half a bow forward, but a bow and a half backward—thinks one of you, and one and a half of himself. Ideality throws the head slightly forward and to one side, as in Washington Irving, a man as gifted in taste and imagination as almost any living writer; and, in his portraits, his finger rests upon this faculty, while in Sterne the finger rests upon Mirthfulness. Very firm men stand straight up and down, inclining not a hair's breadth forward or backward, or to the right or left; hence the expression, "He is an up-and-down man." And this organ is located exactly on a line with the body. Self-Esteem, located in the back and upper portion of the head, throws the head and body upward and backward. Large feeling, pompous persons walk in a very dignified, majestic manner, and throw their heads in the direction of Self-Esteem; while approbative persons throw their heads backward, but to

NO. 41.—WASHINGTON IRVING

63

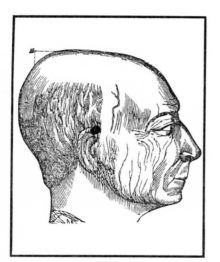

NO. 42.—A CONCEITED SIMPLETON.

one side or both. The difference between the natural language of these two organs being slight, only the practical phrenologist can perfectly distinguish them.

A coxcomb once asking a philosopher, "What makes you hang your head down so? Why don't you hold it up, and look as I do?" was answered: "Look at that field of wheat! The heads that are well filled bend downward, but those that stand up straight are empty."

There is, moreover, a natural language of money-loving, a leaning forward and turning, which carries the head to one side, as if in ardent pursuit of something, and ready to grasp it with outstretched arms; while Alimentiveness, situated lower, hugs itself down to the dainty dish with the greediness of an epicure, better seen than described. The shake of the head is the natural language of Combativeness, and means no, or, I resist you. Those who are combating earnestly shake the head more or less violently, according to the power of the combative feeling, but always shake it slightly inclining *backward*; while Destructiveness, inclining forward, causes a shaking of the head slightly forward, and turning to one side. When a person who threatens you shakes his head violently, and holds it partially backward, and to one side, never fear—he is only barking; but whoever inclines his head to one side, and shakes it violently, will bite, whether possessed of two legs or four. The social affections are located in the *back* part of the head; and, accordingly, woman being more loving than man, when not under the influence of the other faculties, usually inclines her head backward; and when she kisses children, and those she loves, always turns the head directly backward, and rolls it from side to side, on the back of the neck. Thus it is that each of the various postures assumed by individuals expresses the present or permanent activity of their respective faculties.

SECTION II
THE PHRENOLOGICAL FACULTIES

But the highest evidence, most conclusive to a think-ing mind, that Phrenology is true, is this: Whatever is true bears indisputable evidence of its divine origin, in its infinite perfection; while that which is human is im-perfect. If, therefore, Phrenology is true, every part and parcel of it will be perfection itself — in its facts, its philos-ophies, its teachings. And that proposed analysis of the phrenological faculties to which we now proceed will so expound its internal workings as to show whether it is or is not thus perfect or imperfect — true or false.

Its perfection is seen especially in these three aspects:

First, the grouping and location of its organs. Through-out all nature, the *place* of every organ serves to facilitate its function. Thus, foot, eye, heart, each bone and organ, can fulfill its office better, placed where it is, than if placed anywhere else. And if Phrenology is true, each of the phrenological organs will be so located, both absolutely and as regards the others, that their position shall aid the end they subserve. And their being thus placed furnishes additional proof that Phrenology is divine.

Though the phrenological organs were discovered, some in one century and continent, and others in another, yet on casting the analytical eye over them all, we find them *self-*classified by their geographical position in the head. When on first taking a general survey of the phrenological organs, thinking to improve the classification somewhat, I adopted this rule, beginning at the lowest posterior organs in the head, and classifying them in accordance with the *geograph-ical position* upward and forward in the head; and have seen since no chance to improve on this general principle.

And what is more, all those organs are in groups whose faculties perform analogous functions. Thus, all the social affections are grouped in one portion of the head — the back and lower; and their position is beneath and below all, just as their function is basilar, yet comparatively un-seen. Neither do these organs obtrude themselves on our vision; nor do we stand on the corners of the streets to pro-claim how much we love husband, wife, children, or friends. So the animal organs are placed at the top of the spi-nal column and base of the brain, or just where the nerves from the various portions of the body ramify on the brain. Now the office of these organs is to carry forward the various bodily wants. This, nature fulfills, by placing them right at the head of those nerves which enable them to communicate with the body in the most perfect manner possible. So the organs in the top of the head, being the highest of all, fulfill the most exalted functions of all. By a law of structure, as we rise from the sole of the foot to the crown of the head, at every inch of our ascending progress we meet with functions more and more important as their organs are located still higher up. Feet, located lowest of all, perform the menial services of all; while the organs in the lower part of the body proper, higher in position, are also higher in function; for whereas we can live without feet, convenient though they be, yet we can not live long without the visceral organs. Yet longer and better without these than heart or lungs, which, located highest of all in the body proper, fulfill its most important functions, their suspension causing simultaneous death. But even these perform functions less elevated than head, which, located highest of all, fulfills the crowning function of all—mind: that for which the entire body, as well as universal nature, was created. And we might therefore infer that the various parts of this brain would fulfill functions more important, according to their position upward from the base to the top. And so it is. For while the animal and social organs are to man what foundations are to house—absolutely indispensable, yet that there is a higher quality or grade to man's moral faculties than animal—to those which ally him to angels and to God, than to matter, to immortality than mortality—is but the common sentiment of mankind. Is not the good man higher in the human scale than those of powerful animal functions? Are not those great intellectually greater than those great animally? The talented above the rich? or reason above acquisitiveness? Does not the philosophy involved in this position of the respective organs both absolutely, and as regards each other, evince a divine hand in its construction?

Secondly. Equally philosophical and perfect is the analysis of the phrenological faculties, considered both in reference to man's necessary life-requisitions, and as regards universal nature. Man, having a material department to his nature, must needs be linked to matter, and possessed of all its properties. He is so. Then might we not expect some department of his nature to inter-relate him to each prop-

68

erty of matter? These phrenological faculties furnish that relation. And it so is that each phrenological faculty is adapted and adapts man to some great element in matter and arrangement in nature, as also to some special want or requisition of his being. Thus appetite relates him to his need of food, and to that department of nature which supplies this food, or to her dietetic productions. Causality adapts him to nature's arrangements of cause and effect; Comparison, to her classifications; Form, to her configurations[10]; Ideality, to the beautiful; and in like manner each of the other faculties adapt him to some institute of nature. And to point out this adaptation furnishes the finest explanation of the faculties to be found, as well as the strongest proof that "the hand that formed them is divine." That is, Parental Love is adapted, and adapts man to, the infantile and parental relations. Nature must needs provide for the rearing of every individual child; and this she effects by creating in all parents — vegetable, animal, human — the parental sentiment, or love of their *own* young, particularly as infants, thus specifying what adult shall care for each particular child, thus absolutely providing for the rearing of all. Hence, whatever concerns the relations of parents to their children comes under this faculty; and its correct analysis unfolds whatever concerns parents and their children. So Constructiveness adapts man to his need of clothes, houses, and materials for creature comforts, and is adapted to nature's mechanical institutes. And each of the other phrenological organs has a like adaptation to some great fact or provision in the economy of things.

And what is more yet, each phrenological faculty is found to run throughout all animal, all vegetable life, and to be an inherent property of things — of nature, of matter. Thus, the phrenological faculty of Firmness expresses a principle which runs throughout every phase of nature, as seen in the stability of all her operations — the perpetual return of her seasons, the immutability of her laws, the stability of her mountains, the uniformity and reliability or firmness of all her operations. Time, too, expresses a natural institute. For it not only appertains to man and all his habits — the natural period of his life included — but all plants are timed, observe each its own times and seasons.

Each seed, fruit, animal, everything has its time. Some things begin and end their lives, as it were, in a day — others a year; while the cedars of Lebanon or California live through many centuries. But even they have their germination, adolescence, maturity, decline, death, and decay. Given fruits ripen each at its given season; and even flowers and vegetables, transplanted from a southern to a northern latitude, keep up their periodical function in spite of opposite seasons. Has not every rock, even, its age? that is, a time element — appertaining to the earth, and every one of its productions and their functions, as well as to every star — is a universal institute of nature. So is Order. For are not eye, foot, heart, spine, always in their respective places? And so of bark, root, limb, fruit, every organ of every animal and vegetable — that is, method is quite as much an element of universal nature as of man. Color is equally universal. So is Form. And is not conscientiousness in nature's arrangement that, all her laws obeyed, reward — violated, punish? A tree injured inflicts punishment by withholding its fruit. And every wrong done to man, animal, or thing becomes its own avenger, while every right embodies its own reward, showing that the entity we call conscientiousness is a universal institute, not of man alone, but of every phase of life and function of nature. And so of all the other faculties.

Thirdly. Phrenology teaches the true *philosophy of life.* It unfolds the *original* constitution of man. That constitution was right — was as perfect even as its divine Author could render it. And in pointing out the original constitution of humanity, Phrenology shows who departs therefrom, and wherein. That is, by giving a *beau ideal* of human perfection, it teaches one and all, individuals and communities, wherein and how far they conform to, and depart from, this perfect human type, and thereby becomes the great reformer. And as far as individuals and communities live in accordance with its requisitions, they live *perfect* lives. That is, each of its faculties has a normal action. That normal action fulfilled is perfection. Has also an abnormal, which is imperfection. And in teaching us both their normal and abnormal, it thereby teaches us just how to live, even in details; and thereby settles all questions in morals, in ethics, in deal between man and man, in every possible phase and aspect of life, down to its minutest details and requisitions, thereby becoming the great law-giver of humanity.

But to follow out these grand first principles would unduly enlarge our volume. Having stated them, the reader, curious to follow them up, will find in the *American Phrenological Journal*, and in works on Phrenology, these and kindred ideas amplified. Meanwhile, to proceed with the phrenological organs, their groups, and individual functions.

THE SOCIAL GROUP, OR FAMILY AFFECTIONS.

These occupy the back and lower portion of the head, causing it to project behind the ears, and create most of the family affections and virtues.

7. Are pre-eminently attached to family and home, and enjoy them more than any of the other pleasures of life; love companions and children with passionate fondness, and will do and sacrifice anything for them; must have a home and home joys, and pine away without them.

6. Love family, home, country, and the fireside relations devotedly, and regard family as the center of most of life's pleasures or pains; are eminently social and companionable, and strive to make home pleasant and family happy; sacrificing often and much on the domestic altar.

5. Love and enjoy the domestic relations well, but not as life's highest good; and seek other things and pleasures first, though home pleasures much.

4. Have fair, average commonplace family ties, and do much but not over much, for companion, children, and friends.

3. Are rather indifferent in and to the family, and take a little, though no great pleasure, in them; and need to cultivate the domestic virtues.

2. Care little for home, its inmates, or pleasures, and are barren of its virtues.

1. Have scarcely any social ties, and they weak.

SECTION III

THE PHRENOLOGICAL FACULTIES, THEIR ANALYSIS AND CLASSIFICATION

1a. AMATIVENESS.

SEXUALITY; THE LOVE ELEMENT; ATTACHMENT TO THE OPPO-
SITE SEX; DESIRE TO LOVE, BE LOVED, AND MARRY.

Everything in nature is sexed — is male or female. And this sexual institute embodies those means employed by the Author of all life for its inception — for the perpetuity and multiplication of the race, of all forms of life. It creates in each sex admiration and love of the other; renders woman winning, persuasive, urbane, affectionate, loving, and lovely; and develops all the feminine charms and graces; and makes man noble in feeling and bearing; elevated in aspiration; gallant, tender, and bland in manner; affectionate toward woman; pure in feeling; highly susceptible to female charms; and clothes him with that dignity, power, and persuasiveness which accompanies the masculine. Perverted, it occasions grossness and vulgarity in expression and action; licentiousness in all its forms; a feverish state of mind; depraves all the other propensities; treats the other sex merely as a minister to passion — now caressing, and now abusing them; and renders the love-feeling every way gross and animal.

Very Large: Are admirably sexed, or well-nigh perfect as a male or female; literally idolize, almost worship, the opposite sex; treat them with the utmost consideration; cherish for them the most exalted feelings of regard and esteem, as if they were superior beings; have the instincts — the true spirit and tone — of the male or female in a pre-eminent degree; must love and be beloved, and with inexpressible tenderness; are sure to elicit and return love; are winning, attractive to, and attracted by, the other sex; and that by instinct, in behavior, in conversation, in all they say and do; with organic quality 6, and the other social organs large, have the conjugal intuition in a pre-eminent degree; assimilate and conform to those loved, and become perfectly united; and with Conjugality large, manifest the most clinging fondness and utmost devotion, and are made or unmade for life by the state of the affections. For other combinations, see large.

Large: Are well sexed, or *very much* of a man or woman; that is, have the form, carriage, spirit, manners, and mind of the true man or woman in a high degree; are eminently both loving and lovely; are full of love, and with Conjugality large, of the real conjugal sentiment and intuition;

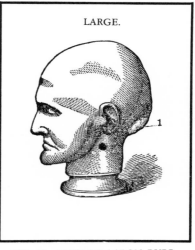

NO. 43. — BUST OF AARON BURR.

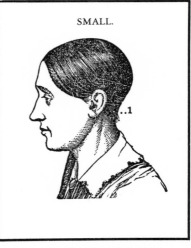

NO. 44. — MISS MODESTY.

75

strongly attract, and are strongly attracted by, the opposite sex; admire and love their beauty and excellences; easily win their affectionate regards, or kindle their love; have many warm friends, if not admirers, among them; love young and most intensely, and are powerfully influenced by the love elements for good or evil, according as it is well or ill placed; with Adhesiveness and Conjugality large, will mingle pure friendship with devoted love; can not flourish alone, but must have a matrimonial mate, with whom to become perfectly identified, and whom to invest with almost superhuman perfections, by magnifying their charms and overlooking their defects; in the sunshine of whose love be perfectly happy, but proportionally miserable without it; with large Ideality and the mental temperament added, will experience a fervor and intensity of love, amounting almost to ecstasy or romance; can marry those only who combine refinement of manners with correspondingly strong attachments; with Parental Love and Benevolence also large, are eminently qualified to enjoy the domestic relations, and be happy in home, as well as render home happy; with Inhabitiveness also large, will set a high value on house and place; long to return home when absent, and consider family and children as the greatest of life's treasures; with large Conscientiousness added, will keep the marriage relations inviolate, and regard unfaithfulness as the greatest of sins; with Combativeness large, will defend the object of love with great spirit, and resent powerfully any indignity offered them; with Alimentiveness large, will enjoy eating with the family dearly; with Approbativeness large, can not endure to be blamed by those beloved; with Cautiousness and Secretiveness large, will express love guardedly, and much less than is experienced; but with Secretiveness small, will show in every look and action the full, unvailed feeling of the soul; with Firmness, Self-Esteem, and Conjugality large, will sustain interrupted love with fortitude, yet suffer much damage of mind and health therefrom; but with Self-Esteem moderate, will feel crushed and broken down by disappointment; with the moral faculties predominant, can love those only whose moral tone is pure and elevated; with predominant Ideality, and only average intellectual faculties, will prefer those who are showy and gay to those who are sensible, yet less beautiful; but with Ideality less than the intellectual and moral organs, will prefer those who are substantial and valuable rather than showy; with Mirthfulness, Time, and Tune, will love dancing, lively company, etc.

Full: Possess quite strong susceptibilities of love for a congenial spirit; are capable of much purity, intensity, and cordiality of love; with Adhesiveness and Benevolence large, will be kind and affectionate in the family; with Secretiveness large, will manifest less love than is felt, and show little in promiscuous society; with a highly susceptible temperament will experience great intensity of love, and evince a good degree of masculine or feminine excellence, etc.

Average: Are capable of fair sexual attachments, and calculated to feel and exhibit a good degree of love, provided it is properly placed and fully called out; experience a greater or less degree of love in proportion to its activity; as a man, are quite attached to mothers and sisters, and fond of female society, and endowed with a fair share of the masculine element, yet not remarkable for its perfection; as a woman, quite winning and attractive, yet not particularly susceptible to love; as a daughter, fond of father and brothers, and desirous of the society of men, yet not extremely so; and capable of a fair share of conjugal devotedness under favorable circumstances; combined with an ardent temperament, and large Adhesiveness and Ideality, have a pure and platonic cast of love, yet can not assimilate with a coarse temperament, or a dissimilar phrenology; are refined and faithful, yet have more friendship than passion; can love those only who are just to the liking; with Cautiousness and Secretiveness large, will express less love than is felt, and that equivocally, and by piecemeal, nor then till the loved one is fully committed; with Cautiousness, Approbativeness, and Veneration large, and Self-Esteem small, are diffident in promiscuous society, yet enjoy the company of a select few of the opposite sex; with Adhesiveness, Benevolence, and Conscientiousness large, and Self-Esteem small, are kind and affectionate in the family, yet not particularly fond of caressing or being caressed; and do much to make family happy, yet will manifest no great fondness and tenderness; with Order, Approbativeness, and Ideality large, seek in a companion personal neatness and polish of manners; with full intellectual and moral faculties, base their conjugal attachments in the higher qualities of the affections, rather than their personal attractiveness or strength of passion; but with a commonplace temperament, and not so full moral and intellectual faculties, are indifferent toward the opposite sex, and rather cool toward them in manners and conversation; neither attract nor are attracted much, and are rather tame in love and marriage, and can live tolerably comfortably without loving or being beloved, etc.

Moderate: Will be rather deficient, though not palpably so, in the love element, and averse to the other sex; and love their mental excellences more than personal charms; show little desire to caress or be caressed; and find it difficult to sympathize with a conjugal partner, unless the natural harmony between both is well-nigh perfect; care less for marriage, and can live unmarried without inconvenience; with Conjugality large, can love but once, and should marry only the first love, because the love-principle will not be sufficiently strong to overcome the difficulties incident to its transfer, or the want of congeniality, and find more pleasure in other things than in the matrimonial relations; with an excitable temperament, will experience greater warmth and ardor than depth and uniformity of love; with Ideality large and organic quality 6, are fastidious and over-modest, and terribly shocked by allusions to love; pronounce love a silly farce, only fit for crack-brained poets; with Approbativeness large, will soon become alienated by rebukes and fault-finding; with Adhesiveness and the moral and intellectual faculties large, can become strongly attached to those who are highly moral and intellectual, yet experience no affinity for any other, and to be happy in marriage, must base it in the higher faculties.

Small: Dislike the opposite sex, and distrust and refuse to assimilate with them; feel little sexual love, or desire to marry; are cold, coy, distant, and reserved toward the other sex; experience but little of the beautifying and elevating influence of love, and should not marry, because incapable of appreciating its relations, and making a companion happy.

Very Small: Are passively continent, and almost destitute of love.

To Cultivate: Mingle much in the society of the other

sex; observe and appreciate their excellences, and overlook their faults; be as gallant, as gentlemanly or lady-like, as inviting, as prepossessing, as lively and entertaining in their society as you know how to be, and always on the alert to please them; say as many complimentary and pretty things, and as few disagreeable things, as possible; that is, feel and play the agreeable; if not married, contemplate its advantages and pleasures, and be preparing to enjoy them; if married, get up a second and an improved edition of courtship; re-enamor both yourself and conjugal partner, by becoming just as courteous, loving, and lovely as possible; luxuriate in the company and conversation of those well sexed, and yield to drink in their inspiriting influence; be less fastidious, and more free and communicative; establish a warm, cordial intimacy and friendship for them, and feast yourself on their masculine or feminine excellences; if not married, marry, and cultivate the feelings, as well as live the life of a right and a hearty sexuality.

To Restrain: Simply *direct* this love element more to the mental, and less to the personal qualities of the other sex; admire and love them more for their minds than bodies, more for their moral purity and conversational powers than instruments of passion; seek the society of the virtuous and good, but avoid that of the vulgar; should mingle in their society but to derive moral elevation and inspiration therefrom, not to feed the fires of passion; to be made better and yield to their molding influences for good; should be content to commune with their *spirits*; should sanctify and elevate the cast and tone of love, and banish its baser forms; expecially should lead a right *physiological* life — avoid tea and meats, and abstain wholly from coffee, tobacco, and all forms and degrees of alcoholic drinks, wines and beer included; exercise much in the open air; abstain wholly from carnal indulgence; work off your vital force on other functions as a relief of this; bathe daily; eat sparingly; study and commune with nature; cultivate the pure, the intellectual, the moral as the best means of rising above the passional, and put yourself on a high human plane throughout. Remember these two things — first, that you require its purification, elevation, and right direction rather than restraint, because it is more perverted than excessive — it can not be too great if rightly exercised — and secondly, that the inflamed state of the body irritates and perverts this passion, of which a cooling regimen is a specific antidote.

1b. CONJUGALITY.

MONOGAMY; UNION FOR LIFE; FIRST LOVE; THE PAIRING INSTINCT; ATTACHMENT TO ONE CONJUGAL PARTNER; DUALITY AND EXCLUSIVENESS OF LOVE. PERVERTED ACTION – A BROKEN HEART JEALOUSY; ENVY TOWARD LOVE RIVALS. LOCATED BETWEEN AMATIVENESS AND ADHESIVENESS AND ADAPTED TO PARENTS LIVING WITH AND EDUCATING ALL THEIR OWN CHILDREN IN THE SAME FAMILY. SOME BIRDS, SUCH AS DOVES, EAGLES, GEESE, ROBINS, ETC., PAIR, AND REMAIN TRUE TO THEIR CONNUBIAL ATTACHMENT; WHILE HENS, TURKEYS, SHEEP, HORSES, AND NEAT CATTLE ASSOCIATE PROMISCUOUSLY, WHICH SHOWS THIS TO BE A FACULTY DISTINCT FROM AMATIVENESS AND ADHESIVENESS.

Very Large: Select some One of the opposite sex as the sole object of love; concentrate the whole soul on the single *one* beloved; magnifying excellences and overlooking faults; long to be always with that one; are exclusive, and require a like exclusiveness; are true and faithful in wedlock, if married in spirit; possess the element of conjugal union, of flowing together of soul, in the highest degree, and with Continuity 6, become broken-hearted when disappointed, and comparatively worthless in this world; seek death rather than life; regard this union as the gem of life, and its loss as worse than death; and should manifest the utmost care to bestow itself only where it can be reciprocated for life.

Large: Seek one, and but one, sexual mate; experience the keenest disappointment when love is interrupted; are restless until the affections are anchored; are perfectly satisfied with the society of that one; and should exert every faculty to win the heart and hand of the one beloved; nor allow anything to alienate the affections.

Full: Can love cordially, yet are capable of changing their object, especially if Continuity is moderate; will love for life, provided circumstances are favorable, yet will not bear everything from a lover or companion, and if one love is interrupted can readily form another.

Average: Are disposed to love but one for life, yet capable of changing their object, and, with Secretiveness and Approbativeness large, and Conscientiousness only full, are capable of coquetry, especially if Amativeness is large, and Adhesiveness only full, and the temperament more powerful than fine-grained; such should cultivate this faculty, and not allow their other faculties to break their first love.

Moderate: Are somewhat disposed to love only one, yet allow other stronger faculties to interrupt that love, and,

81

with Amativeness large, can form one attachment after another with comparative ease, yet are not true as a lover, nor faithful to the connubial union.

Small: Have but little conjugal love, and seek the promiscuous society and affection of the opposite sex, rather than a single partner for life.

Very Small: Manifest none of this faculty, and experience little.

To Cultivate: Do not allow new faces to awaken new loves, but cling to the first one, and cherish its associations and reminiscences; do not allow the affections to wander, but be much in the company of the one already beloved, and both open your heart to love the charms, and keep up those thousand little attentions calculated to revive and perpetuate conjugal love.

To Restrain: Try to appreciate the excellences of others than the first love, remembering that "there are as good fish in the sea as ever were caught;" if a first love dies or is blighted, by no means allow yourself to pore over the bereavement, but transfer affection just as soon as a suitable object can be found, and be industrious in finding one, by making yourself just as acceptable and charming as possible. Above all, do not allow a pining, sad feeling to crush you, nor allow hatred toward the other sex.

2. PARENTAL LOVE. (PHILOPROGENITIVENESS.)

ATTACHMENT TO ONE'S OWN OFFSPRING; LOVE OF CHILDREN, PETS, AND ANIMALS GENERALLY, ESPECIALLY THOSE YOUNG OR SMALL; ADAPTED TO THAT INFANTILE CONDITION IN WHICH MAN ENTERS THE WORLD, AND TO CHILDREN'S NEED OF PARENTAL CARE AND EDUCATION. THIS FACULTY RENDERS CHILDREN THE RICHEST TREASURE OF THEIR PARENTS, CASTS INTO THE SHADE ALL THE TOIL AND EXPENSE THEY CAUSE, AND LACERATES THEM WITH BITTER PANGS WHEN DEATH OR DISTANCE TEARS THEM ASUNDER. IT IS MUCH LARGER IN WOMAN THAN IN MAN; AND NATURE REQUIRES MOTHERS TO TAKE THE PRINCIPAL CARE OF INFANTS. PERVERTED, IT SPOILS CHILDREN BY EXCESSIVE INDULGENCE, PAMPERING, AND HUMORING.

NO. 45.—THE GOOD MOTHER.

Very Large: Experience the parental feeling with the greatest possible intensity and power; almost idolize their own children, grieve immeasurably over their loss, and, with large Continutiy, refuse to be comforted; with very large Benevolence, and only moderate Destructiveness, can not bear to see them punished, and with only moderate Causality, are liable to spoil them by over-indulgence; with large Approbativeness added, indulge parental vanity and conceit; with large Cautiousness and disordered nerves, are always cautioning them, and feel a world of groundless apprehensions about them; with Acquisitiveness moderate, make them many presents, and lavish money upon them; but with large Acquisitiveness, lay up fortunes for them; with large moral and intellectual organs, are indulgent, yet love them too well to spoil them, and do their utmost to cultivate their higher faculties, etc..

NO. 46.—THE UNMOTHERLY.

Large: Love their own children devotedly; value them above all price; cheerfully endure toil and watching for their sake; forbear with their faults; win their love; delight to play with them, and cheerfully sacrifice to promote their interest; with Continuity large, mourn long and incessantly over their loss; with Combativeness, Destructiveness, and Self-Esteem large, are kind, yet insist on being obeyed; with Self-Esteem and Destructiveness moderate, are familiar with, and liable to be ruled by, them; with Firmness only average, fail to manage them with a steady hand; with Cautiousness large, suffer extreme anxiety if they are sick or in danger; with large moral and intellectual organs, and less Combativeness and Destructiveness, govern them more by moral suasion than physical force—by reason than fear; are neither too strict nor over-indulgent; with Approbativeness large, value their moral character as of the utmost importance; with Veneration and Conscientiousness large, are particularly interested in their moral improvement; with large excitability, Combativeness, and Destructiveness, and only average Firmness, will be, by turns, too indulgent, and over-provoked — will pet them one minute, but punish them the next; with larger Approbativeness and Ideality than intellect, will educate them more for show than usefulness — more fashionably than substantially — and dress them off in the extreme of fashion; with a large and active brain, large moral and intellectual faculties, and Firmness, and only full Combativeness, Destructiveness, and Self-Esteem, are well calculated to teach and manage the young. It renders farmers fond of stock, dogs, etc., and women fond of birds, lap dogs, etc.; girls fond of dolls, and boys of being among horses and cattle; and creates a general interest in young and small animals.

Full: Love their own children well, yet not passionately — do much for them, yet not more than necessary — and with large Combativeness, Destructiveness, and Self-Esteem, are too severe, and make too little allowance for their faults; but with Benevolence, Adhesiveness, and Conscientiousness large, do and sacrifice much to supply their wants and render them happy. Its character, however, will be mainly determined by its combinations:

Average: Love their own children tolerably well, yet care but little for those of others; with large Adhesiveness and Benevolence, like them better as they grow older, yet do and care little for infants — are not duly tender to them, or forbearing toward their faults, and should cultivate parental fondness, especially if Combativeness, Destructiveness, and Self-Esteem are large.

Moderate: Are not fond enough of children; can not bear much from them; fail to please or take good care of them, particularly of infants; can not endure to hear them cry, or make a noise, or disturb things; and with an excitable temperament, and large Combativeness, are liable to punish them for trifling offenses, find much fault with them, and be sometimes cruel; yet, with Benevolence and Adhesiveness large, may do what is necessary for their comfort.

Small: Care little for their own children, and still less for those of others; and with Combativeness and Destructiveness large, are liable to treat them unkindly and harshly, and are utterly unqualified to have charge of them.

Very Small: Have little or no parental love or regard for children, but conduct toward them as the other faculties dictate.

To Cultivate: Play with and make much of children; try to appreciate their loveliness and innocence, and be patient and tender and indulgent toward them; and if you have no own children, adopt some, or provide something to pet and fondle.

To Restrain: Set judgment over against affection; rear them intellectually; give yourself less anxiety about them, and if a child dies, by all means turn your mind from that loss by seeking some powerful diversion, and a change of associations, removing clothes and all remembrances, and keep from talking or thinking about them.

3. FRIENDSHIP. (ADHESIVENESS.)

SOCIAL FEELING; LOVE OF SOCIETY; DESIRE TO CONGREGATE, ASSOCIATE, VISIT, SEEK COMPANY, ENTERTAIN FRIENDS, FORM AND RECIPROCATE ATTACHMENTS, AND INDULGE THE FRIENDLY FEELINGS. WHEN PERVERTED IT FORMS ATTACHMENTS FOR THE UNWORTHY, AND LEADS TO BAD COMPANY. ADAPTED TO MAN'S REQUISITION FOR CONCERT OF ACTION, COPARTNERSHIP, COMBINATION, AND COMMUNITY OF FEELING AND INTEREST, AND IS A LEADING ELEMENT OF HIS SOCIAL RELATIONS.

Very Large: Love friends with the utmost tenderness and intensity, and will sacrifice almost anything for their sake; with Amativeness large, are susceptible of the highest order of conjugal love, yet base that love primarily in friendship; with Combativeness and Destructiveness large, defend friends with great spirit, and resent and retaliate their injuries; with Self-Esteem moderate, take character from associates; with Acquisitiveness moderate, allow friends the free use of their purse; but with Acquisitiveness large, will do more than give; with Benevolence and Approbativeness moderate, and Acquisitiveness only full, will spend money freely for social gratification; with Self-Esteem and Combativeness large, must be first or nothing; but with only average Combativeness, Destructiveness, and Self-Esteem, large Approbativeness, Benevolence, Conscientiousness, Ideality, Marvelousness, and reasoning organs, will have many friends, and but few enemies—be amiable and universally beloved; with large Eventuality and Language, will remember, with vivid emotions, bygone scenes of social cheer and friendly converse; with large reasoning organs, will give good advice to friends, and lay excellent plans for them; with smaller Secretiveness and large moral organs, will not believe ill of them, and dread the interruption of friendship as the greatest of calamities; willingly make any sacrifice required by friendship, and evince a perpetual flow of that commingling of soul, and desire to become one with others, which this faculty inspires.

Large: Are warm, cordial, and ardent as friends; readily form friendships, and attract friendly regards in return; must have society of some kind; with Benevolence large, are hospitable, and delight to entertain friends; with Alimentiveness large, love the social banquet, and set the best before friends; with Approbativeness large, set the world by their commendation, but are terribly cut by their rebukes;

with the moral faculties large, seek the society of the moral and elevated, and can enjoy the friendship of no others; with the intellectual faculties large, seek the society of the intelligent; with Language large, and Secretiveness small, talk freely in company; and with Mirthfulness and Ideality also large, are full of fun, and give a lively, jocose turn to conversation, yet are elevated and refined; with Self-Esteem large, lead off in company, and give tone and character to others; but with Self-Esteem small, receive character from friends, and with Imitation large, are liable to copy their faults as well as virtues, with Cautiousness, Secretiveness, and Approbativeness large, are apt to be jealous of regards bestowed upon others, and exclusive in the choice of friends — having a few select, rather than many commonplace; with large Causality and Comparison, love philosophical conversation, literary societies, etc., and are every way sociable and companionable.

Full: Make a sociable, companionable, warm-hearted friend, who will sacrifice much on the altar of friendship, yet offer up friendship on the altar of the stronger passions; with large or very large Combativeness, Destructiveness, Self-Esteem, Approbativeness, and Acquisitiveness, will serve self first, and friends afterward; form attachments, and break them, when they conflict with the stronger faculties; with large Secretiveness and moderate Conscientiousness, will be double-faced, and profess more friendship than possess; with Benevolence large, will cheerfully aid friends, yet it will be more from sympathy than affection; will have a few warm friends, yet only few, but perhaps many speaking acquaintances; and with the higher faculties generally large, will be a true, good friend, yet by no means enthusiastic; many of the combinations under Adhesiveness large, apply to it when full, allowance being made for its diminished power.

Average: Are capable of tolerably strong friendships, yet their character is determined by the larger faculties; enjoy present friends, yet sustain their absence; with large Acquisitiveness, place business before friends, and sacrifice them whenever they conflict with money-making; with Benevolence large, are more kind than affectionate, relish friends, yet sacrifice no great for their sake; with Amativeness large, love the person of the other sex more than their minds, and experience less conjugal love than animal passion; with Approbativeness large, break friendship when ridiculed or rebuked, and with Secretiveness large, and Conscientiousness only average, can not be trusted as friends.

Moderate: Love society somewhat, and form a few, but only few, attachments, and these only partial; may have many speaking acquaintances, but few intimate friends; with large Combativeness and Destructiveness, are easily offended with friends, and seldom retain them long; with large Benevolence, will bestow services, and with moderate Acquisitiveness, money, more readily than affection; but with the selfish faculties strong, take care of self first, and make friendship subservient to interest.

Small: Think and care little for friends; dislike copartnership; are cold-hearted, unsocial, and selfish; take little delight in company, but prefer to be alone; have few friends, and with large selfish faculties, many enemies, and manifest too little of this faculty to exert a perceptible influence upon character.

Very Small: Are perfect strangers to friendship.

To Cultivate: Go more into society; associate freely with those around you; open your heart; don't be so exclusive and distant; keep your room less, but go more to parties, and strive to be as companionable and familiar as you well can; nor refuse to affiliate with those not exactly to your liking, but like what you can, and overlook faults.

To Restrain: Go abroad less, and be more select in choosing friends; besides guarding yourself against those persuasions and influences friends are apt to exercise over you, and trust friends less, as well as properly direct friendship by intellect.

4. INHABITIVENESS.

THE HOME FEELING; LOVE OF HOUSE, THE PLACE WHERE ONE WAS BORN OR HAS LIVED, AND OF HOME ASSOCIATIONS. ADAPTED TO MAN'S NEED OF AN ABIDING PLACE, IN WHICH TO EXERCISE THE FAMILY FEELINGS; PATRIOTISM. PERVERSION—HOMESICKNESS WHEN AWAY FROM HOME, AND NEEDLESS PINING AFTER HOME.

Very Large: Are liable to homesickness when away from home, especially for the first time, and the more so if Parental Love and Adhesiveness are large; will suffer almost any inconvenience, and forego bright prospects rather than leave home; and remain in an inferior house or place of business rather than change. For combinations, see Inhabitiveness large:

Large: Have a strong desire to locate young, to have a home or room exclusively; leave home with great reluctance, and return with extreme delight; soon become attached to house, sleeping-room, garden, fields, furniture, etc.; and highly prize domestic associations; are not satisfied without a place on which to expend this home instinct; with Parental Love, Adhesiveness, Individuality, and Locality large, will love to travel, yet be too fond of home to stay away long at a time; may be a cosmopolite in early life, and see much of the world, but will afterward settle down; with Approbativeness and Combativeness large, will defend national honor, praise own country, government, etc., and defend both country and fireside with great spirit; with Ideality large, will beautify home; with Friendship large, will delight to see friends at home rather than abroad; with Alimentiveness large, will enjoy food at home better than elsewhere, etc..

Full: Prefer to live in one place, yet willingly change it when interest or the other faculties require it; and with large Parental Love, Adhesiveness, and Amativeness, will think more of family and friends than of the domicile.

Average: Love home tolerably well, yet with no great fervor, and change the place of abode as the other faculties may dictate; take some, but no great interest in house or place, as such, or pleasure in their improvement, and are satisfied with ordinary home comforts; with Acquisitiveness large, spend reluctantly for its improvement; with Constructiveness moderate, take little pleasure in building additions to home; with Individuality and Locality large, love traveling more than staying in one place, and are

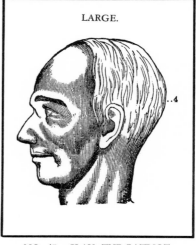

LARGE.

NO. 47.—CLAY, THE PATRIOT.

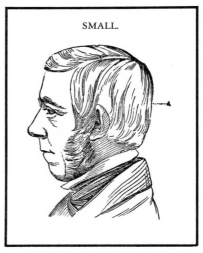

SMALL.

NO. 48.—THE RAMBLER.

89

satisfied with inferior home accommodations.

Moderate or Small: Care little for home; leave it without much regret; contemplate it with little delight; take little pains with it; and with Acquisitiveness large, spend reluctantly for its improvement.

Very Small: Feel little, and show less, love of domicile as such.

To Cultivate: Stay more at home, and cultivate a love of home, and its associations and joys, and the love of country.

To Restrain: Go from home, and banish that feeling of homesickness experienced away from home.

5a. CONTINUITY.

A PATIENT DWELLING UPON ONE THING TILL IT IS DONE; CON-SECUTIVENESS AND CONNECTEDNESS OF THOUGHT AND FEEL-ING. ADAPTED TO MAN'S NEED OF DOING ONE THING AT A TIME. PERVERSION—PROLIXITY, REPETITION, AND EXCESSIVE AMPLIFICATION.

Very Large: Fix the mind upon objects slowly, yet can not leave them unfinished; have great application, yet lack intensity or point: are tedious, prolix, and thorough in a few things rather than an amateur in many.

Large: Give the whole mind to the one thing in hand till it is finished; complete at the time; keep up one common train of thought, or current of feeling, for a long time; are disconcerted if attention is directed to a second object, and can not duly consider either; with Adhesiveness large, pore sadly over the loss of friends for months and years; with the moral faculties large, are uniform and consistent in religious exercises and character; with Combativeness and Destructiveness large, retain grudges and dislikes for a long time; with Ideality, Comparison, and Language large, amplify and sustain figures of speech; with the intellectual faculties large, con and pore over one thing, and impart a unity and completeness to intellectual investigations; become thorough in whatever study is commenced, and rather postpone than commence, unless sure of completing.

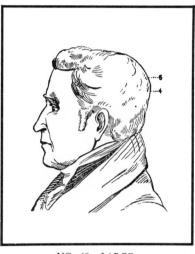

NO. 49.—LARGE.

Full: Dwell continuously upon subjects, unless especially called to others; prefer to finish up matters in hand, yet can, though with difficulty, give attention to another thing; with the business organs large, make final settlements; with the feelings strong, continue their action, yet are not monotonous, etc..

Average: Can dwell upon things, or divert attention to others, as occasion requires; are not confused by interruption, yet prefer one thing at a time; with the intellectual organs large, are not a smatterer, nor yet profound; with the mental temperament, are clear in style, and consecutive in idea, yet never tedious; with Comparison large, manufacture expressions and ideas consecutively, and connectedly, and always to the point, yet never dwell unduly.

NO. 50.—SMALL.

Moderate: Love and indulge variety and change of thought, feeling, occupation, etc.; are not confused by them; rather lack application; with a good intellectual lobe, and an active temperament, know a little about a good many things, rather than much about any one thing; with an active organization, think clearly, and have unity and intensity of thought and feeling, yet lack connectedness; with large Language and small Secretiveness, talk easily, but not long at a time upon any one thing; do better on the spur of the moment than by previous preparation; and should cultivate consistency of character and fixedness of mind, by finishing all begun.

Small: With activity great, commence many things, yet finish few; crave novelty and variety; have many irons in the fire; lack application; jump rapidly from premise to conclusion, and fail to connect and carry out ideas; lack steadiness and consistency of character; may be brilliant, yet can not be profound; humming-bird like, fly rapidly from thing to thing, but do not stay long; have many good thoughts, yet they are scattered; and talk on a great variety of subjects in a short time, but fail sadly in consecutiveness of feeling, thought, and action. An illustrative anecdote. An old and faithful servant to a passionate, petulant master finally told him he could endure his testiness no longer, and must leave, though with extreme reluctance. "But," replied the master, "you know I am no sooner angry than pleased again." "Aye, but," replied the servant, "you are no sooner pleased than angry again."

Very Small: Are restless, and given to perpetual change; with activity great, are composed of gusts and counter-gusts of passion, and never one thing more than an instant at a time.

To Cultivate: Dwell on, and pore over, till you complete the thing in hand; make thorough work; and never allow your thoughts to wander, or attention to be distracted, or indulge diversity or variety in anything

To Restrain: Engage in what will compel you to attend to a great many different things in quick succession, and break up that prolix, long-winded monotony caused by an excess of this faculty.

5b. SELFISH PROPENSITIES.

THESE PROVIDE FOR MAN'S ANIMAL WANTS; CREATE THOSE DE-
SIRES AND INSTINCTS AND SUPPLY THOSE WANTS WHICH RE-
LATE MORE ESPECIALLY TO HIS ANIMAL EXISTENCE AND PHYSI-
CAL NECESSITIES.

Very Large: Experience these animal impulses with great intensity; enjoy animal existence and
pleasures with the keenest relish, and with great excitability
or a fevered state of body, are strongly predisposed to
sensual gratification and sinful desires; yet if properly directed, and sanctified by the higher faculties, have tremendous force of character and energy of mind.

Large: Have strong animal desires; and that selfishness
which takes good care of number one; are strongly attached to this world and its pleasures; and with activity
great, use vigorous exertions to accomplish worldly and personal ends; with the moral organs less than the selfish,
connected with bodily disease, are liable to their depraved
and sensual manifestation; but with the moral and intellectual large, and a healthy organization, have great force,
energy, determination, and that efficiency which accomplishes wonders.

Full: Have a good share of energy and physical force,
yet no more than is necessary to cope with surrounding
difficulties; and, with large moral and intellectual faculties,
manifest more mental than physical power.

Average: Have a fair share of animal force, yet hardly
enough to grapple with life's troubles and wrongs; with
large moral and intellectual faculties, have more goodness
than efficiency, and enjoy quiet more than conflict with
men; and fail to manifest what goodness and talent are
possessed.

Moderate: Rather lack efficiency; yield to difficulties;
want fortitude and determination; fail to assert and maintain rights; and with large moral organs, are good-hearted,
moral, etc.; yet border on tameness.

Small: Accomplish little; lack courage and force, and
with large intellectual organs, are talented, yet utterly fail
to manifest that talent; and with large moral organs, so
good as to be good for nothing.

To Cultivate: Keep a sharp eye on your own interests;
look out well for number one; fend off imposition; harden
up; don't be so good; and in general cultivate a burly, driv-
ing, self-caring, physical, worldly spirit; especially increase
the physical energies by observing the health laws, as this

LARGE.

NO. 51.—YANKEE SULLIVAN.

SMALL.

NO. 52.—REV. DR. BOND.

93

will re-increase these animal organs.

To Restrain: First and most, obviate all causes of physical inflammation and false excitement; abstain from spirituous liquors, wines, tobacco, mustards, spices, all heavy and rich foods; eat lightly, and of farinaceous rather than of flesh diet, for meat is directly calculated to inflame the animal passions; avoid temptation and incentives to anger and sensuality; especially associate only with the good, never with those who are vulgar or vicious; but most of all, cultivate the higher, purer moral faculties, and aspire to the high and good; also cultivate love of nature's beauties and works, as the very best means of restraining the animal passions.

5c. VITATIVENESS.

TENACITY OF LIFE; RESISTANCE TO DEATH; LOVE OF EXISTENCE AS SUCH; DREAD OF ANNIHILATION; LOVE OF LIFE, AND CLINGING TENACIOUSLY TO IT FOR ITS OWN SAKE.

Very Large: Shrink from death, and cling to life with desperation; struggle with the utmost determination against disease and death; nor give up to die till the very last, and then by the hardest; with Cautiousness very large, and Hope moderate, shudder at the very thought of dying, or being dead; but with Hope large, expect to live against hope and experience. The combinations are like those under large, allowance being made for the increase of this faculty.

Large: Struggle resolutely through fits of sickness, and will not give up to die till absolutely compelled to do so. With large animal organs, cling to life on account of this world's gratifications; with large moral organs, to do good—to promote human happiness, etc.; with large social faculties, love life both for its own sake and to bless family; with very large Cautiousness, dread to change the present mode of existence, and with large and perverted Veneration and Conscientiousness, and small Hope, have an indescribable dread of entering upon an untried future state; but with Hope large, and a cultivated intellect, expect to exist hereafter, etc.

Full: Love life, and cling tenaciously to it, yet not extravagantly; hate to die, not from the fear of being dead, but yield to disease and death, though reluctantly.

Average: Enjoy life, and cling to it with a fair degree of earnestness, yet by no means with passionate fondness; and with a given constitution and health, will die easier and sooner than with this organ large.

Moderate or Small: Like to live, yet care no great about existence for their own sake; with large animal or domestic organs, may wish to live on account of family, or business, or worldly pleasures, yet care less about it for their *own sake*, and yield up existence with little reluctance or dread.

Very Small: Have no desire to live merely for the sake of living, but only to gratify other faculties.

To Cultivate: Think on the value of life, and plan things to be done and pleasures to be enjoyed that are worthy to live for.

To Restrain: Guard against a morbid love of life, or

dread of death. Regard death as much as possible as a natural institution, and this life as the pupilage for a better state of being.

6. COMBATIVENESS.

RESISTANCE; OPPOSITION; DEFENSE; DEFIANCE; BOLDNESS; COURAGE; SPIRIT; DESIRE TO ENCOUNTER; SELF-PROTECTION; PRESENCE OF MIND; DETERMINATION; GET-OUT-OF-MY-WAY; LET-ME-AND-MINE-ALONE. ADAPTED TO MAN'S REQUISITION FOR OVERCOMING OBSTACLES, CONTENDING FOR RIGHTS, ETC. PERVERSION—ANGER; CONTRARIETY; FAULT-FINDING; CONTENTION; ILL-NATURE; AND FIGHTING.

Very Large: Show always and everywhere the utmost heroism, boldness, and courage; can face the cannon's mouth coolly, and stare death in the face without flinching; put forth remarkable efforts in order to carry measures; grapple right in with difficulties with a real relish, and dash through them as if mere trifles; love pioneer, adventurous, even hazardous expeditions; shrink from no danger; are appalled by no hardships; prefer a rough and daring life — one of struggles and hair-breadth escapes — to a quiet, monotonous business; are determined never to be conquered, even by superior odds, but incline to do battle single-handed against an army; with Cautiousness only roused, which will be but seldom; with large Approbativeness, and small Acquisitiveness, will defend character, but not pecuniary rights; with large Cautiousness, may be courageous where danger is far off, yet will run rather than fight; with smaller Cautiousness, will show some resentment when imposed upon, but submit rather tamely to injuries; with very large Parental Love, and only average friendship, will resent any injuries offered to children with great spirit, yet not those offered to friends, etc.

Moderate: Rather lack efficiency; with only fair muscles, are poor workers, and fail to put forth even what little strength they have; with good moral and intellectual organs, possess talent and moral worth, yet are easily overcome by opposition or difficulty; should seek some quiet occupation, where business comes in of itself, because loth to intrude unbidden upon the attention of others; are too good to be energetic; with weak Acquisitiveness, allow virtual robbery without resentment; with large Cautiousness, are tame and pusillanimous; with large Approbativeness, can not stand rebuke, but wilt under it; with moderate Self-Esteem and Hope, are all "I can't, it's hard," etc., and will do but little in life.

Small: Are inert and inefficient; can accomplish little; never feel self-reliant or strong; and with large moral and

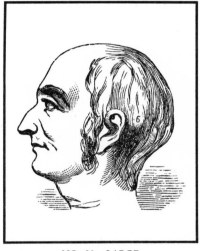

NO. 53.—LARGE.

NO. 54.—SMALL.

97

intellectual organs, are too gentle and easily satisfied; with large Cautiousness, run to others for protection, and are always complaining of bad treatment.

Very Small: Possess scarcely any energy, and manifest none.

To Cultivate: Encourage a bold, resistant, defiant, self-defending spirit; fend off imposition like a real hero; rather encourage than shrink from encounter; engage in debate, and the mental conflict of ideas and sentiments in politics, in religion, in whatever comes up, and take part in public meetings; take sides in everything; say and try to feel, None shall provoke me with impunity.

To Restrain: Do just the opposite of the preceding advice; whenever you find anger rising, turn on your heel; avoid debate, and say mildly and pleasantly whatever you have to say; bear with imposition rather than resent it; cultivate a turn-the-other-cheek spirit; never swear, or scold, or blow up anybody, and restrain temper and wrath in all their manifestations.

7. DESTRUCTIVENESS.

EXECUTIVENESS; SEVERITY; STERNNESS; THE DESTROYING AND PAIN-CAUSING FACULTY; HARSHNESS; EXTERMINATION, INDIGNATION; DISPOSITION TO BREAK, CRUSH, AND TEAR DOWN; THE WALK-RIGHT-THROUGH-SPIRIT. ADAPTED TO MAN'S DESTROYING WHATEVER IS PREJUDICIAL TO HIS HAPPINESS; PERFORMING AND ENDURING SURGICAL OPERATIONS; UNDERGOING PAIN, ETC. PERVERSION—WRATH; REVENGE; MALICE; DISPOSITION TO MURDER, ETC.

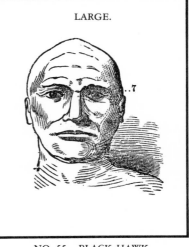

NO. 55.—BLACK HAWK.

Very Large: Experience the most powerful indignation, amounting even to rage and violence, when thoroughly provoked; and with large or very large Combativeness, act like a chafed lion, and feel like rushing into the midst of perilous dangers; tear up and destroy what ever is in the way; are harsh and often morose in manner, and should cultivate pleasantness; with large Combativeness, Firmness, Self-Esteem, and Approbativeness moderate, are exceedingly repulsive, hating and hateful when angry, and much more provoked than occasion requires; with large intellectuals, put forth tremendous mental energy; and should offset this faculty by reason and moral feeling, and cultivate blandness instead of wrath.

Large: Impart the determination, energy, and force which remove or destroy whatever impedes progression; with Firmness large, give that iron will which adheres till the very last, in spite of everything, and carry points anyhow; with large Combativeness, impart a harsh, rough mode of expression and action, and a severity, if not fierceness, to all encounters; with large Acquisitiveness and Conscientiousness, will have every cent due, though it cost two to get one, yet want no more, and retain grudges against those who have injured the pocket; with large Approbativeness and Combativeness, experience determination and hostility toward those who trifle with reputation or impeach character; with large Self-Esteem, upon those who conflict with its interests, or detract from its supposed merits; with large Adhesiveness, when angry with friends, are very angry; with large Benevolence and Conscientiousness, employ a harsh mode of showing kindness; with large Comparison and Language, heap very severe and galling epithets upon enemies; with large Ideality, polish and refine expression of anger, and put a keen edge upon sarcasms, yet they cut to the very bone, etc. Such should avoid and turn from whatever provokes.

Full: Evince a fair degree of this faculty, yet its tone

NO. 56.—JAUP, PRES. FIRST PEACE CONG.

99

and direction depend upon the larger organs; with large propensities, manifest much animal force; with large moral organs, evince moral determination and indignation; with large intellectual organs, possess intellectual might and energy, and thus of its other combinations; but with smaller Combativeness, are peaceful until thoroughly roused, but then rather harsh and vindictive; if boys, attack only when sure of victory, yet are then harsh; with smaller Self-Esteem, exercise this faculty more in behalf of others than of self; with large Cautiousness and moderate Combativeness, keep out of danger, broils, etc., till compelled to engage in them, but then become desperate, etc.:

Average: Are like full, only less so.

Moderate: Evince but little harshness or severity, and shrink from pain; with large Benevolence, are unable to witness suffering or death, much less to cause them; possess but little force of mind, or executiveness of character, to drive through obstacles; with large moral organs added, are more beloved than feared, manifest extreme sympathy, amounting sometimes even to weakness, and secure ends more by mild than severe measures; with moderate Combativeness and Self-Esteem, are irresolute, unable to stand ground, or take care of self; fly to others for protection; can do little, and feel like trying to do still less; fail to realize or put forth strength; and with large Cautiousness added, see lions where there are none, and make mountains of mole-hills; and with small Hope added, are literally good for nothing; but with large Hope and Firmness, and full Self-Esteem and Combativeness, accomplish considerable, yet in a quiet way, and by perseverance more than force — by siege rather than by storm — and with large intellectual and moral faculties added, are good, though not tame; exert a good influence, and that always healthful, and are mourned more when dead than prized while living. The combinations under this organ large, reversed, apply to it when moderate.

Small: With large moral faculties, possess too tender a soul to enjoy our world as it is, or to endure hardships or bad treatment; can neither endure nor cause suffering, anger being so little as to provoke only ridicule, and need hardness and force:

Very Small: Experience little, and manifest none of this faculty.

To Cultivate: Destroy anything and everything in your way; killing weeds, blasting rocks, felling trees, using edge tools, tearing up roots, plowing new ground, cultivating new farms, hunting, exercising indignation when wronged, and against public wrongs; espousing the cause of the oppressed; fighting public evils, such as intemperance and the like, are all calculated to cultivate and strengthen this faculty. Still, care should be taken to exercise it under the control of the higher faculties, and then no matter how great that exercise.

To Restrain: Kill nothing; and offset destructiveness by benevolence; never indulge a rough, harsh spirit, but cultivate instead a mild and forgiving spirit; never brood over injuries or indulge revengeful thoughts or desires, or aggravate yourself by brooding over wrongs; cultivate good manners; and when occasion requires you to reprove, do it in a bland, gentle manner rather than roughly; never tease, even children, or scourge animals, but be kind to both, and offset by benevolence and the higher faculties.

8a. ALIMENTIVENESS.

APPETITE; THE FEEDING INSTINCT; RELISH FOR FOOD; HUNGER. ADAPTED TO MAN'S NEED OF FOOD, AND CREATING A DISPOSITION TO EAT. PERVERTED, IT PRODUCES GORMANDIZING AND GLUTTONY, AND CAUSES DYSPEPSIA AND ALL ITS EVILS.

NO. 57.—LARGE.

NO. 58.—SMALL.

Very Large: Often eat more than is requisite; enjoy food exceedingly well; and hence are liable to clog body and mind by over-eating; should restrain appetite; will feel better by going without an occasional meal, and are liable to dyspepsia. This faculty is liable to take on a diseased action, and crave a much greater amount of food than nature requires and hence is the great cause of dyspepsia. Its diseased action may be known by a craving, hankering, gone sensation before eating; by heart-burn, pain in the stomach, belching of wind, a dull, heavy, or painful sensation in the head, and a desire to be always nibbling at something; lives to eat, instead of eating to live, and should at once be eradicated by omitting one meal daily, and, in its stead, drinking abundantly of cold water.

Large: Have a hearty relish for food; set high value upon table enjoyments, and solid, hearty food; with Acquisitiveness large, lay up abundance of food for future use — perhaps keep so much on hand that some of it spoils; with Ideality large, must eat from a clean plate, and have food nicely cooked; with large Language and intellect, enjoy table-talk exceedingly, and participate in it; with large social faculties, must eat with others; can cook well, if practiced in culinary arts; and with larger Approbativeness and Ideality than Causality, apt to be ceremonious and over-polite at table, etc. Such should restrain this faculty by eating less, more slowly, and seldom.

Full: With a healthy stomach, eat freely what is offered, asking no questions; enjoying it, but not extravagantly; rarely over-eat, except when the stomach is disordered, and then experience that hankering above described, which a right diet alone can cure. For combinations, see large.

Average: Enjoy food well, and eat with a fair relish; yet rarely over-eat, except when rendered craving by dyspeptic complaints.

Moderate: Rather lack appetite; eat with little relish, and hence require to pamper and cultivate appetite by dainties, and enjoying rich flavors; can relish food only when other circumstances are favorable; feel little hunger, and eat to live, instead of living to eat; with Eventuality small, can not remember from one meal to another what was eaten at the last.

Small: Eat "with long teeth," and little relish; hardly know or care what or when they eat; and should pay more attention to duly feeding the body.

Very Small: Are almost wholly destitute of appetite.

This faculty is more liable to perversion than any other, and excessive and fast eating occasions more sickness, and depraves the animal passions more than all other causes combined. Properly to feed the body is of the utmost importance. Whenever this faculty becomes diseased, the first object should be to restore its natural function by abstinence. Medicines rarely do it.

To Cultivate: Consider before you provide or order your meals what would relish best, and as far as possible provide what seems to you will taste good; pamper appetite; eat leisurely, and as if determined to extract from your food all the rich flavors it may contain, and in eating be governed more by flavor than quantity; endeavor to get up an appetite, even when you feel none, by eating some dainty, as if to see if it were not good; do by food and drinks as wine connoisseurs do in testing viands — that is, taste things with a view of ascertaining their relative flavors; in short, exercise and indulge appetite; also, do as directed in order to cultivate digestion.

To Restrain: Eat but seldom — for by keeping away from table this faculty remains comparatively quiet; and when you eat, eat slowly, leisurely, quietly, pleasurably, as if determined to enjoy eating, for this satisfies appetite with much less food than to eat voraciously; mingle pleasant conversation with meals; direct attention more to how good your food than how much you eat; always leave the table with a good appetite, and stop the moment you have to resort to condiments or desserts to keep up appetite; eat like the epicure, but not like the gourmand — as if you would enjoy a little rather than devour so much; eat sparingly, for the more you eat the more you re-inflame the stomach, and thereby re-increase that hankering you need to restrain.

FONDNESS FOR LIQUIDS; DESIRE TO DRINK; LOVE OF WATER, WASHING, BATHING, SWIMMING, SAILING, ETC. ADAPTED TO THE EXISTENCE AND UTILITY OF WATER. PERVERSION—DRINKING IN EXCESSIVE QUANTITIES; DRUNKENNESS; AND UNQUENCHABLE THIRST.

Very large: Are excessively fond of water, whether applied internally or externally, and a natural swimmer; and with Individuality and Locality, a natural seaman; with large Adhesiveness and Approbativeness, and small Self-Esteem and Acquisitiveness, should avoid the social glass, for fear of being overcome by it.

Large: Love to drink freely, and frequently; experience much thirst; enjoy washing, swimming, bathing, etc., exceedingly, and are benefited by them; with Ideality large, love water prospects.

Full: Enjoy water well, but not extravagantly; drink freely when the stomach is in a fevered state, and is benefited by its judicious external application.

Average: Like to drink at times, after working freely or perspiring copiously, yet ordinarily care little about it.

Moderate: Partake of little water, except occasionally, and are not particularly benefited by its external application, further than is necessary for cleanliness; dislike shower or plunge-baths, and rather dread than enjoy sailing, swimming, etc., especially when Cautiousness is large.

Small: Care little for liquids in any of their forms, or for any soups, and, with large Cautiousness, dread to be on or near the water; with Alimentiveness large, prefer solid, hard food to puddings or broth, etc.

Very Small: Have an unqualified aversion to water and all fluids.

9. ACQUISITIVENESS.

ECONOMY; FRUGALITY; THE ACQUIRING, SAVING, AND HOARD-
ING INSTINCT; LAYING UP A SURPLUS, AND ALLOWING NOTH-
ING TO BE WASTED; DESIRE TO POSSESS AND OWN; THE MINE-
AND-THINE FEELING; CLAIMING OF ONE'S OWN THINGS; LOVE
OF TRADING AND AMASSING PROPERTY. ADAPTED TO MAN'S
NEED OF LAYING UP THE NECESSARIES AND COMFORTS OF LIFE
AGAINST A TIME OF FUTURE NEED. PERVERSION – A MISERLY,
GRASPING, CLOSE-FISTED PENURIOUSNESS.

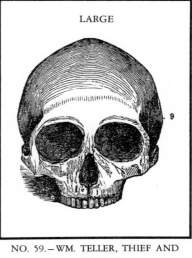

NO. 59. – WM. TELLER, THIEF AND
MURDERER.

Very Large: Hasten to be rich; are too eager after wealth;
too industrious; too close in making bargains; too small
in dealing; with large Cautiousness, are penny wise, but
pound foolish; hold the sixpence too close to the eye to
see the dollar farther off, and give entire energies to amassing property; with smaller Secretiveness and large Conscientiousness, are close, yet honest, will have due, yet
want no more, and never employ deception; but, with
large Secretiveness and but average Conscientiousness,
make money anyhow; palm off inferior articles for good
ones, or at least over-praise what is on sale, but run down
in buying; and with large Parental Love and Perceptives
added, can make a finished horse-jockey; with small Self-
Esteem, are small and mean in deal, and stick for the half
cent; with very large Hope, and only full Cautiousness,
embark too deeply in business, and are liable to fail; with
large Adhesiveness and Benevolence, will *do* for friends
more than give, and *circulate* the subscription-paper rather
than sign it; with large Hope and Secretiveness, and only
average Cautiousness, buy – more than can be paid for, pay
more in promises than in money, should adopt a cash business, and check the manifestations of this faculty by being
less penurious and industrious, and more liberal.

Large: Save for future use what is not wanted for present; allow nothing to go to waste; turn everything to a
good account; buy closely, and make the most of everything; are industrious, economical, and vigorously employ
all means to accumulate property, and desire to own and
possess much; with large social organs, industriously acquire property for domestic purposes, yet are saving in the
family; with very large Adhesiveness and Benevolence, are
industrious in acquiring property, yet spend it too freely
upon friends; with large Hope added, are too apt to indorse for them; with small Secretiveness, and activity
greater than power, are liable to overdo, and take on too

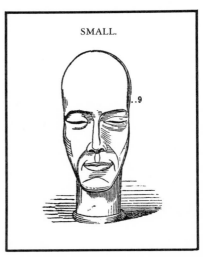

NO. 60. – MR. GOSSE – GAVE AWAY TWO
FORTUNES.

105

much work in order to save so much, as often to incur sickness, and thus lose more than gain; with large Approbativeness and small Secretiveness, boast of wealth, but with large Secretiveness, keep pecuniary affairs secret; with large Constructiveness, incline to make money by engaging in some mechanical branch of business; with large Cautiousness, are provident; with large Ideality, keep things very nice, and are tormented by whatever mars beauty; with large intellectual organs, love to accumulate books, and whatever facilitates intellectual progress; with large Veneration and Self-Esteem, set great store by antique and rare coins, and specimens, etc.

Full: Take good care of possessions, and use vigorous exertions to enhance them; value property for itself and its uses; are industrious, yet not grasping; and saving, without being close; with large Benevolence, are too ready to help friends; and with large Hope added, too liable to indorse; and with an active temperament, too industrious to come to want; yet too generous ever to be rich.

Average: Love property; yet the other faculties spend quite as fast as this faculty accumulates; with Cautiousness large or very large, love property in order to be safe against future want; with large Approbativeness, desire it to keep up appearances; with large Conscientiousness, to pay debts; with large intellectual organs, will pay freely for intellectual attainments; yet the kind of property and objects sought in its acquisition depends upon other and larger faculties.

Moderate: Value and make property more for its uses than itself; seek it as a means rather than an end; with Cautiousness large, may evince economy from fear of coming to want, or with other large organs, to secure other ends, yet care little for property on its own account; are rather wasteful; do not excel in bargaining, or like it; have no great natural pecuniary tact, or money-making capability, and are in danger of living quite up to income; with Ideality large, must have nice things, no matter how costly, yet do not take first-rate care of them; disregard small expenses; purchase to consume as soon as to keep; prefer to enjoy earnings now to laying them up; with large domestic organ, spend freely for family; with strong Approbativeness and moderate Cautiousness, are extravagant, and contract debts to make a display; with Hope large, run deeply in debt, and spend money before it is earned.

Small: Hold money loosely; spend it often without getting its value; care little how money goes; with Hope very large, enjoy money to-day without saving for to-morrow; and with large Approbativeness and Ideality added, and only average Causality, are prodigal, and spend money to poor advantage; contract debts without providing for their payment, etc.

Very Small: Neither heed nor know the value of money; are wasteful; spend all they can get; lack industry, and will be always in want.

The back part of this organ, called Acquisition, accumulates property; the fore part, called Accumulation, saves; the former large and latter small, encompass sea and land to make a dollar, and then throw it away, which is an American characteristic; and get many things, but allow them to go to waste. Properly to spend money implies a high order of wisdom. Every dollar should be made an instrument of the highest happiness.

To Cultivate: Try to estimate the value of money intellectually, and save up as a philosophy; economize time and means; cultivate industry; engage in some mercenary business; determine to get rich, and use the means for so doing, and be what you consider even small in expenditures; lay by a given sum at stated times, without thinking to use it except in extreme want; and when enough is laid by, make a first payment on real estate, or launch into business, thus compelling yourself both to save the driblets, and earn what you can in order to save yourself, and do by intellect what you are not disposed to do by intuition.

To Restrain: Think less of dollars; study means for enjoying your property; often quit business for recreation; attend more relatively to other life ends, less to mere money-getting; that is, cultivate the other faculties, and be more generous.

10. SECRETIVENESS.

SELF-GOVERNMENT; ABILITY TO RESTRAIN FEELINGS; POLICY; MANAGEMENT; RESERVE; EVASION; DISCRETION; CUNNING; ADAPTED TO MAN'S REQUISITION FOR CONTROLLING HIS ANIMAL NATURE. PERVERTED, IT CAUSES DUPLICITY, DOUBLE-DEALING, LYING, DECEPTION, AND ALL KINDS OF FALSE PRETENSIONS.

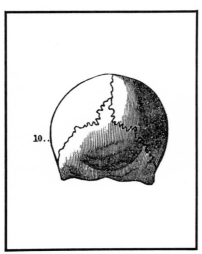

NO. 61.—LARGE.

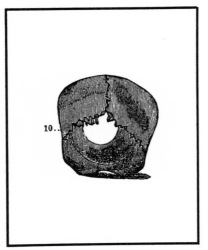

NO. 62.—SMALL.

Very Large: Are non-committal and cunning in the extreme, and with only average Conscientiousness, deceptive, tricky, foxy, double-dealing, and unworthy to be trusted; with large Acquisitiveness added, will both cheat and lie; with large Cautiousness, are unfathomable even by acknowledged friends; with very large moral organs, and only average or full propensities, are not dangerous, and have a good moral basis, yet instinctively employ many stratagems calculated to cover up the real motives; and should cultivate openness and sincerity.

Large: Throw a vail over countenance, expression, and conduct; appear to aim at one thing, while accomplishing another; love to surprise others; are enigmatical, mysterious, guarded, politic, shrewd, managing, employ humbug, and are hard to be found out; with Cautiousness large, take extra pains to escape detection; with Conscientiousness also large, will not tell a lie, yet will not always tell the truth; evade the direct question, and are equivocal, and though honest in purpose, yet resort to many little cunning devices; with large intellectual organs and Cautiousness, express ideas so guardedly as to lack distinctness and directness, and hence to be often misunderstood; with large Approbativeness, take many ways to secure notoriety, and hoist some false colors; with large Acquisitiveness, employ too much cunning in pecuniary transactions, and unless checked by still larger Conscientiousness, are not always strictly truthful or honest; with large social organs, form few friendships, and those only after years of acquaintance, nor evince half the attachment felt; are distant in society, and communicate even with friends only by piecemeal; divulge very few plans or business matters to acquaintances, or even to friends; lack communicativeness, and have little or no fresh-hearted expression of feeling, but leave an impression of uncertainty as to character and intention.

Full: Evince much self-government; yet, if the temperament is active, when the feelings do break forth, manifest them with unusual intensity; with large Acquisitiveness and Cautiousness, communicate but little respecting pecuniary affairs; with large Approbativeness, take the popular side of subjects, and sail only with the current of public opinion; with Conscientiousness large, are upright in motive, and tell the truth, but not always the whole truth; and though never hoist false colors, yet do not always show true ones.

Average: Maintain a good share of self-government, except when under excitement, and then let the whole mind out fully; with large Combativeness and an active temperament, though generally able to control resentment, yet, when once provoked, show the full extent of their anger; with large Cautiousness, see that there is no danger before allowing the feelings to burst forth; but with an excitable temperament, and especially a deranged stomach, show a general want of policy and self-government, because the feelings are too strong to be kept in check; but if this faculty is manifested in connection with stronger faculties, it evinces considerable power, yet is wanting when placed in opposition to them.

Moderate: Express feelings with considerable fullness; pursue an open, direct course; are sincere and true; employ but little policy, and generally give full vent to thoughts and feelings; with Cautiousness large, evince prudence in deeds, but imprudence in words; express opinions unguardedly, yet are safe and circumspect in conduct; with large Acquisitiveness and Conscientiousness, prefer the one-price system in dealing, and can not bear to banter; with large Adhesiveness, are sincere and open-hearted in friendship, and communicate with perfect freedom; with large Conscientiousness and Combativeness added, are truthful, and speak the whole mind too bluntly; with fine feelings, and a good moral organization, manifest the higher, finer feelings, without restraint or reserve, so as to be the more attractive; are full of goodness, and show all that goodness without any intervening vail; manifest in looks and actions what is passing within; express all mental operations with fullness, freedom, and force; choose direct and unequivocal modes of expression; disclose faults as freely as virtues, and leave none at a loss as to the real character; but with the harsher elements predominant, appear more hating and hateful than they really are, because all is blown right out.

Small: Are perfectly transparent; seem to be just what, and all they really are; disdain concealment in all forms; are no hypocrite, but positive and unequivocal in all said and done; carry the soul in the hands and face, and make way directly to the feelings of others, because expressing them so unequivocally; with large Cautiousness, are guarded in action, but unguarded in expression; free the mind regardless of consequences, yet show much prudence in other respects; with Conscientiousness large, love the truth wherever it exists, and open the mind freely to evidence and conviction; are open and above-board in everything, and allow all the mental operations to come right out, unvailed and unrestrained, so that their full force is seen and felt.

Very Small: Conceal nothing, but disclose everything.

To Cultivate: Supply by intellect that guardedness and policy lacked by instinct, for you are too spontaneous; try to "lie low, and keep dark," and suppress your natural out-gushings of feeling and intellect, cultivate self-control by subjecting all you say and do to judgment, instead of allowing momentary impulses to rule conduct; do not tell all you know or intend to do, and occasionally pursue a round-about course; be guarded, politic, and wary in everything; do not make acquaintances or confide in people as much as is natural, but treat everybody as if they needed watching.

To Restrain: Cultivate a direct, straightforward, above-board, and open way, and pursue a course just the opposite from the one suggested for its cultivation.

11. CAUTIOUSNESS.

CAREFULNESS; WATCHFULNESS; PRUDENCE; PROVISION AGAINST WANT AND DANGER; SOLICITUDE; ANXIETY; APPREHENSION; SECURITY; PROTECTION; AVOIDING PROSPECTIVE EVILS, THE SENTINEL. ADAPTED TO WARD OFF SURROUNDING DANGERS, AND MAKE THOSE PROVISIONS NECESSARY FOR FUTURE HAPPINESS PERVERSION – IRRESOLUTION; TIMIDITY; PROCRASTINATION; INDECISION; FRIGHT; PANIC.

Very Large: Are over-anxious; always on the look-out; worried about trifles; afraid of shadows; forever getting ready, because so many provisions to make; are careful in business; often revise decisions, because afraid to trust the issue; live in perpetual fear of evils and accidents; take extra pains with everything; lack promptness and decision, and refuse to run risks; put off till tomorrow what ought to be done to-day; with excitability 7, live in a constant panic; procrastinate; are easily frightened; see mountains of evil where there are only molehills; are often unnerved by fright, and overcome by false alarms; with only average or full Combativeness, Self-Esteem, and Hope, and large Approbativeness, accomplish literally nothing, but should always act under others; with large but more risky ones, and safe investments to active business.

NO. 63.—DEACON TERRY.

Large: Are always on the look-out; take ample time to get ready; provide against prospective dangers; make everything safe; guard against losses and evils; incur no risks; sure bind that they may sure find; with large Combativeness, Hope, and an active temperament, drive, Jehu-like, whatever is undertaken, yet drive cautiously; lay on the lash, yet hold a tight rein, so as not to upset plans; with large Approbativeness, are doubly cautious as to character; with large Approbativeness and small Acquisitiveness, are extra careful of character, but not money; with large Acquisitiveness and small Approbativeness, take special care of all money matters, but not of reputation; with large Adhesiveness and Benevolence, experience the greatest solicitude for the welfare of friends; with large Conscientiousness, are careful to do nothing wrong; with large Causality, lay safe plans, and are judicious; with large Combativeness and Hope, combine judgment with energy and enterprise, and often seem reckless, yet are prudent; with large intellectual organs and Firmness, are cautious in coming to conclusions, and canvass well all sides of all

NO. 64.—CHARLES XII. OF SWEDEN.

111

questions, yet, once settled, are unmoved; with small Self-Esteem, rely too much on the judgment of others, and too little on self; with large Parental Love and disordered nerves, experience unnecessary solicitude for children, and take extra care of them, often killing them with kindness, etc.

Full: Show a good share of prudence and carefulness, except when the other faculties are powerfully excited; with large Combativeness and very large Hope, have too little prudence for energy; are tolerably safe, except when under considerable excitement; with large Acquisitiveness, are very careful whenever money or property are concerned; yet, with only average Causality, evince but little general prudence, and lay plans for the present rather than future, etc.:

Average: Have a good share of prudence, whenever this faculty works in connection with the larger organs, yet evince but little in the direction of the smaller; with large Combativeness and Hope, and an excitable temperament, are practically imprudent, yet somewhat less so than appearances indicate; with large Causality, and only average Hope and Combativeness, and a temperament more strong than excitable, evince good general judgment, and meet with but few accidents; but with an excitable temperament, large Combativeness and Hope, and only average or full Causality, are always in hot water, fail to mature plans, begin before ready, and are luckless and unfortunate in everything, etc.

Moderate: With excitability great, act upon the spur of the moment, without due deliberation; meet with many accidents caused by imprudence; with large Combativeness, are often at variance with neighbors; with large Approbativeness, seek praise, yet often incur criticism; with average Causality and large Hope, are always doing imprudent things, and require a guardian; with small Acquisitiveness, keep money loosely, and are easily over-persuaded to buy more than can be paid for; with large Parental Love, play with children, yet often hurt them; with large Language and small Secretiveness, say many very imprudent things, etc.; and with large Combativeness, have many enemies, etc.:

Small: Are rash, reckless, luckless; and with large Hope, always in trouble; with large Combativeness, plunge headlong into difficulties in full sight, and should assiduously cultivate this faculty.

Very Small: Have so little of this faculty, that its influence on conduct is rarely ever perceived.

To Cultivate: Count the advantages against, but not for; look out for breakers; think how much indiscretion and carelessness have injured you, and be careful and watchful in everything. Imprudence is your fault — be judicious; and remember that danger is always much greater than you anticipate — so keep aloof from every appearance of it.

To Restrain: Offset its workings by intellect; remember that you perpetually magnify dangers; let intellect tell Cautiousness to keep quiet; offset it by cultivating a bold, combative, daring spirit; encourage a don't-care feeling, and a let-things-take-their-course — why-should-I-worry-about-them; do not indulge so much anxiety when children or friends do not return as expected; never allow a frightened, panic-stricken state of mind, but face apprehended evils, instead of quailing before them; and remember that you magnify every appearance of evil.

12. APPROBATIVENESS.

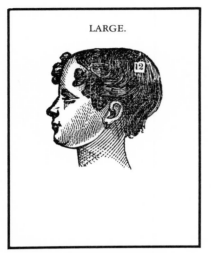

LARGE.

NO. 65.—CLARA FISHER.

114

REGARD FOR CHARACTER, APPEARANCES, ETC.; LOVE OF PRAISE; DESIRE TO EXCEL AND BE ESTEEMED; AMBITION; AFFABILITY; POLITENESS; DESIRE TO DISPLAY AND SHOW OFF; SENSE OF HONOR; DESIRE FOR A GOOD NAME, FOR NOTORIETY, FAME, EMINENCE, DISTINCTION, AND TO BE THOUGHT WELL OF; PRIDE OF CHARACTER; SENSITIVENESS TO THE SPEECHES OF PEOPLE; AND LOVE OF POPULARITY. ADAPTED TO THE REPUTABLE AND DISGRACEFUL. PERVERSION—VANITY; AFFECTATION; CEREMONIOUSNESS; ARISTOCRACY; POMPOSITY; EAGERNESS FOR POPULARITY, OUTSIDE DISPLAY, ETC.

Very Large: Set everything by the good opinion of others; are ostentatious, if not vain and ambitious; love praise, and are mortified by censure inordinately; with moderate Self-Esteem and Firmness, can not breast public opinion, but are over-fond of popularity; with only average Conscientiousness, seek popularity without regard to merit; but with large Conscientiousness, seek praise mainly for virtuous doings; with large Ideality, and only average Causality, seek praise for fashionable dress and outside appearances rather than internal merit; are both vain and fashionable as well as aristocratic; starve the kitchen to stuff the parlor; with large Acquisitiveness, boast of riches; with large Adhesiveness, of friends; with large Language, are extra forward in conversation, and engross much of the time, etc. This is the main organ of aristocracy, exclusiveness, fashionableness, so-called pride, and nonsensical outside show.

Large: Love commendation, and are cut by censure; are keenly alive to the smiles and frowns of public opinion; mind what people say; strive to show off to advantage, and are affable, courteous, and desirous of pleasing; love to be in company; stand on etiquette and ceremony; aspire to do and become something great; set much by appearances, and are mortified by reproach; with large Cautiousness and moderate Self-Esteem, are careful to take the popular side, and fear to face the ridicule of others; yet, with Conscientiousness and Combativeness large, stick to the right, though unpopular, knowing that it will ultimately confer honor; with large Benevolence, seek praise for works of philanthropy and mercy; with large intellectual organs, love literary and intellectual distinctions; with large Adhesiveness, desire the good opinion of friends, yet care little for that of others; with large Self-Esteem, Combativeness, and excitability, are very touchy when criticised, seek public life, want all the praise, and hate rivals; with large perceptives, take a forward part in literary and debating societies; with large Combativeness, Hope, and activity, will not be outdone, but rather work till completely exhausted, and are liable to over-do, in order to eclipse rivals.

Full: Value the estimation of others, yet will not go far after it; seek praise in the direction of the larger organs, yet care little for it in that of the smaller; are not aristocratic, yet like to make a fair show in the world; with large Adhesiveness, love the praise and can not endure the censure of friends; with large Conscientiousness, set much by moral character, and wish to be praised for correct motives; yet, with moderate Acquisitiveness, care little for the name of being rich; with large Benevolence and intellectual organs, desire to be esteemed for evincing talent in doing good, etc.

Average: Show only a respectable share of this faculty, except when it is powerfully wrought upon by praise or reproach; are mortified by censure, yet not extremely so, and call the other faculties to justify; are not particularly ambitious, yet by no means deficient, and not insensible to compliments, yet can not well be inflated by praise:

Moderate: Feel some, but no great, regard for popularity; and evince this faculty only in connection with the larger organs; with large Self-Esteem and Firmness, are inflexible and austere; and with large Combativeness and small Agreeableness, lack civility and complaisance to others; disdain to flatter, and can not be flattered, and should cultivate a pleasing, winning mode of address.

Small: Care little for the opinions of others, even of friends; are comparatively insensible to praise; disregard style and fashion; despise etiquette and formal usages; never ask what will persons think, and put on no outside appearances for their own sake; with large Self-Esteem, Firmness, and Combativeness, are destitute of politeness, devoid of ceremony, and not at all flexible or pleasing in manners; with large Combativeness and Conscientiousness, go for the right regardless of popularity, and are always making enemies; say and do things in so graceless a manner as often to displease; with large Acquisitiveness and Self-Esteem, though wealthy, make no boast of it, and are as commonplace in conduct as if poor, etc.

Very Small: Care almost nothing for reputation, praise, or censure.

To Cultivate: Remember that you often stand in your own light by caring little for the speeches of people, for appearance and character; and cherish a higher regard for public opinion, for your character and standing among men, for a good name, and do nothing in the least to tarnish your reputation, but cultivate a winning, politic, pleasant manner toward all, as if you would ingratiate yourself into their good-will.

To Restrain: Remember that you are infinitely too sensitive to reproof; that your feelings are often hurt when there is no occasion; that you often feel neglected or reproved without cause; that evil speaking breaks no bones, and will ultimately thwart itself; lay aside that affected, artificial, nippy style of manners and speaking; be more natural; walk, act, feel as if alone, not forever looked at; be less particular about dress, style, appearance, etc., and less mindful of praise and blame; subject Approbativeness to conscience — that is, do what is right, and let people say what they like; be more independent, and less ambitious and sensitive to praise and flattery.

13. SELF-ESTEEM.

SELF-APPRECIATION AND VALUATION; SELF-RESPECT AND RELI-
ANCE; MAGNANIMITY; NOBLENESS; INDEPENDENCE; DIGNITY
SELF-SATISFACTION AND COMPLACENCY; LOVE OF LIBERTY AND
POWER; AN ASPIRING, SELF-ELEVATING, RULING INSTINCT; PRIDE
OF CHARACTER; MANLINESS; LOFTY-MINDEDNESS, AND DESIRE
FOR ELEVATION. ADAPTED TO THE SUPERIORITY, GREATNESS,
AND EXALTED DIGNITY OF HUMAN NATURE. PERVERSION: EGO-
TISM; HAUTEUR; FORWARDNESS; TYRANNY; SUPERCILIOUSNESS;
IMPERIOUSNESS.

NO. 66.—SUBMISSION.

Very Large: Have the highest respect for *self*; place
special stress on the personal pronouns; carry a high head,
and walk so straight as to lean backward; have a restless,
boundless ambition to be and do some great thing; with
only full intellect, have more ambition than talents, and
are proud, pompous, supercilious, and imperious, and with
Hope large, must operate on a great scale or none, and
launch out too deeply; with Approbativeness large, are
most aristocratic; and with only fair intellect, are a swell-
head and great brag, and put self above everybody else;
with only average Approbativenes and Agreeableness, take
no pains to smooth off the rougher points of character, but
are every way repulsive; with average Parental Love, are
very domineering in the family, and insist upon being
waited upon, obeyed, etc.; and should carry the head a little lower, and cultivate humility.

Large: Put a high estimate upon self—sayings, doings,
and capabilities; fall back upon their own unaided resources; will not take advice, but insist upon being their
own master; are high-minded; will never stoop, or demean
self; aim high; are not satisfied with moderate success, or a
petty business, and comport and express with dignity, and
perhaps with majesty; are perfectly self-satisfied; with large
Parental Love, pride self in children, yet with Combativeness large, require implicit obedience, and are liable to be
stern; with large Adhesiveness, seek society, yet must lead;
with large Acquisitiveness added, seek partnership, but
must be the head of the firm; with large Firmness and
Combativeness, can not be driven, but insist upon doing
their *own* will and pleasure, and are sometimes contrary
and headstrong with large Hope, think that anything they
do can not possibly fail, because done so well; with large
moral organs, impart a tone, dignity, aspiration, and elevation of character which command universal respect; and
with large intellectual faculties added, are desirous of, and

NO. 67.—AUTHORITY.

117

well calculated for, public life; are a natural leader, but seek moral distinction, and lead the public *mind*; with large Combativeness. Destructiveness, Firmness, and Approbativeness, love to be captain or general, and speak with that sternness and authority which enforce obedience; with large Acquisitiveness, aspire to be rich — the richest man in town — partly on account of the power wealth confers; with large Language, Individuality, Firmness, and Combativeness, seek to be a political leader; with large Constructiveness, Perceptives, Causality, and Combativeness, are well calculated to have the direction of men, and oversee large mechanical establishments; with only average brain and intellect, and large selfish faculties, are proud, haughty, domineering, egotistical, overbearing, greedy of power and dominion, etc.

Full: Evince a good degree of dignity and self-respect; yet are not proud or haughty; with large Combativeness, Firmness, and Hope, rely fully upon their own energies in cases of emergency, yet are willing to hear advice, though seldom take it; conduct becomingly, and secure respect; and with large Combativeness and Firmness, and full Destructiveness and Hope, evince much power of this faculty, but little when these faculties are moderate:

Average: Show this faculty mainly in combination with those that are larger; with large Approbativeness and Firmness, and a large brain and moral organs, rarely trifle or evince meanness, yet are rarely conceited, and think neither too little nor too much of self, but place a just estimate upon their own capabilities; with large Adhesiveness, both receive and impart character to friends, yet receive most; with large Conscientiousness, pride self more on moral worth than physical qualities, wealth, titles, etc.; and with large intellectual and moral organs, mainly for intellectual and moral excellence.

Moderate: Rather underrate personal capabilities and worth; feel rather inferior, unworthy, and humble; lack dignity and manliness, and are apt to say and do trifling things, and let self down; with large intellectual and moral organs, lead off well when once placed in a responsible position, yet at first distrust their own capabilities; with large Conscientiousness, Combativeness, and activity, often appear self-sufficient and positive, because certain of being right, yet it is founded more on reason than egotism; with large Approbativeness, love to show off, yet are not satisfied with self; go abroad after praise, rather than feel internally conscious of personal merits; are apt to boast, because more desirous of the estimation of others than conscious of personal worth; with large moral and intellectual powers, have exalted thoughts and aspirations, and communicate well, yet often detract from them by commonplace phrases and undignified expressions; will be too familiar to be respected in proportion to merit, and should vigorously cultivate this faculty by banishing mean, and cultivating high, thoughts of self.

Small: Feel diminutive lack elevation and dignity of tone and manner; place too low estimate on self; and, with Approbativeness large, are too anxious to appear well in the eyes of others; with large Combativeness and Destructiveness, show some self-reliance when provoked or placed in responsible positions, yet lack that dignity and tone which command universal respect, and give a capability to lead off in society; lack self-confidence and weight of character; shrink from responsible and great undertakings, from a feeling of unworthiness; underrate self, and are therefore undervalued by others, and feel insignificant, as if in the way, or trespassing upon others, and hence often apologize, and should cultivate this faculty.

Very Small: Feel little, and manifest none of this faculty.

To Cultivate: Say of yourself what Black Hawk said to Jackson—"I am a man"—one endowed with the ennobling elements of humanity; try to realize how exalted those human endowments conferred on you, and hence duly to estimate yourself, physically, intellectually, morally; recount your good traits, and cultivate self-valuation in view of them; pride yourself on what you are; but never indulge self-abasement because not dressed, because not as rich or stylish as others; be less humble toward men, but hold up your head among them, as if good enough for any; assume the attitude of self-esteem; study its phrenological definition, and cultivate the self-esteem feeling.

To Restrain: Bear in mind that you esteem yourself much better than you really are; that you overrate all your powers, and are too forward and self-confident; that more modesty would improve you; that you incline too much to be arbitrary, and domineer; that you are more faulty than you suppose, and need humility.

14a. FIRMNESS.

STABILITY; DECISION; PERSEVERANCE; FIXEDNESS OF PURPOSE; TENACITY OF WILL, AND AVERSION TO CHANGE. ADAPTED TO MAN'S REQUISITION FOR HOLDING OUT TO THE END. PERVERSION—OBSTINACY; WILLFULNESS; MULISHNESS; STUBBORNNESS; UNWILLINGNESS TO CHANGE, EVEN WHEN REASON REQUIRES.

Very Large: Are well-nigh obstinate, stubborn, and with large Combativeness and Self-Esteem, as unchangeable as the laws of the Medes and Persians, and can neither be persuaded nor driven; with large activity, power, brain, and intellectual organs, are well calculated to carry forward some great work which requires the utmost determination and energy; with large Causality, can possibly be turned by potent reasons, yet by nothing else.

Large: Are set and willful; stick to and carry out what is commenced; hold on long and hard; continue to the end, and may be fully relied upon; with full Self-Esteem and large Combativeness, can not be driven, but the more they are forced the more they resist; with large Combativeness and Destructiveness, add perseverance to stability, and not only hold on, but drive forward determinedly through difficulties; with large Hope, undertake much, and carry all out; with large Cautiousness and Causality, are careful and judicious in laying plans and forming opinions, yet rarely change; may seem to waver until the mind is fully made up, but are afterward the more unchanging; with Hope very large, and Cautiousness and Causality only average, decided quickly, even rashly, and refuse to change; with Adhesiveness and Benevolence large, are easily persuaded, especially by friends, yet can not be driven; and with large Cautiousness, Combativeness, Causality, perceptives, activity, and power, will generally succeed, because wise in planning and persevering in execution; with Combativeness and Self-Esteem large, and Causality only average, will not see the force of opposing arguments, but tenaciously adhere to affirmed opinions and purposes; with large Conscientiousness and Combativeness, are doubly decided wherever right or justice are concerned, and in such cases will never give one inch, but will stand out in argument, effort, or as a juryman till the last.

Full: Like Firmness large, show a great degree of decision when this faculty works with large organs, but not otherwise; with Combativeness and Conscientiousness large, show great fixedness where right and truth are con-

NO. 68.—LARGE.

NO. 69.—SMALL.

cerned, yet with Acquisitiveness moderate, lack perseverance in money matters; with moderate Combativeness and Self-Esteem, are easily turned; and with large Adhesiveness and Benevolence, too easily persuaded, even against their better judgment; with Cautiousness and Approbativeness large, or very large, often evince fickleness, irresolution, and procrastination; and with an uneven head, and an excitable temperament, often appear deficient in this faculty.

Average: When supported by large Combativeness or Conscientiousness, or Causality, or Acquisitiveness, etc., show a good degree of this faculty; but when opposed by large Cautiousness, Approbativeness, or Adhesiveness, evince its deficiency, and have not enough for great undertakings.

Moderate: Rather lack perseverance, even when the stronger faculties support it; but when they do not, evince fickleness, irresolution, indecision, and lack perseverance; with Adhesiveness large, are too easily persuaded and influenced by friends; with large Cautiousness and Approbativeness, and moderate or small Self-Esteem, are flexible and fickle, and go with the current.

Small: With activity great, and the head uneven, are fitful, impulsive, and, like the weather-vane, shift with every changing breeze, and are ruled by the other faculties, and as unstable as water.

Very Small: Are changed by the slightest motives, and a perfect creature of circumstances, and accomplishes nothing requiring perseverance.

To Cultivate: Have more a mind of your own; make up your mind wisely, and then stand to your purpose; be sure you are right, then hold on; surmount difficulties, instead of turning aside to avoid them; resist the persuasions of others; begin nothing not worthy of finishing, and finish all you begin.

To Restrain: Remember that you are too obstinate and persistent—often to your own loss; at least listen to the advice of others, and duly consider it, and govern Firmness by Intellect and Conscience, not allow it to govern them.

14b. MORAL SENTIMENTS.

THESE RENDER MAN A MORAL, ACCOUNTABLE, AND RELIGIOUS BEING—HUMANIZE, ADORN, AND ELEVATE HIS NATURE; CONNECT HIM WITH THE MORAL NATURE OF THINGS; CREATE HIS HIGHER AND NOBLER FACULTIES; BEGET ASPIRATIONS AFTER GOODNESS, VIRTUE, PURITY AND MORAL PRINCIPLE, AND ALLY HIM TO ANGELS AND TO GOD.

LARGE.

NO. 70.—REV. DR. TYNG.

SMALL.

NO. 71.—MALEFACTOR.

Very Large: Have a most exalted sense and feeling of the moral and religious, with a high order of practical goodness, and the strongest aspirations for a higher and holier state, both in this life and that which is to come.

Large: Experience a high regard for things sacred and religious; have an elevated, moral, and aspiring cast of feelings and conduct, right intentions, and a desire to become good, holy, and moral in feeling and conduct; and, with weak animal feelings, are a rose in the shade.

Full: Have a good moral and religious tone, and general correctness of motive, so as to render feelings and conduct about right; but with strong propensities, and only average intellectual faculties, are sometimes led into errors of belief and practice; mean right, yet sometimes do wrong, and should cultivate these faculties, and restrain the propensities.

Average: Surrounded by good influences, will be tolerably moral and religious in feeling, yet not sufficiently so to withstand strong propensities; with disordered nerves, are quite liable to say and do wrong things, yet afterward repent, and require much moral cultivation.

Moderate: Have a rather weak moral tone; feel but little regard for things sacred and religious; are easily led into temptation; feel but little moral restraint; and, with large propensities, especially if circumstances favor their excitement, are exceedingly liable to say and do what is wrong.

Small: Have weak moral feeling; lack moral character; and with large organs of the propensities, are liable to be depraved, and a bad member of society.

To Cultivate: Yield implicit obedience to the higher, better sentiments of your nature; cultivate a respect for religion; lead a moral, spotless life; cultivate all the human virtues; especially study and contemplate nature, and yield yourself to those elevating influences enkindled thereby; cultivate adoration and love of the Deity in His works; study natural religion, and make your life as pure, right, true, and good as possible.

To Restrain: To avoid becoming morbid in the action of the moral sentiments, and to obviate it when it exists, subject Benevolence or generosity, justice or conscientious scruples, Veneration or devotion, Spirituality or faith, to the guidance of intellect; and be more selfish, or at least less self-sacrificing — think more of material things.

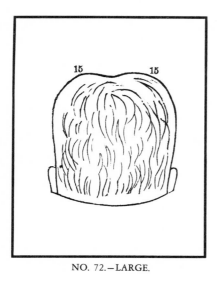

NO. 72.—LARGE.

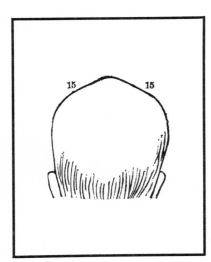

NO. 73.—SMALL.

124

MORAL PRINCIPLE; INTEGRITY; PERCEPTION AND LOVE OF RIGHT; INNATE SENSE OF ACCOUNTABILITY AND OBLIGATION; LOVE OF JUSTICE AND TRUTH; REGARD FOR DUTY; DESIRE FOR MORAL PURITY AND EXCELLENCE; DISPOSITION TO FULFILL PROMISES, AGREEMENTS, ETC.; THAT INTERNAL MONITOR WHICH APPROVES THE RIGHT AND CONDEMNS THE WRONG; SENSE OF GUILT; PENITENCE; CONTRITION; DESIRE TO REFORM. ADAPTED TO THE RIGHTNESS OF RIGHT, AND THE WRONGNESS OF WRONG, AND TO THE MORAL NATURE AND CONSTITUTION OF THINGS. PERVERTED, IT MAKES ONE DO WRONG FROM CON-SCIENTIOUS SCRUPLES, AND TORMENTS WITH UNDUE SELF-CONDEMNATION.

Very Large: Place moral excellence at the head of all excellence; make duty everything; are governed by the highest order of moral principle; would on no account knowingly do wrong; are scrupulously exact in all matters of right; perfectly honest in motive; always condemning self and repenting, and very forgiving to those who evince penitence, but inexorable without; with Combativeness large, evince the utmost indignation at the wrong, and drive the right with great force; are censorious, make but little allowance for the faults and follies of mankind, and show extraordinary moral courage and fortitude; with small Secretiveness and an active temperament, are liable to denounce evil-doers; with large Friendship, can not tolerate the least thing wrong in friends, and are liable to reprove them; with large Parental Love, exact too much from children, and with large Combativeness, are too liable to blame them; with large Cautiousness, are often afraid to do, for fear of doing wrong; with large Veneration, reason-ing faculties, and Language, are a natural theologian, and take the highest pleasure in reasoning and conversing upon all things having a moral and religious bearing; with Ven-eration average, and Benevolence large or very large, can not well help being a thorough-going reformer, etc.

Large: Love the right as right, and hate the wrong be-cause wrong are honest, faithful, upright in motive; mean well; consult duty before expediency; feel guilty when con-scious of having done wrong ask forgiveness for the past, and try to do better in future; with strong propensities, will sometimes do wrong, but be exceedingly sorry there-for; and, with a wrong education added, are liable to do wrong, thinking it right, because these propensities warp conscience, yet mean well; with large Cautiousness, are so-licitous to know what is right, and careful to do it; with weaker Cautiousness, sometimes do wrong carelessly or indifferently, yet afterward repent it; with large Cautiousness and Destructiveness, are severe on wrong-doers, and unrelenting until they evince penitence, and then cordially forgive; with large Approbativeness, keep the moral character pure and spotless — value others on their morals more than wealth, birth, etc., and make the word the bond; with large Benevolence, Combativeness, and Destructiveness, feel great indignation and severity against oppressors, and those who cause others to suffer by wronging them; with large Ideality, have strong aspirations after moral purity and excellence; with large reasoning organs, take great pleasure, and show much talent in reasoning upon and investigating moral subjects, etc.

Full: Have good conscientious feelings, and correct general intentions, yet are not quite as correct in action as intentions; mean well, yet with large Combativeness, Destructiveness, Amativeness, etc., may sometimes yield to these faculties, especially if the system is somewhat inflamed; with large Acquisitiveness, make very close bargains, and will take such advantages as are common in business, yet do not intend to wrong others out of their just dues, still have more regard for money than justice; with large intellectual organs, love to reason upon subjects where right and duty are involved, yet too often take the ground of expediency, and fail to allow right its due weight; and should never allow conscience to be in any way weakened, but cultivate it assiduously.

Average: When not tempted by stronger faculties, do what is about right; generally justify self, and do not feel particularly indignant at the wrong, or commendatory of the right; with large Approbativeness and Self-Esteem, may do the honorable thing, yet where honor and right clash, will choose the former; with only average Combativeness and Destructiveness, allow many wrong things to pass unrebuked, or even unresented, and show no great moral indignation or force; with moderate or small Secretiveness and Acquisitiveness, and large Approbativeness, Benevolence, and Ideality, will do as nearly right, and commit as few errors as those with Secretiveness, Acquisitiveness, and Conscientiousness all large, and may be trusted, especially on honor, yet will rarely feel guilty, and should never be blamed, because Approbativeness will be mortified before conscience is convicted; with large propensities, especially Secretiveness and Acquisitiveness, and only full Benevolence, are selfish; should be dealt with cautiously, and thoroughly bound in writing, because liable to be slippery, tricky, etc.; and should cultivate this faculty by never allowing the propensities to overcome it, and by always considering things in the moral aspect.

Moderate: Have some regard for duty in feeling, but less in practice; justify self; are not very penitent or forgiving; even temporize with principle, and sometimes let interest rule duty.

Small: Have few conscientious scruples, and little penitence, gratitude, or regard for moral principle, justice, duty, etc., and are governed mainly by the larger faculties; with large propensities, and only average Veneration and Spirituality, evince a marked deficiency of moral principle; with moderate Secretiveness and Acquisitiveness, and only full Destructiveness and Combativeness, and large Adhesiveness, Approbativeness, Benevolence, Ideality, and Intellect, and a fine temperament, may live a tolerably blameless life, yet, on close scrutiny, will lack the moral in feeling, but may be safely trusted, because true to promises; that is, conscience having less to contend with, its deficiency is less observable. Such should most earnestly cultivate this faculty:

Very Small: Are almost wholly destitute of moral feeling, and wholly controlled by the other faculties.

To Cultivate: Always ask yourself what is right and wrong, and adhere closely to the former, and studiously avoid the latter; make everything a matter of principle; do just as nearly right as you know how in everything, and never allow conscience to be borne down by any of the other faculties, but keep it supreme; maintain the right everywhere and for everybody; cultivate a high sense of duty and obligation, and try to reform every error; in short, "let justice be done, though the heavens fall."

To Restrain: Remember that you are too exact and exacting in everything; that you often think you see faults where there are none; that you carry duty and right to a boundless extreme, and so far as to make it wrong; that you are too condemnatory, and need to cultivate a lenient, forbearing, forgiving spirit; that you trouble yourself un-

126

duly about the wrong-doing of others; that you often accuse people of meaning worse than they really intend — look at minor faults as mountains of wrong; are too censorious; too apt to throw away the gold on account of dross; to discard the greater good on account of lesser attendant evils; too liable to a feeling of guilt and unworthiness, as if unfit to live, and too conscience-stricken. Extreme Conscientiousness, with 6 or 7 organic quality, and large Combativeness, along with disordered nerves or dyspepsia, makes one of the most unpleasant of characters — querulous, eternally grumbling about nothing, magnifying everybody's faults, thus making mischief among neighbors; perpetually accusing everybody, and chiding children for mere trifles; too rabid in matters of reform, and violent in denouncing its opponents — of whom rabid radicals, punctilious religionists, and old maids furnish examples.

16. HOPE.

EXPECTATION; ANTICIPATION OF FUTURE SUCCESS AND HAPPI-NESS. ADAPTED TO MAN'S RELATIONS WITH THE FUTURE. PER-VERTED, IT BECOMES VISIONARY AND CASTLE-BUILDING.

Very Large: Have unbounded expectations; build a world of castles in the air; live in the future; enjoy things in anticipation more than possession; with small Continuity, have too many irons in the fire; with an active temperament added, take on more business than can be worked off properly; are too much hurried to do things in season; with large Acquisitiveness, are grasping, count chickens before they are hatched, and often two to the egg at that; with only average Cautiousness, are always in hot water; never stop to enjoy what is possessed, but grasp after more, and will never accomplish much, because undertake too much, and in taking one step forward, often slip two steps back.

Large: Expect much from the future; contemplate with pleasure the bright features of life's picture; never despond; overrate prospective good, and underrate and overlook obstacles and evils; calculate on more than the nature of the case will warrant; expect, and hence attempt, a great deal, and are therefore always full of business; are sanguine, and rise above present trouble by hoping for better things in future, and though disappointed, hope on still; build some air-castles, and live in the future more than present; with large Combativeness, Firmness, and Causality, are enterprising, never give up the ship, but struggle manfully through difficulties; and with large Approbativeness, and full Self-Esteem added, feel adequate to difficulties, and grapple with them spiritedly; with large Self-Esteem, think that everything attempted must succeed, and with large Causality added, consider their plans well-nigh perfect; with large Acquisitiveness, lay out money freely in view of future gain; with large Approbativeness and Self-Esteem, hope for renown, honor, etc.; with large Veneration and Spirituality, hope to attain exalted moral excellence, and should check it by acting on only half it promises, and reasoning against it.

Full: Expect considerable, yet realize more; undertake no more than can be accomplished; are quite sanguine and enterprising, yet with Cautiousness large are always on the safe side; with large Acquisitiveness added, invest money freely, yet always safely; make good bargains, if any, and count all the cost, yet are not afraid of expenses where they will more than pay; with larger animal organs than moral, will hope more for this world's goods than for another, and with larger moral than animal, for another state of being than this, etc.

Average: Expect and attempt too little, rather than too much; with large Cautiousness, dwell more on difficulties than encouragements; are contented with the present rather than lay out for the future; with large Acquisitiveness added, invest money very safely, if at all, and prefer to put it out securely on interest rather than risk it in business, except in a perfectly sure business; will make money slowly, yet lose little; and with large intellectual organs, in the long run may acquire considerable wealth.

Moderate: With large Cautiousness, make few promises; but with large Conscientiousness, scrupulously fulfill them, because promise only what can be performed; with small Self-Esteem, and large Veneration, Conscientiousness, and Cautiousness, if a professed Christian, will have many fears as to his future salvation; with only average propensities, will lack energy, enterprise, and fortitude; with large Firmness and Cautiousness, are very slow to embark, yet once committed, rarely give up; with large reasoning faculties, may be sure of success, because see *why and how* it is to be brought about; with large Acquisitiveness, will hold on to whatever money is once acquired, or at least spend very cautiously, and only where sure to be returned with interest; should cheer up, never despond, count favorable, but not unfavorable chances, keep up a lively, buoyant state of mind, and "hope on, hope ever."

Small: Expect and undertake very little; with large Cautiousness, put off till it is too late; are always behind; may embark in projects after everybody else has succeeded, but will then be too late, and in general knock at the door just after it has been bolted; with large Cautiousness, are forever in doubt; with large Approbativeness and Cautiousness, though most desirous of praise, have little hopes of obtaining it, and therefore exceedingly backward in society, yet fear ridicule rather than hope for praise; are easily discouraged; see lions in the way; lack enterprise; magnify obstacles, etc.

Very Small: Expect next to nothing, and undertake less.

To Cultivate: Look altogether on the bright side, the dark none; calculate all the chances for, none against you; mingle in young and lively society; banish care, and cultivate juvenility; cheer up; venture more in business; cultivate trust in the future, and "look aloft!"

To Restrain: Offset excessive expectation by intellect; say to yourself, "My hope so far exceeds realities that I shall not get half I expect," and calculate accordingly; do business on the *cash* principle in both buying and selling, otherwise you are in danger of being swamped — of buying more than you can pay for, and indorsing too much; build no castles in the air; indulge no revelings of hope; shoulder only half the load you feel confident you can carry, and balance your visionary anticipations by cool judgment.

17. SPIRITUALITY.

FAITH; PRESCIENCE; THE "LIGHT WITHIN;" TRUST IN PROPHETIC GUIDINGS; PERCEPTION AND FEELING OF THE SPIRITUAL; INTERIOR PERCEPTION OF TRUTH, WHAT IS BEST, WHAT IS ABOUT TO TRANSPIRE, ETC. ADAPTED TO MAN'S PROPHETIC GIFT AND A FUTURE LIFE. PERVERSION—SUPERSTITION; WITCHCRAFT; AND WITH CAUTIOUSNESS LARGE, FEAR OF GHOSTS.

Very Large: Are led and governed by a species of prophetic guiding; feel by intuition what is right and best; are forewarned of danger, and led by spiritual monition into the right way; feel internally what is true and false, right and wrong, best and not best; unless well regulated, are too credulous, superstitious, and a believer in dreams, ghosts, and wonders, and liable to be misled by them and so-called prophecies, as well as to become fanatical on religion.

Large: Perceive and know things independent of the senses or intellect, or, as it were, by prophetic intuition; experience an internal consciousness of what is best, and that spiritual communion which constitutes the essence of true piety; love to meditate; experience a species of waking clairvoyance, as it were "forewarned;" combined with large Veneration, hold intimate communion with the Deity, who is profoundly adored; and take a world of pleasure in that calm, happy, half-ecstatic state of mind caused by this faculty; with large Causality, perceive truth by intuition, which philosophical tests prove correct; with large Comparison added, have a deep and clear insight into spiritual subjects, and embody a vast amount of the highest order of truth; and clearly perceive and fully realize a spiritual state of being after death.

Full: Have a full share of high, pure, and spiritual feeling; many premonitions or interior warnings and guidings, which, implicitly followed, conduct to success and happiness through life; and an inner test or touchstone of truth, right, etc., in a kind of interior consciousness, which is independent of reason, yet, unperverted, in harmony with it; are quite spiritual-minded, and, as it were, "led by the spirit."

Average: Have some spiritual premonitions and guidings, yet they are not always sufficiently distinct to secure being followed; but when followed, they lead correctly; see this light within, and feel what is true and best with tolerable distinctness, and should cultivate this faculty by following its light.

131

Moderate: Have some, but not very distinct perception of spiritual things; rather lack faith; believe mainly from evidence, and little from intuition; with large Causality, say "Prove it," and take no man's say unless he gives good *reasons*.

Small: Perceive spiritual truths so indistinctly as rarely to admit them; are not guided by faith, because so weak; like disbelieving Thomas, must see the fullest proof before believing; have very little credulity, and doubt things of a superhuman origin or nature; have no premonitions, and disbelieve in them.

Very Small: Have no spiritual guidings or superstitions:

To Cultivate: Muse and meditate on divine things — the Deity, a future existence, the state of man after death, immortality, and that class of subjects; and, especially, *follow* your innermost impressions or presentiments in everything, as well as open your mind to the intuitive reception of truth.

To Restrain: Cultivate the terrestrial more and celestial less; abstain from and restrain spiritual musings and contemplations, and confine yourself more to the practical, tangible, and real; keep away from fanatical meetings, and confine yourself more to life as it is — to what and where you are, instead of are to be — to earth, its duties and pleasures.

18. VENERATION.

DEVOTION; ADORATION OF A SUPREME BEING; REVERENCE FOR RELIGION AND THINGS SACRED; DISPOSITION TO PRAY, WORSHIP, AND OBSERVE RELIGIOUS RITES. ADAPTED TO THE EXISTENCE OF A GOD, AND THE PLEASURES AND BENEFITS EXPERIENCED BY MAN IN WORSHIPING HIM. PERVERTED, IT PRODUCES IDOLATRY, SUPERSTITIOUS REVERENCE FOR AUTHORITY, BIGOTRY, RELIGIOUS INTOLERANCE, ETC.

Very Large: Experience the highest degree of Divine love and worship; place God as supreme upon the throne of the soul, and make His worship a central duty; manifest extreme fervor, anxiety, and delight in divine worhsip and are pre-eminently fervent in prayer; obsequious reverence for age, for time-honored forms, ceremonies, and institutions; with moderate Self-Esteem, and large Conscientiousness and Cautiousness, and a disordered temperament, experience the utmost unworthiness and guiltiness in His sight, and are crushed by a sense of guilt and vileness, especially before God, yet should never cherish these feelings; are always dreading the wrath of Heaven, no matter whether the actions are right or wrong; and should cultivate religious cheerfulness and hope of future happiness.

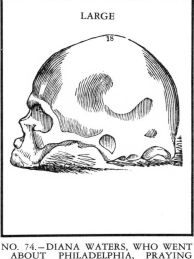

NO. 74.—DIANA WATERS, WHO WENT ABOUT PHILADELPHIA, PRAYING AND EXHORTING ALL SHE MET TO REPENT AND PRAY TO GOD.

Large: Experience an awe of God and things sacred; love to adore the Supreme Being, especially in His works; feel true devotion, fervent piety, and love of divine things; take great delight in religious exercises; have much respect for superiority; regard God as the center of hopes, fears, and aspirations; with large Hope and Spirituality, worship Him as a spirit, and hope to be with and like Him; with large Ideality, contemplate His works with rapture and ecstasy; with large Sublimity, adore Him as infinite in everything; with large reasoning organs have clear, and, if the faculties are unperverted, correct ideas of the Divine character and government, and delight to reason thereon: with large Parental Love, adore Him as a friend and father; and with large Benevolence, for His infinite *goodness*, etc.; with large Causality added, as securing the happiness of sentient beings by a wise institution of *law*, and as the great first cause of all things; with large and perverted Cautiousness, mingle fear and dread with worship; with large Constructiveness and Causality, admire the system evinced in His architectural plans, contrivances, etc.

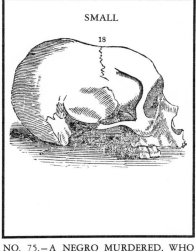

NO. 75.—A NEGRO MURDERED, WHO IGNORED ALL RELIGION.

Full: Experience a good degree of religious worship whenever cicumstances excite this faculty, and allow the

133

stronger faculties frequently to divert it, yet pray at least internally; with large or very large Conscience or Benevolence, place religion in doing right and doing good more than in religious observances, and esteem duties higher than ceremonies; with strong propensities, may be devout upon the Sabbath, yet will be worldly through the week, and experience some conflict between the religious and worldly aspirations.

Average: Will adore the Deity, yet often make religion subservient to the larger faculties; with large Adhesiveness, Benevolence, and Conscience, may love religious meetings, to meet friends, and pray for the good of mankind, or because duty requires their attendance; yet are not habitually and innately devotional, except when this faculty is especially excited by circumstances.

Moderate: Will not be particularly devout or worshipful; with large Benevolence and Conscientiousness, if religiously educated, may be religious, yet will place religion more in works than faith, in duty than prayer, and be more moral than pious; in prayer will supplicate blessings upon mankind, and with Conscientiousness large, will confess sin more than express an awe of God; with large reflectives, worship no further than *reason* precedes worship; with moderate Spirituality and Conscientiousness, care little for religion as such, but with large Benevolence, place religion mainly in doing good, etc.; and are by no means conservative in religion, but take liberal views of religious subjects; and are religious only when this faculty is considerably excited.

Small: Experience little devotion or respect, and are deficient in fervor; care little for religious observances, and are not easily impressed with the worshiping sentiment.

Very Small: Are almost destitute of the feeling and practice of this sentiment.

To Cultivate: Study and admire the divine in nature, animate and inanimate, heaven and earth, man and things, present and future; cultivate admiration and adoration of the Divine character and government, of this stupendous order of things, of the beauties and perfections of nature, as well as a regard for religion and things sacred; but contemplate the Divine *mercy* and goodness rather than austerity, and salvation than condemnation.

134

To Restrain is rarely, if ever, necessary, unless where religious excitement endangers religious fanaticism and hallucination. In such cases avoid religious meetings, conversations, etc., as much as possible; cultivate the other faculties, and especially those which relate to this world and its pleasures; take those physical remedies, exercise, bathing, etc., which will withdraw blood from the head, and promote health; and especially do not think of the Deity with feelings of awe, fear, or terror, but as a kind and loving heavenly Father, good to all His creatures.

19a. BENEVOLENCE.

SYMPATHY; KINDNESS; HUMANITY; DESIRE TO MAKE OTHERS HAPPY; A SELF-SACRIFICING DISPOSITION; PHILANTHROPY; GENEROSITY; THE ACCOMMODATING, NEIGHBORLY SPIRIT. ADAPTED TO MAN'S CAPABILITY OF MAKING HIS FELLOW-MEN HAPPY. PERVERSION—MISPLACED SYMPATHIES.

Very Large: Are deeply and thoroughly imbued with a benevolent spirit, and do good spontaneously; with large Adhesiveness and moderate Acquisitiveness, are too ready to help friends; and with large Hope added, especially inclined to indorse for them; with large Acquisitiveness, bestow time more freely than money, yet will also give the latter; but with only average or full Acquisitiveness, freely bestow both substance and personal aid; with large Veneration and only full Acquisitiveness, give freely to religious objects; with large Combativeness and Destructiveness, are more severe in word than deed, and threaten more than execute; with larger moral than animal organs, literally overflow with sympathy and practical goodness, and reluctantly cause others trouble; with large reasoning organs, are truly philanthropic, and take broad views of reformatory measures; with large Adhesiveness and Parental Love, are pre-eminently qualified for nursing; with large Causality, give excellent advice, etc., and should not let sympathy overrule judgment.

Large: Delight to do good; make personal sacrifices to render others happy; can not witness pain or distress, and do what can well be done to relieve them; manifest a perpetual flow of disinterested goodness; with large Adhesiveness, Ideality, and Approbativeness, and only average propensities and Self-Esteem, are remarkable for practical goodness; live more for others than self; with large domestic organs, make great sacrifices for family; with large reflectives, are perpetually reasoning on the evils of society, the way to obviate them, and to render mankind happy; with large Adhesiveness, are hospitable; with moderate Destructiveness, can not witness pain or death, and revolt at capital punishment; with moderate Acquisitiveness, give freely to the needy, and never exact dues from the poor; with large Acquisitiveness, help others to help themselves rather than give money; with large Combativeness, Destructiveness, Self-Esteem, and Firmness, at times evince harshness, yet generally are kindly disposed.

Full: Show a good degree of kind, neighborly, and humane feeling, except when the selfish faculties overrule it, yet are not remarkable for disinterestedness; with large Adhesiveness, manifest kindness toward friends; and with large Combativeness and Destructiveness, are unrelenting toward enemies; with large Acquisitiveness, are benevolent when money can be made thereby; with large Conscientiousness, are more just than kind, and with large Combativeness and Destructiveness, are exacting and severe toward offenders.

Average: Manifest kindness only in conjunction with Adhesiveness and other large organs; and with only full Adhesiveness, if kind, are so for selfish purposes; with large Acquisitiveness, give little or nothing, yet may sometimes do favors; with large Veneration, are more devout than humane; and with only full reasoning organs are neither philanthropic nor reformatory.

Moderate: Allow the selfish faculties to infringe upon the happiness of others; with large Combativeness, Destructiveness, Self-Esteem, and Firmness, are comparatively hardened to suffering; and with Acquisitiveness and Secretiveness added, evince almost unmitigated selfishness.

Small: Care little for the happiness of man or brute, and do still less to promote it; make no disinterested self-sacrifices; are callous to human woe; do few acts of kindness, and those grudgingly, and have unbounded selfishness:

Very Small: Feel little and evince none of this sentiment, but are selfish in proportion as the other faculties prompt.

To Cultivate: Be more generous and less selfish; more kind to others, the sick included; interest yourself in their wants and woes, as well as their relief; and cultivate general philanthropy and practical goodness in sentiment and conduct; indulge benevolence in all the little affairs of life, in every look and action, and season your whole conduct and character with this sentiment.

To Restrain: Lend and indorse only where you are willing and can afford to lose; give and do less freely than you naturally incline to; bind yourself solemnly not to indorse beyond a given sum; harden yourself against the woes and sufferings of mankind; avoid waiting much on the sick, lest you make yourself sick thereby, for your Benevolence is in danger of exceeding your strength; be selfish first and generous afterward, and put Benevolence under bonds to judgment.

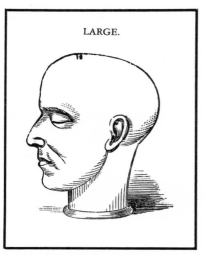

NO. 76.—MR. GOSSE—GAVE AWAY TWO FORTUNES.

NO. 77.—JUDAS, JR.

137

LOVE OF, AND TALENT FOR, THE FINE ARTS; AND FOR IMPROVE-MENT IN SELF-PERFECTION, AND OBTAINING AND ACQUIRING WHATEVER IS BEAUTIFUL AND PERFECT.

This group elevates and chastens the animal faculties, prevents the propensities, even when strong, from taking on the grosser sensual forms of action, and hence is rarely found in criminals; elevates even the moral sentiments, and constitute a stepping-stone from the animal to the moral, and a connecting link between the moral and the intellectual in man.

Very Large: Perfectly abhor the coarse, low, sensual, carnal, and animal action of the propensities, and follow after the beautiful and perfect in nature and art; with strong propensities, manifest them in a proper manner; with a large moral lobe, adopt imposing and eloquent forms of religion, as the Episcopalian, etc.

Large: Aspire after a higher and more perfect state or style of feeling and character and conduct; and discard the imperfect and sensual in all their forms; and are like very large, only less so.

Full: Like style, but can live without it; are like large in quality, only less in degree.

Average: Have only commonplace aspirations after a high life, and love of the fine arts, etc.

Moderate: Are comparatively indifferent to the beauties of nature and art, fail both to appreciate and adopt them, and prefer common houses, clothes, furniture, and style of living to the artistical and stylish, and feel out of place when surrounded by the elegances of life; with large Veneration, have a rude religion, etc.

Small: Are rude, uncultivated, contented with few and plain articles of dress, furniture, property, etc., and prefer the rudeness of savage to the elegances of civic life.

Very Small: Are almost destitute of these perfecting aspirations and sentiments.

To Cultivate: Associate with persons of wit, ingenuity, and refinement; visit galleries of art and mechanism, scenes of beauty and perfection, and read poetry and other works of the most polished and refined writers.

To Restrain: Give more attention to the common affairs of life, and refrain from fostering esthetic subjects; read history, science, and metaphysics rather than poetry, romance, etc.

20. CONSTRUCTIVENESS.

THE MAKING INSTINCT; THE TOOL-USING TALENT; SLEIGHT OF HAND IN CONSTRUCTING THINGS. ADAPTED TO MAN'S NEED OF THINGS MADE, SUCH AS HOUSES, CLOTHES, AND MANUFACTURED ARTICLES OF ALL KINDS. PERVERTED, IT WASTES TIME AND MONEY ON PERPETUAL MOTION, AND OTHER LIKE FUTILE INVENTIONS.

Very Large: Show extraordinary mechanical ingenuity, and a perfect passion for making everything; with large Imitation, Form, Size, and Locality, have firstrate talents as an artist, and for drawing, engraving, etc.; and with Color added, are excellent limners.

Large: Love to make, are able and disposed to tinker, mend, and fix up, build, manufacture, employ machinery, etc.; show mechanical skill and dexterity in whatever is done with the hands; with large Causality and perceptives, are inventive; and with large Imitation added, can make after a pattern, and both copy the improvements of others, and supply defects by original inventions, as well as improve on the mechanical contrivances of others; with the mental temperament, and large intellectual organs and Ideality, employ ingenuity in constructing sentences and arranging words, and forming essays, sentiments, books, etc.:

Full. Can, when occasion requires, employ tools and use the hands in making, tinkering, and fixing up, and turn off work with skill, yet have no great natural passion or ability therein; with practice, can be a good workman; without it, would not excel.

Average: Like full, only less gifted in this respect:

Moderate: Are rather awkward in the use of tools, and in manual operations of every kind; with large Causality and perceptives, show more talent to invent than execute, yet no great in either; with the mental temperament, evince some mental construction, yet no great physical ingenuity:

Small: Are deficient in the tool-using capability; awkward in making and fixing up things; poor in understanding and managing machinery; take hold of work awkwardly and wrong end first; write poorly and lack both mental and physical construction.

Very Small: Can make nothing, except in the most awkward manner.

To Cultivate: Try your hand in using tools, and turning off work of any and every kind; if in any writing business, in writing well and cutting flourishes; if a mechanic, in doing with skill and dexterity what you undertake, etc.;

NO. 78.—JACOB JORDAN.

NO. 79.—LORD LIVERPOOL.

139

observe and study machinery and inventions, and call out this faculty in its various phases — that is, *work.*

To Restrain: Give yourself more to the exercise of your other faculties, and less to mechanical inventions and executions; especially abstain from chimerical inventions, perpetual motion, and the like; and spend no more time or money on inventions than you can spare without inconvenience.

21a. IDEALITY.

PERCEPTION AND ADMIRATION OF THE BEAUTIFUL AND PER-
FECT; GOOD TASTE AND REFINEMENT; PURITY OF FEELING;
SENESE OF PROPRIETY, ELEGANCE, AND GENTILITY; POLISH AND
IMAGINATION. ADAPTED TO THE BEAUTIFUL IN NATURE
AND ART. PERVERTED, IT GIVES FASTIDIOUSNESS AND EXTRA
NICENESS.

Very Large: Have the highest order of taste and refinement; love the exquisite and perfect beyond expression,
and are correspondingly dissatisfied with the imperfect,
especially in themselves; admire beauty in bird and insect,
flower and fruit, animal and man, the physical and mental;
are perfectly enraptured with the impassioned, oratorical,
and poetical in speech and action, in nature and art, and
live much in an ideal world; have a most glowing and vivid
imagination, and give a delicate finish and touch of perfection to every act, word, thought, and feeling, and find
few things to come up to their exalted standard of taste;
with only average Causality, have more taste than solidity
of mind and character, and more exquisiteness than sense;
but with large reflectives, add the highest artistical style
of expression to the highest conceptions of reason, and with
organic quality 6 or 7, are always and involuntarily eloquent.

Large: Appreciate and enjoy beauty and perfection
wherever found, especially in nature; give grace, purity,
and propriety to expression and conduct, gracefulness and
polish to manners, and general good taste to all they say
and do; are pure-minded; enjoy the ideal of poetry and
romance; long after perfection of character, and desire to
obviate blemishes, and with Conscientiousness large, moral
imperfections; with large social organs, evince a nice sense
of propriety in friendly intercourse; eat in a becoming and
genteel manner; with large moral organs, appreciate most
highly perfection of character, or moral beauties and excellences; with large reflectives, add a high order of sense and
strength of mind to beauty and perfection of character;
with large perceptives, are gifted with a talent for the
study of nature, etc.

Full: Evince a good share of taste and refinement, yet
not a high order of them, except in those things in which
it has been vigorously cultivated; with large Language,
Eventuality, and Comparison, may compose with elegance,
and speak with much natural eloquence, yet will have more

NO. 80.—FANNY FORRESTER.

NO. 81.—JACOB JORDAN.

141

force of thought than beauty of diction; with large Constructiveness, will use tools with considerable taste, yet more skill; with large Combativeness and Destructiveness, show general refinement, except when provoked, but are then grating and harsh; with large moral organs, evince more moral beauty and harmony than personal neatness; with large intellectual organs, possess more beauty of mind than regard for looks and outside appearances, and prefer the sensible to the elegant and nice, etc.

Average: Prefer the plain and substantial to the ornamental, and are utilitarian; with large intellectual organs, prefer sound, solid matter to the ornaments of style, and appreciate logic more than eloquence; with Benevolence and Adhesiveness large, are hospitable, and evince true cordiality, yet care nothing for ceremony; with Approbativeness large, may try to be polite, but make an awkward attempt, and are rather deficient in taste and elegance; with Constructiveness large, make things that are solid and serviceable, but do not polish them off; with Language large, talk directly to the purpose, without paying much attention to the mode of expression, etc.

Moderate: Rather lack taste in manners and expression; have but little of the sentimental or finished; should cultivate harmony and perfection of character, and endeavor to polish up; with strong propensities, evince them in rather a coarse and gross manner, and are more liable to their perverted action than when this organ is large, and are homespun in everything.

Small: Show a marked deficiency in whatever appertains to taste and style, also to beauty and sentiment:

Very Small: Are almost deficient in taste, and evince none.

To Cultivate: First, avoid all disgusting habits—swearing, chewing, and drinking, low conversation, vulgar expressions and associates; and dress and appear in good taste, and cultivate personal neatness, good behavior, refinement and style in manners, purity in feeling, the poetical and sentimental, an elegant and classical style of conversation, expression, and writing, and love of the fine arts and beautiful forms; of the beauties of nature, of sunrise, sunset, mountain, lawn, river, scenery, beautiful birds, fruits, flowers, mechanical fabrics and productions—in short, the beautiful and perfect in nature, in general, and yourself in particular.

To Restrain: Remember that in you the ideal and imaginative exceed the practical; that your building airy castles out of bubbles prevents your building substantial structures, and attaining useful life ends; that you are too symbolical, fastidious, and ornamental, too much tormented by a spot and wrinkle, too apt to discard things that are *almost* perfect, because not *quite* so, and hold in check the revelings of Ideality, and learn to prize what is right, instead of discarding the greater good because of minor faults. Especially do not refuse to associate with others because they are not in all particulars just to your fastidious tastes.

21b. SUBLIMITY.

PERCEPTION AND APPRECIATION OF THE VAST, ILLIMITABLE, ENDLESS, OMNIPOTENT, AND INFINITE. ADAPTED TO THAT INFINITUDE WHICH CHARACTERIZES EVERY DEPARTMENT OF NATURE. PERVERTED, IT LEADS TO BOMBAST, AND A WRONG APPLICATION OF EXTRAVAGANT WORDS AND IDEAS.

Very Large: Have a literal passion for the wild, romantic, boundless, endless, infinite, eternal, and stupendous, and are like large, only more so.

Large: Appreciate and admire the grand, sublime, vast, and magnificent in nature and art; admire and enjoy exceedingly mountain scenery, thunder, lightning, tempests, vast prospects, and all that is awful and magnificent, also the foaming, dashing cataract, a storm at sea, the lightning's vivid flash, and its accompanying thunder; the commotion of the elements, and the star-spangled canopy of heaven, and all manifestations of omnipotence and infinitude; with large Veneration, are particularly delighted by the infinite as appertaining to the Deity, and His attributes and works; and with large Time added, have unspeakably grand conceptions of infinitude as applicable to devotion, the past and future, and the character and works of the Deity; with large intellectual organs, take a comprehensive view of subjects, and give illimitable scope to all mental investigations and conceptions, so that they will bear being carried out to any extent; and with Ideality large, add the beautiful and perfect to the sublime and infinite.

Full: Enjoy grandeur, sublimity, and infinitude quite well, and impart considerable of this element to thoughts, emotions, and expressions, and evince the same qualities as large, only in a less degree.

Average: Possess considerable of this element, when it is powerfully excited, yet, under ordinary circumstances, manifest only an ordinary share of it.

Moderate: Are rather deficient in the conception and appreciation of the illimitable and infinite; and with Veneration moderate, fail to appreciate this element in nature and her Author.

Small: Show a marked deficiency in this respect, and should earnestly cultivate it.

Very Small: Are almost destitute of sublime emotions and conceptions.

To Cultivate: Mount the lofty summit to contemplate

144

the outstretched landscape; admire the grand and stupen-dous in towering mountain, rolling cloud, rushing wind and storm, loud thunder, majestic river, raging sea, roaring cataract, burning volcano, and the boundless, endless, infinite, and eternal in nature and her Author.

To Restrain: which is rarely ever necessary— refrain from the contemplation of the sublime.

22. IMITATION.

ABILITY AND DISPOSITION TO COPY, TAKE PATTERN, AND IMI-
TATE. ADAPTED TO MAN'S REQUISITION FOR DOING, TALKING,
ACTING, EW., LIKE OTHERS. PERVERTED, IT COPIES EVEN THEIR
FAULTS.

Very Large: Can mimic, act out, and pattern after almost anything; with large Mirthfulness, relate anecdotes
to the very life; have a theatrical taste and talent; gesticulate almost constantly while speaking; and with large
Language, impart an uncommon amount of expression
to countenance, and everything said; with large Individuality, Eventuality, Language, Comparison, and Ideality,
can make a splendid speaker; and with large Mirthfulness,
and full Secretiveness added, can keep others in a roar of
laughter, yet remain serious; with an uneven head, are droll
and humorous in the extreme; with large Approbativeness,
delight in being the sport-maker at parties, etc., and excel
therein; with large Constructiveness, Form, Size, Locality,
and Comparison, full Color, and a good temperament, and
a full-sized brain, can make a very superior artist of almost
any kind; but with Color small, can engrave, draw, carve,
model, etc., better than paint.

Large: Have a great propensity and ability to copy and
take pattern from others, and do what is seen done; describe and act out well; with large Language, gesticulate
much; with large perceptives, require to be shown but
once; with large Constructiveness, easily learn to use tools,
and to make things as others make them; and with small
Continuity added, are a jack-at-all-trades, but thorough in
none; begin many things, but fail to finish; with large
Causality, perceptives, and an active temperament added,
may make inventions or improvements, but never dwell on
one till it completes it, or are always adding to them; with
large Approbativeness, copy after renowned men; with
large Adhesiveness, take pattern from friends; with large
Language, imitate the style and mode of expression of
others; with large Mirthfulness and full Secretiveness, create laughter by taking off the oddities of people; with
large Form, Size, and Constructiveness, copy shape and
proportions; with large Color, imitate colors, and thus of
all the other faculties.

Full: copy quite well, yet not remarkably so; with large
Causality, had rather invent a new way of doing things
than copy the ordinary mode, and evince considerable imi-

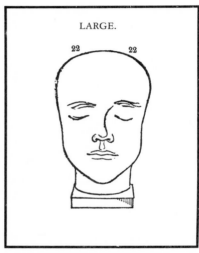

NO. 82.—CLARA FISHER.

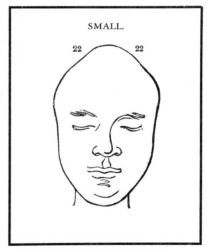

NO. 83.—JACOB JERVIS.

tating talent when this faculty works in conjunction with large organs, yet but little otherwise.

Average: Can copy tolerably well when this faculty is strongly excited, yet are not a mimic, nor a natural copyist; with only full Constructiveness, evince little manual dexterity; yet with large Causality, can originate quite well, and show no great disposition or ability to copy either the excellences or deficiencies of others, but prefer to be original.

Moderate: Have little inclination to do what and as others do; but with large Causality, prefer to strike out a new course, and invent an original plan of their own; with large Self-Esteem added, have an excellent conceit of that plan; but if Causality is only fair, are full of original devices, yet they do not amount to any great things.

Small: Copy even commonplace matter with extreme difficulty and reluctance, and generally do everything in their own way.

Very Small: Possess scarcely any, and manifest no disposition or ability to copy anything, not even enough to learn to talk well.

To Cultivate: Study and practice copying from others in manners, expressions, sentiments, ideas opinions, everything, and try your hand at drawing, and in every species of copying and imitation, as well as conforming to those around you; that is, try to become what they are, and do what and as they do.

To Restrain: Maintain more your own personality in thought, doctrine, character, everything, and be less a parrot, an echo, and cultivate the original and inventive in everything.

INTUITIVE PERCEPTION OF THE ABSURD AND RIDICULOUS; DISPOSITION AND ABILITY TO JOKE AND MAKE FUN, AND LAUGH AT WHAT IS IMPROPER, ILL-TIMED, OR UNBECOMING; PLEASANTNESS; FACETIOUSNESS. ADAPTED TO THE ABSURD, INCONSISTENT, AND LAUGHABLE. PERVERTED, IT MAKES FUN ON SOLEMN OCCASIONS, AND WHERE THERE IS NOTHING RIDICULOUS AT WHICH TO LAUGH.

LARGE

NO. 84.—LAURENCE STERNE.

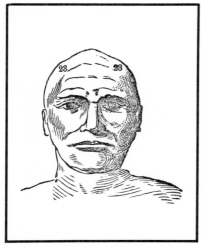

NO. 85.—INDIAN CHIEF

Very Large: Show an extraordinary disposition and capacity to make fun; are always laughing and making others laugh; with large Language, Comparison, Imitation, Perceptives, and Adhesiveness, and moderate Self-Esteem and Secretiveness, are "the fiddle of the company," with only average Ideality added, are clownish, and often say undignified, and perhaps low things, to raise a laugh; and with only moderate Causality, things that lack sense, etc.

Large: Enjoy a hearty laugh at the absurdities of others exceedingly, and delight to make fun out of everything not exactly proper or in good taste, and are always ready to give as good joke as get; with large Amativeness, love to joke with and about the other sex; and with large Imitation and Language added, to talk with and tell stories to and about them; with large Combativeness and Ideality added, make fun of their imperfections in dress, expression, manners, etc., and hit them off to admiration; with large Adhesiveness, Language, and Imitation, are excellent company; with large Causality, comparison, and Combativeness, argue mainly by ridicule or by showing up the absuridty of the opposite side, and excel more in exposing the fallacy of other systems than in propounding new ones; with large Ideality, show taste and propriety in witticisms, but with this faculty average or less, are often gross, and with large Amativeness added, vulgar in jokes; with large Combativeness and Destructiveness, love to tease, and are sarcastic, and make many enemies; and with large Comparison added, compare those disliked to something mean, disgusting, and ridiculous.

Full: Possess and evince considerable of the fun-making disposition, especially in the direction of the larger organs; with large or very large Comparison, Imitation, and Approbativeness, and moderate Self-Esteem, manifest more of the laughable and witty than is really possessed; may make much fun and be called witty, yet it will be owing more to what may be called drollery than pure wit; with moderate

Secretiveness and Self-Esteem, and an excitable temperament, let fly witty conceptions on the spur of the moment, and thus increase their laughableness by their being well-timed, unexpected, sudden, etc.

Average: Are generally serious and sedate, except when this faculty is excited, yet then often laugh heartily, and evince considerable wit; with large Individuality and Language, often say many laughable things, yet they owe their wit more to argument or the criticism they embody than to this faculty.

Moderate: Are generally serious, sedate, and sober, and with large Self-Esteem, stern and dignified, nor companionable except when Adhesiveness is large, and in company with intimate friends; with only average Ideality and Imitation, are very poor in joking, have to expand witticisms, and thereby spoil them; have some witty ideas, yet lack in perceiving and expressing them; fail to please others in witticisms, and with large Approbativeness and Combativeness, are liable to become angry when joked, and should cultivate this faculty by laughing and joking more.

Small: Make little fun; are slow to perceive, and still slower to turn jokes; seldom laugh, and think it foolish or wrong to do so; with only average Adhesiveness, are uncompanionable; with large reflectives and Language, may do well in newspaper diction, yet not in debate.

Very Small: Have few, if any, witty ideas and conceptions.

To Cultivate: Get rid of the idea that it is sinful or undignified to laugh; try to perceive the witty and the facetious aspects of subjects and things; cultivate the acquaintance of mirthful people, and read witty books, and as much as may be imbibe their spirit.

To Restrain: Cease hunting for something to laugh at and make fun of; observe in the conduct and appearance of others all that is congruous, correct, and proper, and not that merely which is droll or ridiculous; avoid turning everything into ridicule, punning, playing upon words, *double entendre*, etc.

23b. INTELLECTUAL FACULTIES.

KNOWING, REMEMBERING, AND REASONING POWERS; GENERAL INTELLECTUAL CAPABILITY AND DESIRE. ADAPTED TO THE PHYSICAL AND METAPHYSICAL. PERVERTED, THEY APPLY THEIR RESPECTIVE POWER TO ACCOMPLISH WRONG ENDS.

Very Large: Have natural greatness of intellect and judgment, and a high order of talents and sound sense, with originality, capaciousness, and comprehensiveness of mind which can hardly fail to make their mark.

Large: Confer sufficient natural talent and intellectual capability to take a high stand among men; give strength of mind, superior judgment, and power both of acquiring knowledge easily and reasoning profoundly. Their direction depends upon the other faculties; with large animal organs and weak morals, they make philosophical sensualists; with large moral and weaker animal organs, moral and religious philosophers, etc.

Full: Have good intellectual capabilities and much strength of mind, provided it is well cultivated; with large Acquisitiveness, a talent to acquire property; with large moral organs, to enlighten and improve the moral character; with large Constructiveness, mechanical intelligence, etc.

Average: Evince fair mental powers, provided they are cultivated, otherwise only moderate intellectual capabilities; with an excitable temperament, allow the feelings and stronger faculties to control judgment; with large moral organs, have more piety than talents, and allow religious prejudices and preconceived doctrines to prevent impartial intellectual examination; with moderate Acquisitiveness, will never acquire property; with average Constructiveness, will be a poor mechanic, etc.

Moderate: Are rather deficient in sense and judgment, yet not palpably so; can be easily imposed upon; are deficient in memory, and rather wanting in judgment, comprehension, and intellectual capacity.

Small: Are decidedly deficient in mind; slow and dull of comprehension; lack sense, and have poor powers of memory and reason.

Very Small: Are naturally idiotic.

These faculties are divided into three classes — the Perceptive, the Literary, and the Reflective — which, when large, confer three kinds of talent.

To Cultivate: Exercise the whole mind in diversified studies and intellectual exercises. See specific directions in "Fowler on Memory." And probably nothing is so well calculated to discipline and improve intellect as the study and practice of Phrenology.

To Restrain: Divert the flow of blood from the brain to the body by vigorous exercise, an occasional hot bath, frequent ablutions, and a general abstinence from intellectual exercises, especially reading and writing.

LARGE.

NO. 86.—GOVERNEUR MORRIS.

SMALL.

NO. 87.—MEDITATION.

THESE BRING MAN INTO DIRECT INTERCOURSE WITH THE PHYS-
ICAL WORLD; TAKE COGNIZANCE OF THE PHYSICAL QUALITIES
OF MATERIAL THINGS; GIVE CORRECT JUDGMENT OF THE MATE-
RIAL PROPERTIES OF THINGS, AND A PRACTICAL CAST OF MIND.

Very Large: Are pre-eminent in these respects; know by
intuition the proper conditions, fitness, value, etc., of
things; have extraordinary power of observation, and ability
to acquire knowledge, and a natural taste for examining,
collecting statistics, studying the natural sciences, etc.
For combinations see large.

Large: Judge correctly of the various qualities and relations of material things; with Acquisitiveness large, form
correct ideas of the value of property, goods, etc., and what
kinds are likely to rise in value, and make good bargains;
with large Constructiveness, can conduct mechanical operations, and have very good talents for building machinery,
superintending workmen, etc.; with the mental temperament, and large intellectuals added, are endowed by nature
with a truly scientific cast of mind, and a talent for studying the natural sciences, and are useful in almost every
department and situation in life; with an active tem-
ment and favorable opportunities, know a good deal about
matters and things in general; are quick of observation and
perception and matter-of-fact, common-sense tact, and will
show off to excellent advantage; appear to know all that
they really do, perhaps more; have superior talents for acquiring and retaining knowledge with facility, and attending to the details of business; becoming an excellent scholar,
etc.; and have a strong thirst after knowledge.

Full: Have fair perceptive powers, and a good share of
practical sense; learn and remember most things quite
well; love reading and knowledge, and with study can
become a good scholar, yet not without it; with large
Acquisitiveness, judge of the value of things with sufficient
correctness to make good bargains, but with moderate Acquisitiveness, lack such judgment; with large Constructiveness, aided by experience, have a good mechanical
mind, but without experience, or with only moderate
Constructiveness, are deficient in this respect.

Average: Are endowed with only fair perceptive and
knowing powers, but, well cultivated, know considerable
about matters and things, and learn with tolerable ease; yet
without cultivation are deficient in practicability of talent,

and capability of gathering and retaining knowledge. For combinations see full.

Moderate: Are rather slow and dull of observation and perception, require some time to understand things, and even then lack specific knowledge of detail; are rather deficient in matter-of-fact knowledge, and show off to poor advantage; learn slowly, and fail in off-hand judgment and action; with only average Acquisitiveness, are deficient in judging of the value of things, and easily cheated; and with moderate Language, are rather wanting in practical talent, and can not show advantageously what is possessed.

Small: Are very deficient in remembering and judging; lack practical sense, and should cultivate the knowing and remembering faculties.

Very Small: See few things, and know almost nothing about the external world, its qualities, and relations.

To Cultivate: *Exercise* each separately, and all together, in examining closely all the material properties of physical bodies; study the natural sciences, especially Phrenology; examine the natural qualities of all natural objects.

To Restrain is never necessary.

24. INDIVIDUALITY.

NO. 88.—EPHRAIM BYRAM.

NO. 89.—DEACON SETH TERRY.

OBSERVATION; DESIRE TO SEE AND EXAMINE; COGNIZANCE OF INDIVIDUAL OBJECTS. ADAPTED TO INDIVIDUAL EXISTENCE, OR THE THINGNESS OF THINGS. IT IS THE DOOR THROUGH WHICH MOST FORMS OF KNOWLEDGE ENTER THE MIND. PERVERTED, IT MAKES THE STARER AND THE IMPUDENTLY OBSERVING.

Very Large: Have an insatiable desire to see and know all about everything, together with extraordinary powers of observation; can not rest satisfied till all is known; individualize everything, and are very minute and particular in observation of things; with large Ideality, employ many allegorical and like figures; with large Human Nature and Comparison, observe every little thing which people say and do, and read character correctly from what smaller Individuality would not notice.

Large: Have a great desire to see, know, examine, experience, etc; are a great and practical observer of men and things; see whatever is transpiring around, what should be done, etc.; are quick of perception, knowing, and with large Acquisitiveness, quick to perceive whatever appertains to property; with large Parental Love, whatever concerns children; with large Alimentiveness, whatever belongs to the flavor or qualities of food, and know what things are good by looking at them; with large Approbativeness or Self-Esteem, see quickly whatever appertains to individual character, and whether it is favorable or unfavorable; with large Conscientiousness, perceive readily the moral, or right and wrong of things; with large Veneration, "see God in clouds, and hear him in the winds;" with large Ideality, are quick to perceive beauty, perfection, and deformity; with large Form, notice the countenances and looks of all met; with small Color, fail to observe tints, hues, and shades; with large Order and moderate Ideality, perceive disarrangement at once, yet fail to notice the want of taste or niceness. These and kindred combinations show why some persons are very quick to notice some things, but slow to observe others.

Full: Have good observing powers, and much desire to see and know things, yet are not remarkable in these respects; with large Acquisitiveness, but moderate Ideality, are quick to notice whatever appertains to property, yet fail to observe instances of beauty and deformity; but with large Ideality and moderate Acquisitiveness, quickly see beauty and deformity, yet do not quickly observe the qualities of things or value of property; with large Parental Love and Ideality, see at once indices of beauty and perfection in children; but if Ideality and Language are moderate, fail to perceive beauty of expression or sentiment, etc.:

Average: Observe only the more conspicuous objects, and these more in general than detail, and what especially interests the stronger faculties.

Moderate: Are rather deficient in observing disposition and capability, and should cultivate this faculty; with large Locality, may observe places sufficiently to find them again; with large Order, observe when things are out of place; with large Causality, see that it may find materials for reasoning, etc.

Small: Observe only what is thrust upon the attention, and are quite deficient in this respect.

Very Small: See scarcely anything.

To Cultivate: Notice whatever comes within the range of your vision; observe attentively all the little things done and said by everybody, all their minor manifestations of character — in short, keep a sharp look-out.

To Restrain: of which there is little, if any need — look and stare less, and think more.

COGNIZANCE, AND RECOLLECTION OF SHAPE: MEMORY OF COUNTENANCES AND THE LOOKS OF PERSONS AND THINGS SEEN; PERCEPTION OF RESEMBLANCES, FAMILY LIKENESSES, ETC. ADAPTED TO SHAPE. PERVERTED, SEES IMAGINARY SHAPES OF PERSONS, THIN ETC., AS IN DELIRIUM TREMENS.

NO. 90.—REUBENS.

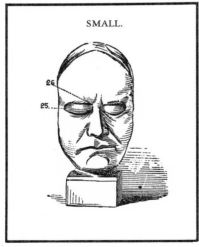

NO. 91.—GEORGE BELL.

Very Large: Possess this capability in an extraordinary degree; recognize persons not seen for many years; with large Ideality, take extreme delight in beautiful forms; with large Spirituality, see the spirits of the departed; with disordered nerves, see horrid images, etc.

Large: Notice, and for a long time remember, the faces, countenances, forms, looks, etc., of persons, beasts, and things once seen; know by sight many whose name is not remembered; with Individuality large, both observe and recollect persons and things, but with Individuality moderate, fail to notice them, and hence to remember them, unless business or something special draws attention to them; with large Parental Love, notice and recollect children, favorite animals, etc.; with large Acquisitiveness, Individuality, and Locality, readily detect counterfeits, etc.

Full: Have a good recollection of the countenances of persons and shape of things, yet not remarkably good unless this faculty has been quickened by practice, or invigorated by some strong incentive to action; with large Ideality, will recollect beautiful shapes; with large Locality and Sublimity, beautiful and magnificent scenery, etc.; and should endeavor to impress the recollection of shape upon the mind.

Average: Have only a fair natural recollection of shapes, countenances, etc.; yet with practice may do tolerably well, but without practice will be only fair in these respects, and should cultivate this faculty.

Moderate: Are rather deficient in recognizing persons and things seen; fail to recognize by their looks those who are related to each other by blood, and should cultivate this faculty by trying to remember persons and things.

Small: Have a poor recollection of persons, looks, etc.; often meet persons the next day after an introduction, or an evening interview, without knowing them; with Eventuality large, may remember their history, but not their faces; with Locality large, where they were seen, but not their looks, etc.

Very Small: Manifest scarcely any of this faculty.

To Cultivate: Scan the shape of everything you would remember; study botany, conchology, Phrenology, and especially those studies which involve configuration; when talking to persons, scan eyes, nose, mouth, chin, forehead, looks, expression of countenance, especially of eye, as if you were determined ever afterward to remember them — looking at them critically, as a police detective looks at a rogue, as if saying to himself, "I'll know you, my man, next time I see you."

To Restrain is never necessary.

26. SIZE.

COGNIZANCE OF BULK, MAGNITUDE, QUANTITY, PROPORTION, ETC.; ABILITY TO MEASURE BY THE EYE. ADAPTED TO THE ABSOLUTE AND RELATIVE MAGNITUDE OF THINGS. PERVERTED, IT IS PAINED BY DISPROPORTION AND ARCHITECTURAL INACCURACIES.

Very Large: Are endowed with an extraordinarily accurate architectural eye; detect at one glance any departure from perfect accuracy and proportion; often detect errors in the work of good workmen; can tell how high, wide, long, far, much, heavy, etc., with perfect accuracy; judge correctly, as if by intuition, the texture, finess, coarseness, qualities, etc., of goods; excel in judging of property where bulk and value are to be estimated by eye; with Constructiveness, can fit nice machinery, and in many things dispense with measuring instruments because accurate enough without, and do best on work requiring the most perfect accuracy.

Large: Have an excellent eye for measuring angles, proportions, disproportions, and departures therefrom, and with large Constructiveness, a good mechanical eye, and judge correctly of quantity in general; love harmony of proportion, and are pained by disproportion. This faculty is necessary to artisans, mechanics, all kinds of dealers, students, etc.

Full: Possess a good share of this eye-measuring power, yet are not remarkable; with practice, do well; without it, only fairly, and in this respect succeed well in their accustomed business.

Average: Have a fair eye for judging of bulk, distance, weight by the size, etc., and with practice do tolerably well in this respect.

Moderate: Measure by eye rather inaccurately, and have poor judgment of bulk, quanity, distance, and whatever is estimated by this faculty.

Small: Are obliged always to rely on actual measurements, because the eye is too imperfect to be trusted.

Very Small: Are almost destitute of this faculty.

To Cultivate: Pass judgment on whatever involves how much, how heavy, how far, the center, the amount, architectural accuracy, guessing the weight, the quantity of groceries, of everything by eye; judging how much grain to the acre, and everything involving the exercise of this faculty.

To Restrain: Do not allow architectural inaccuracies or any disproportion to distrub you as much as it naturally does — that is, put up with things not regulated by size and proportion.

27. WEIGHT.

INTUITIVE PERCEPTION AND APPLICATION OF THE LAWS OF GRAVITY, MOTION, ETC. ADAPTED TO MAN' REQUISITION FOR KEEPING HIS BALANCE. PERVERTED, IT RUNS IMMINENT RISK OF FALLING BY VENTURING TOO FAR.

Very Large: Have control over the muscular system, hence can climb or walk anywhere with safety; can not be thrown by fractious horses; are sure-footed; never slip or fall; are a dead shot, even "on the wing;" have an intuitive gift for skating, swimming, balancing, circus-acting, hurling, everything requiring muscular control; are an excellent judge of perpendiculars and levels; can plumb anything by the eye; as a sculptor or other artist, always make the picture or statue in an easy, natural, and well-balanced attitude, and are annoyed if the mirror or pictures, etc., do not hang plumb; with Constructiveness large, will succeed in any mechanical avocation requiring a steady hand, as in surgery, dental operations, sleight-of-hand performances, fancy glass-blowing, etc.

Large: Have an excellent faculty for preserving and regaining balance, riding a fractious horse, skating, carrying a steady hand, etc.; easily keep from falling when aloft, or in dangerous places; throw a stone, ball, or arrow straight; are pained at seeing things out of plumb; judge of perpendiculars very exactly; love to climb, walk on the edge of a precipice, etc.; with Form and Size large, are an excellent marksman; with Constructiveness large, possess an excellent faculty for understanding and working machinery; with Approbativeness large, are venturesome, etc., to show what risks can be run without falling.

Full: Have a good degree of this faculty, and with practice excel, yet without it are not remarkable.

Average: Like full, only less gifted in this respect; with only average Constructiveness and perceptives, should never engage in working machinery, because deficient in this talent.

Moderate: Can keep the balance under ordinary circumstances, yet have rather imperfect control over the muscles in riding a fractious horse, or walking a narrow beam aloft, hurling, etc.; with large Cautiousness, are timid in dangerous places, and dare not venture far; are rather poor in shooting, skating, throwing, etc., unless rendered so by practice, and should cultivate this faculty by climbing, balancing, hurling, etc.

Small: Are quite liable to sea-sickness, dizziness when aloft, etc. with large Cautiousness, are afraid to walk over water, even on a wide plank, and where there is no danger; never feel safe while climbing, and fall easily.

Very small: Can hardly stand erect, and have very little control over the muscles.

To Cultivate: Skate, slide down hill, practice gymnastic feats, balance a long pole on your hand, walk a fence, climb, ride on horse-back, go to sea, practice gunnery, archery, throwing stones, pitching quoits — anything to call this faculty into exercise.

To Restrain: Do not allow yourself to climb aloft, and walk narrow, dangerous places as much as naturally inclined to. Persons often lose their lives by ambitiously showing what extraordinary feats they can accomplish.

28. COLOR.

PERCEPTION, RECOLLECTION, AND APPLICATION OF COLORS, AND DELIGHT IN THEM. ADAPTED TO THAT INFINITE VARIETY OF COLORING INTERSPERSED THROUGHOUT NATURE. PERVERTED, ARE OVER – PARTICULAR TO HAVE COLORS JUST RIGHT.

Very Large: Have a natural taste and talent, as well as a perfect passion, for whatever appertains to colors; can carry colors perfectly in the eye, and match them from memory; take the utmost delight in viewing harmonious colors, and with very large Constructiveness, Imitation, Form, and Size, and large Weight, a full or large-sided brain, and organic quality 6 or 7, have a natural taste and talent for painting, and are a real genius in this line. For combinations see large.

Large: Can discern and match colors by the eye with accuracy; with Comparison large, can compare them closely, and detect similarities and differences; with Constructiveness, Form, Size, and Imitation large or very large, can excel in painting; but with Form and Size only average, can paint better than draw; with Ideality large, are exceedingly delighted with fine paintings, and disgusted with imperfect coloring; with large Form and Size, manage the perspective and lights and shades of painting admirably.

Full: Possess a good share of coloring ability and talent, provided it has been cultivated; take much pleasure in beautiful flowers, variegated landscapes, beautifully colored fruits, etc.

Average: Possess a fair share of this talent, yet are not extraordinary.

Moderate: With practice, may judge of colors with considerable success, yet without it will be deficient in this respect; with large Form, Size, Constructiveness, Ideality, and Imitation, may take an excellent likeness, yet will fail in the coloring.

Small: May tell the primitive colors from each other, yet rarely notice the color of dress, eyes, hair, etc; can not describe persons and things by them, and evince a marked deficiency in coloring, taste, and talent.

Very Small: Can hardly tell one color from another, or form any idea of colors.

To Cultivate: Observe color in general, and its shadings in particular; try to appreciate their beauties; relish, revel in their richness, as seen in flower, bird, fruit, lawn, twilight, everywhere, and cultivate an appreciation of fine paintings.

To Restrain is rarely necessary; go less into rapturous ecstasy over a new flower or painting, but give more attention to other things.

29. ORDER.

METHOD, SYSTEM, ARRANGEMENT. ADAPTED TO HEAVEN'S FIRST LAW. PERVERTED, IT OVERWORKS, ANNOYS OTHERS TO KEEP THINGS IN ORDER, AND IS TORMENTED BY DISARRANGEMENT.

Very Large: Are perfectly systematic, and are very particular about order, even to old-maidishness; work far beyond strength to have things just so; and with large Ideality, and an active temperament, and only fair Vitality, are liable to break down health and constitution by overworking in order to have things extra nice, and take more pains to keep things in order than this order is worth; with large Ideality, are fastidious about personal appearance, and extra particular to have every little thing very nice; and with Aquisitiveness added, can not bear to have garments soiled, and are pained in the extreme by greasespots, ink-blots, and like deformities.

Large: Have a desire to conduct business on methodical principles, and to be systematic in everything; with large Acquisitiveness and Causality, have good business talents; with large Locality, have a place for everything, and everything in its place; with large Time, have a time for everything, and everything in season; with large Continuity, Comparison, and the mental temperament, have every idea, paragraph, and head of a subject in its proper place; with large Constructiveness, have tools always in place, so that they can be found in the dark; with large Combativeness, are excessively vexed by disarrangement; with large Language, place every word exactly right in the sentence; with large Approbativeness, are inclined to conform to established usages; with large Size, must have everything in rows, at proper distances, straight, etc.; and with large Ideality, must have everything neat and nice as well as methodical, etc.

Full: If educated to business habits, evince a good degree of method, and disposition to systematize, but without practice may sometimes show laxity; with a powerful mentality, but weaker muscles, may like to have things in order, yet do not always keep them so; with large Causality added, show more mental than physical order; with large moral organs, like to have religious matters, codes of discipline, etc., rigidly observed, and have more moral than personal method; with Acquisitiveness and perceptives large, are sufficiently methodical for all practical business purposes, yet not extra particular.

Average: Like order, yet may not always keep it, and desire more than practically secure:

Moderate: Are very apt to leave things where they were last used, and lack method; with Ideality moderate, lack personal neatness, and should cultivate this desirable element by being more particular.

Small: Have a very careless, inaccurate way of doing everything; leave things where it happens; can never find what is wanted; take a long time to get ready, or else go unprepared, and have everything in perpetual confusion:

Very Small: Are almost wholly destitute of this arranging power and desire.

To Cultivate: Methodize and arrange everything; be regular in all your habits; cultivate system in business; have a place for everything, and keep everything in place, so that you could find it in the dark — in short, exercise order.

To Restrain: Work and worry less to keep order, for it costs more to keep it than it is worth; you waste your very life and strength in little niceties of order which, after all, amount to little, but are costing you your sweetness of temper and very life itself.

NO. 92. — ZERAH COLBURN AT NINE.*

NO. 93. — GEORGE COMBS.*

COGNIZANCE OF NUMBERS; ABILITY TO RECKON FIGURES IN THE HEAD; MENTAL ARITHMETIC. ADAPTED TO THE RELATIONS OF NUMBERS.

Very Large: Possess this calculating capability in a most extraordinary degree; can add several columns at once very rapidly and correctly, and multiply and divide with the same intuitive powers; love mental arithmetic exceedingly, and with large reflectives, are a natural mathematician.

Large: Excel in mental arithmetic, in adding, subtracting, multiplying, dividing, reckoning figures, casting accounts, etc., in the head; with large perceptives, have excellent business talents; and large Locality and Causality added, excel in the mathematics.

Full: Possess good calculating powers; with practice, can calculate in the head or by arithmetical rules easily and accurately, yet without practice are not remarkable; with large Form, Size, Comparison, Causality, and Construtiveness, can be a good geometrician or mathematician, yet will do better in the higher branches than merely the arithmetical.

Average: Can learn arithmetic and do quite well by practice, yet are not naturally gifted in mental arithmetic:

Moderate: Add, subtract, divide, and calculate with difficulty; and with large Acquisitiveness and perceptives, will make a better salesman than book-keeper.

Small: Are dull and incorrect in adding, subtracting, dividing, etc.; dislike figuring; are poor in arithmetic, both practical and theoretical, and should cultivate this faculty:

Very Small: Can hardly count, much less calculate.

To Cultivate: Add, subtract, divide, multiply, count, and reckon figures in the head as far as possible, and learn and practice arithmetic.

To Restrain is rarely ever necessary. Avoid counting everything.

*Zerah Colburn, at the age of nine years, without education, astonished the world by his great calculating talent. George Combe, though he studied mathematics seven years, never could master the multiplication table.

31a. LOCALITY.

COGNIZANCE OF PLACE; RECOLLECTION OF THE LOOKS OF PLACES, ROADS, SCENERY, AND THE LOCATION OF OBJECTS; WHERE ON A PAGE IDEAS ARE TO BE FOUND, AND POSITION GENERALLY; THE GEOGRAPHICAL FACULTY; DESIRE TO SEE PLACES, AND THE ABILITY TO FIND THEM. ADAPTED TO NATURE'S ARRANGEMENT OF SPACE AND PLACE. PERVERTED, IT CREATES A COSMOPOLITIC DISPOSITION AND WOULD SPEND EVERYTHING IN TRAVELING.

Very Large: Always keep a correct idea of the relative and absolute position, either in the deep forests or the winding street; can not be lost; are perfectly enamored of traveling; have literally a passion for it.

Large: Remember the whereabouts of whatever they see; can carry the points of the compass easily in the head, and are lost with difficulty either in the city, woods, or country; desire to see places, and never forget them; study geography and astronomy with ease; and rarely forget where things are seen; with Constructiveness remember the arrangement of the various parts of a machine; with Individuality, Eventuality, and Human Nature, love to see men and things as well as places, and hence have a passion for traveling.

Full: Remember places well, yet not extraordinarily so; can generally find the way, yet may sometimes be lost or confused; with large Eventuality, remember facts better than places.

Average: Recollect places and positions seen several times, yet in city or roads are occasionally lost; have no great geographical talent, yet by study and practice can do tolerably well.

Moderate: Recollect places rather poorly; dare not trust to local memory in strange places or large cities; are not naturally good in geography, and to excel in it must study hard; should energetically cultivate this faculty by localizing everything, and remembering just how things are placed.

Small: Are decidedly deficient in finding places, and recollect them with difficulty even when perfectly familiar with them.

Very Small: Must stay at home unless accompanied by others, because unable to find the way back.

To Cultivate: Notice, as you go, turns in the road, landmarks, and objects by the way, geography, and the points of compass, when you see things, and charge your memory

167

where on a page certain ideas or accounts stand recorded, and position in general, and study geography by maps and traveling, the location of anatomical and phrenological organs, and position or place in general.

To Restrain: Settle down, and give over your restless, roving desire to travel.

THESE COLLECT INFORMATION, ANECDOTES, AND REMEMBER MATTERS OF FACT AND KNOWLEDGE IN GENERAL, AND GIVE WHAT IS CALLED A GOOD MEMORY. ADAPTED TO FACTS, DATES, AND THE COMMUNICATION OF IDEAS AND FEELINGS.

Very Large: Have a most remarkable memory; are extraordinarily well informed, if not learned and brilliant; according to advantages are a first-rate scholar; have a literal passion for literary pursuits, and a remarkably knowing mind.

Large: Are smart, knowing, and off-hand; can show off to good advantage in society; with large Ideality, are brilliant as well as talented.

Full: Have a fair, matter-of-fact cast of mind and knowing powers, fair scholarship, and a good general memory.

Average: If cultivated, have a good general memory, and store up considerable knowledge; yet without cultivation, only a common place memory and no great general knowledge.

Moderate: Know more than you can think of at the time, or tell; with large reflective faculties, have more judgment than memory, and strength of mind than ability to show off.

Small or Very Small: Have a poor memory of most things, and inferior literary capabilities.

To Cultivate: Read, study, inform yourself, read the papers; keep pace with the improvements of the day; study history and the experimental sciences; and pick up and store up whatever kinds of knowledge, of your line of business, and of matter-of-fact knowledge comes in your way; write your thoughts in a daily journal or for the press; join a lyceum or debating society, and read history or science with a view to remember its substance, for the purpose of using it in argument; remember the news, and tell it to friends; in short, read, write, and talk.

To Restrain: Read and study less, but divert your mind from books and business by cultivating the other, and especially physical faculties, and never read, or study, or write nights.

32. EVENTUALITY.

MEMORY OF FACTS; RECOLLECTION OF CIRCUMSTANCES, NEWS, OCCURENCES, AND HISTORICAL SCIENTIFIC, AND PASSING EVENTS; WHAT HAS BEEN SAID, SEEN, HEARD, AND ONCE KNOWN. ADAPTED TO ACTION, OR THOSE CHANGES CONSTANTLY OCCURRING AROUND OR WITHIN US.

NO. 94.—LARGE.

NO. 95.—SMALL.

Very Large: Possess a wonderfully retentive memory of everything like facts and incidents; with large Language and Imitation, tell a story admirably, and excel in fiction, etc.; have a craving thirst for knowledge, and literally devour books and newspapers, nor allow any thing once in the mind to escape it.

Large: Have a clear and retentive memory of historical facts, general knowledge, what has been seen, heard, read, done, etc., even in detail; considering advantages, are well informed and knowing; desire to witness and institute experiments; find out what is and has been, and learn anecdotes, particulars, and items of information, and readily recall to mind what has once entered it; have a good general matter-of-fact memory, and pick up facts readily; with Calculation and Acquisitiveness, remember business matters, bargains, etc.; with large social feelings, recall friends to mind, and what they have said and done; and with large Locality, associate facts with the place where they transpired, and are particularly fond of reading, lectures, general news, etc., and can become a good scholar.

Full: Have a good general memory of matters and things, yet it is considerably effected by cultivation—that is, have a good memory if it is habitually exercised—if not, only an indifferent one; with large Locality, recollect facts by associating them with the place, or by recollecting where on a page they are narrated; with large reflectives, remember principles better than facts, and facts by associating them with their principles; and with large Language, tell a story quite well.

Average: Recollect leading events and interesting particulars, yet are rather deficient in memory of items and details, except when it is well cultivated.

Moderate: Are rather forgetful, especially in details; and with moderate Individuality and Language tell a story very poorly, and should cultivate memory by its exercise.

Small: Have a treacherous and confused memory of circumstances; often forget what is wanted, what was intended to be said, done, etc.; have a poor command of knowledge, are unable to swear positively to details, and should strenuously exercise this remembering power.

Very Small: Forget almost everyting, both generals and particulars.

To Cultivate: *Charge* your mind with whatever transpires; remember what you read, see, hear, and often recall and re-impress it, so that you can swear definitely in a court of justice; also, impress on your mind what you intend to do and say at given times; read history and study mythology with a view of weaving such knowledge into the every-day affairs of life; tell anecdotes, recount incidents in your own life, putting in all the little particulars; write down what you would remember, yet only to impress it, but trust to memory rather than to manuscript.

To Restrain: Read less; never allow yourself to recount the painful vicissitudes of life, or to renew past pain by remembrance, for this does only damage; but when you find your mind running on painful subjects, change it to something else, and forget whatever in the past is saddening.

33. TIME.

COGNIZANCE AND RECOLLECTION OF DURATION AND SUCCES-
SION, THE LAPSE OF TIME, WHEN THINGS OCCURRED, ETC., AND
ABILITY TO CARRY THE TIME OF THE DAY IN THE HEAD; PUNC-
TUALITY. ADAPTED TO PERIODICITY. PERVERTED, IT IS EXCES-
SIVELY PAINED BY BAD TIME IN MUSIC NOT KEEPING STEPS IN
WALKING, ETC.

Very Large: Can wake up at any pre-appointed hour,
tell the time of day by intuition almost as correctly as
with a time-piece, and the time that transpired between
one event and another, and are a natural chronologist.

Large: Can generally tell when things occurred, at least
the order of events, and the length of time between one
occurrence and another, etc.; tell the time of day without
time-piece or sun, well; and keep an accurate chronology in
the mind of dates general and particular; with large Eventuality, rarely forget appointment, meetings, etc., and are a
good historian.

Full: With cultivation, can keep time in music, and also
the time of day in the head quite correctly, yet not exceedingly so.

Average: With practice, have a good memory of dates
and successions, yet without it are rather deficient: p. 214.

Moderate: Have a somewhat imperfect idea of time and
dates; with moderate Individuality, Eventuality, and Language, are a poor historian.

Small: Fail to keep the correct time in the head, or
awaken at appointed times; have a confused and indistinct
idea of the time when things transpired, and forget dates.

Very Small: Are almost wholly destitute of this faculty.

To Cultivate: Periodize everything; rise, retire, prosecute
your business, everything, by the clock; appropriate particular times to particular things, and deviate as seldom as
possible; in short, cultivate perfect regularity in all your
habits, as it respects time.

To Restrain: Break in upon your tread-mill monotony,
and deviate now and then, if only for diversion, from your
monotonous routine.

34. TUNE.

THE MUSIC INSTINCT AND FACULTY; ABILITY TO LEARN AND REMEMBER TUNES BY ROTE. ADAPTED TO THE MUSICAL OCTAVE. PERVERSION — EXCESSIVE FONDNESS FOR MUSIC TO THE NEGLECT OF OTHER THINGS.

Very Large: Possess extraordinary musical taste and talent, and are literally transported by good music; and with large Imitation and Constructiveness, fair time, and a fine temperament, are an exquisite performer; learn tunes by hearing them sung once; sing in spirit and with melting pathos; show intuitive taste and skill; sing *from* the soul *to* the soul.

Large: Love music dearly have a nice conception of concord, discord, melody, etc., and enjoy all kinds of music; and with large Imitation, Constructiveness, and Time, can make most kinds, and play well on, musical instruments; with large Ideality, impart a richness and exquisiteness to musical performances; have a fine ear for music, and are tormented by discord, but delighted by concord, and take a great amount of pleasure in the exercise of this faculty; with large Combativeness and Destructiveness, love martial music; with large Veneration, sacred music; with large Adhesiveness and Amativeness, social and parlor music; with large Hope, Veneration, and disordered nerves, plaintive, solemn music, etc.

Full: Have a good musical ear and talent; can learn tunes by rote quite well; and with large Ideality, Imitation, and Firmness, can be a good musician, yet will require practice.

Average: Have fair musical talents, yet, to be a good musician, require considerable practice; can learn tunes by rote, yet with some difficulty; with large Ideality and Imitation, may be a good singer or player, yet are indebted more to art than nature, show more taste than skill, and love music better than can make it.

Moderate: Have no great natural taste or talent for music, yet aided by notes and practice, may sing and play quite well, but will be rather mechanical; lack that pathos and feeling which reach the soul.

Small: Learn to sing or play tunes with great difficulty, and that mechanically, without emotion or effect:

Very Small: Have scarcely any musical idea or feeling, so little as hardly to tell Yankee Doodle from Old Hundred.

To Cultivate: Try to sing; learn tunes by ear; practice vocal and instrumental music, and give yourself up to the spirit and sentiment of the piece; attend concerts, listen appreciatingly and feelingly to gifted performers, and cultivate the soul of music.

To Restrain: Give relatively less time and feeling to music, and more to other things.

35a. LANGUAGE.

THE EXPRESSION OF ALL MENTAL OPERATIONS BY WORDS, WRITTEN OR SPOKEN, BY GESTURES, LOOKS, AND ACTIONS; THE COMMUNICATING FACULTY AND INSTINCT IN GENERAL. ADAPTED TO MAN'S REQUISITION FOR HOLDING COMMUNICATION WITH MAN. PERVERSION, VERBOSITY, PLEONASM, CIRCUMLOCUTION, GARRULITY, EXCESSIVE TALKATIVENESS, TELLING WHAT DOES HARM, ETC.

Very Large: Are exceedingly expressive in all they say and do; have a most expressive countenance, eye, and manner in everything; have a most emphatic way of saying and doing everything, and thoroughly impress the various operations of their own minds on the minds of others; use *the very* word required by the occasion; are intuitively grammatical, even without study, and say oratorically whatever they attempt to say at all; commit to memory by reading or hearing once or twice; learn languages with remarkable facility; are both fluent and copious, even redundant and verbose; with large or very large Imitation, add perfect action, natural language, and gesticulation to perfect verbal expression; with large Ideality, are elegant and eloquent; and with large Individuality, Eventuality, Comparison, and organic quality· added, possess natural speaking talents of the highest order; say the very thing, and in the very way; choose words almost as by inspiration, and evince the highest order of communicating capacity.

Large: Express ideas and feelings well, both verbally and in writing; can learn to speak languages easily; recollect words, and commit to memory well; have freedom, copiousness, and power of expression; with large Amativeness, use tender, winning, persuasive words; with large Combativeness and Destructiveness, severe and cutting expressions; with large moral faculties, words expressive of moral sentiments; with large Acquisitiveness, describe in glowing colors what is for sale; with large Ideality, employ richness and beauty of expression, and love poetry and oratory exceedingly; with large Imitation, express thoughts and emotions by gesticulation; with activity great and Secretiveness small, show in the looks the thoughts and feelings passing in the mind; with large reflective faculties, evince thought and depth in the countenance; with large Comparison, use just the words which convey the meaning intended; with large Ideality, Individuality, Eventuality, Comparison, and the mental temperament, can make an

NO. 96.—CHARLES DICKENS.

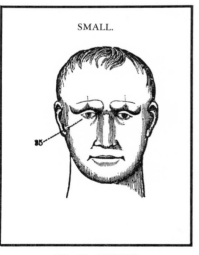

NO. 97.—BRUNEL.

175

excellent editor or newspaper writer; and with large Causality added, a philosophical writer:

Full: Say well what is said at all, yet are not garrulous; with small Secretiveness, speak without qualification, and also distinctly and pointedly; express the manifestations of the larger faculties with much force, yet not of the smaller ones; with large Secretiveness and Cautiousness, do not always speak to the purpose, and make ideas fully understood, but use rather non-committal expressions; with large Comparison, Human Nature, Causality, Ideality, activity, organic quality, and power, have first-rate writing talents, and can speak well, yet large Secretiveness impairs speaking and writing talents by rendering them wordy and non-committal.

Average: Have fair communicating talents, yet not extra; with activity great and Secretiveness small, speak right out, and to the purpose, yet are not eloquent, and use commonplace words and expressions; with large Individuality, Eventuality, and Comparison, and moderate Secretiveness, can make an excellent writer by practice; use none too many words, but express itself clearly and to the point; with large Causality, have more thought than language; with moderate Individuality and Eventuality, find it difficult to say just what is desired, and are not fully and easily understood; with large Ideality, have more beauty and elegance than freedom.

Moderate: Are not particularly expressive in words, actions, or countenance, nor ready in communicating ideas and sentiments; with large Ideality, Eventuality, Comparison, activity, and power, may succeed well as a writer, yet not as a speaker; with large Causality and moderate Eventuality, have abundance of thoughts, but find it quite difficult to cast them into sentences, or bring in the right adjectives and phrases at the right time; are good in matter, yet poor in delivery; commit to memory with difficulty, and fail to make ideas and feelings fully understood, and to excite like organs in others; with large Eventuality, Locality, Form, and Comparison, may be fair as a linguist, and learn to read foreign languages, yet learn to speak them with difficulty, and are barren in expression, however rich in matter.

Small: Have poor lingual and communicative talents; hesitate for words; speak with extreme difficulty and very awkwardly, and should cultivate this faculty by talking and writing much.

Very Small: Can hardly remember or use words at all, or even remember their meaning.

To Cultivate: Talk, write, speak as much, as eloquently, as well as you can; often change clauses with a view to improving sentences; erase unnecessary and improper words, and choose the very words exactly expressive of the desired meaning; throw feeling and expression into all you say—into action, and expressions of countenance; study languages and the classics, but especially fluency in your mother tongue; narrate incidents; tell what you have heard, seen, read, done; debate; if religious, lead in religious exercises—anything, everything to discipline and exercise this faculty.

To Restrain: Talk less; never break in when others are talking; lop off redundancies, pleonasms, and embellishments, and use simple instead of bombastic expressions.

NO. 98.—GALILEO.

NO. 99.—INDIAN WOMAN.

THESE GIVE A PHILOSOPHIZING, PENETRATING, INVESTIGATING, ORIGINATING CAST OF MIND; ASCERTAIN CAUSES AND ABSTRACT RELATIONS; CONTRIVE, INVENT, ORIGINATE IDEAS, ETC. ADAPTED TO THE FIRST PRINCIPLES, OR LAWS OF THINGS.

Very Large: Possess extraordinary depth of reason and strength of understanding; and with large perceptives, extraordinary talents, and manifest them to good advantage; with perceptives small, have great strength of mind, yet a poor mode of manifesting it; are not appreciated, and lack intellectual balance, and are more plausible than reliable, and too deep to be clear.

Large: Possess the higher capabilities of intellect; reason clearly and strongly on whatever data is furnished by the other faculties; have soundness of understanding, depth of intellect, and that weight which carries conviction, and contributes largely to success in everything; with perceptives small, possess more power of mind than can be manifested, and fail to be appreciated and understood, because more theoretical than practical.

Full: Possess fair reflective powers, and reason well from the data furnished by the other faculties; and with activity great, have a fair flow of ideas and good general thoughts.

Average: Resaon fairly on subjects fully understood, yet are not remarkable for depth or clearness of idea; with cultivation, will manifest considerable reasoning power —without it, only ordinary.

Moderate: Are rather deficient in power and soundness of mind; but with large perceptives, evince less deficiency of reason than is possessed.

Small: Have inferior reasoning capabilities.

Very Small: Are almost destitute of thought, idea, and sense.

To Cultivate: Muse, meditate, ponder, reflect on, think, study, and pry deep into the abstract principles and nature of things.

To Restrain: Theorize less, and give more time to the other faculties.

36. CAUSALITY.

PERCEPTION AND APPLICATION OF CAUSATION; THOUGHT ORIGINALITY; COMPREHENSIVENESS OF MIND; FORETHOUGHT THE RESOURCE-CREATING POWER; ADAPTATION OF WAYS AND MEANS TO ENDS. ADAPTED TO NATURE'S INSTITUTES, PLANS, CAUSE, AND EFFECT. PERVERTED, IT REASONS IN FAVOR OF UN-TRUTH AND INJURIOUS ENDS.

Very Large: Possess this cause-seeking and applying power to an extraordinary degree; perceive by intuition those deeper relations of things which escape common minds; are profound in philosophy, and deep and powerful in reasoning, and have great originality of mind and strength of understanding.

Large: Desire to know the why and wherefore of things, and to investigate their laws; reason clearly and correctly from causes to effects, and from facts to their causes; have uncommon capabilities of planning, contriving, inventing, creating resources, and making the head save the hands; kill two birds with one stone; predicate results and arrange things so as to succeed; synthesize, and put things together well; with large Combativeness, love to argue; with large perceptives, are quick to perceive facts and conditions, and reason powerfully and correctly from them; with Comparison and Conscientiousness large, reason forcibly on moral truths; with the selfish faculties strong, will so adapt ways and means as to serve personal purposes; with moderate perceptives, excel more in principles and philosophy than facts, and remember laws better than details; with Comparison and Human Nature large, are particularly fond of mental philosophy, and excel therein; with Individuality and Eventuality only moderate, are guided more by reason than experience, by laws than facts, and arrive at conclusions more from reflection than observation; with large perceptives, possess a high order of practical sense and sound judgment; with large Comparison and moderate Eventuality, remember thoughts, inferences, and subject-matter, but forget items; with the mental temperament and Language moderate, make a much greater impression upon mankind by action than expressions, by deeds than words, etc.

Full: Have good cause-seeking and applying talents; reason, and adapt ways and means to ends, well; with large perceptives, Comparison, activity, and thought, possess excellent reasoning powers, and show them to first-rate

LARGE.

NO. 100.—DR. GALL.

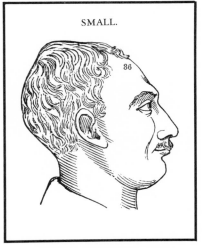

SMALL.

NO. 101.—HEWLETT, ACTOR.

179

advantage; with moderate perceptives and large Secretiveness, can plan better than reason; with large Acquisitiveness and moderate Constructiveness, lay excellent money-making, but poor mechanical plans, etc.

Average: Plan and reason well in conjunction with the larger faculties, but poorly with the smaller ones; with moderate Acquisitiveness, lay poor money-making plans; but with large Conscientiousness, reason well on moral subjects, especially if Comparison is large, etc.

Moderate: Are rather deficient in discerning and applying causes; perceive them when presented by other minds, yet do not originate them; with activity and perceptives large, may do well in the ordinary routine of business, yet fail in difficult matters.

Small: Are deficient in reasoning and planning power; need perpetual telling and showing; seldom arrange things beforehand, and then poorly; should work under others; lack force of idea and strength of understanding.

Very Small: Are idiotic in reasoning and planning:

To Cultivate: First and mainly, study nature's causes and effects, adaptations, laws, both in general and in those particular departments in which you may feel any special interest; think, muse, meditate, reason; give yourself up to the influxes of new ideas; plan; adapt ways and means to ends; endeavor to think up the best ways and means of overcoming difficulties and bringing about results; especially study Phrenology and its philosophy, for nothing is equally suggestive of original ideas, or as explanative of nature's laws and first principles.

To Restrain: which is rarely necessary—divert your mind from abstract thought by engaging more in the practical and real, nor allow any one thing, as inventing perpetual motion, or reasoning on any particular subject, to engross too much attention.

37a. COMPARISON.

INDUCTIVE REASONING; ABILITY AND DISPOSITION TO ANA-
LYZE, CLASSIFY, COMPARE, DRAW INFERENCES, ETC. ADAPTED TO
NATURE'S CLASSIFICATIONS OF ALL HER WORKS. PERVERTED, IS
TOO REDUNDANT IN PROVERBS, FABLES, AND FIGURES OF
SPEECH.

Very Large: Possess this analyzing, criticising, and inductive faculty in a truly wonderful degree; illustrate with
great clearness and facility from the known to the unknown; discover the deeper analogies which pervade nature,
and have an extraordinary power of discerning new truths;
with large Individuality, Eventuality, and activity, have
a great faculty of making discoveries; with large Language,
use words in their exact meaning, and are a natural phi-
lologist; with full Language, explain things plausibly and
correctly.

Large: Reason clearly and correctly from conclusions
and scientific facts up to the laws which govern them; discern the known from the unknown; detect error by its in-
congruity with facts; have an excellent talent for comparing, explaining, expounding, criticising, exposing, etc.;
employ similes and metaphors well; put this and that together, and draw correct inferences from them; with large
Continuity, use well-sustained figures of speech, but with
small Continuity, drop the figure before it is finished; with
large Individuality, Eventuality, activity, and power, have a
scientific cast of mind; with large Veneration, reason about
God and His works; with large Language, use words in
their exact signification; with large Mirthfulness, strike the
nail upon the head in all criticisms, and hit off the oddities
of people to admiration; with large Ideality, evince beauty,
taste, and propriety of expression, etc.

Full: Possess a full share of clearness and demonstrative
power, yet with large Causality, and only moderate Language, can not explain to advantage; with large Eventuality,
reason wholly from facts; with moderate Language, fail
in giving the precise meaning to words; and make good
analytical discriminations.

Average: Show this talent in a good degree in conjunction with the larger organs, but poorly in reference to the
smaller ones.

Moderate: Rather fail in explaining, clearing up points,
putting things together, drawing inferences, and even use
words incorrectly; with Individuality and Eventuality

LARGE.

NO. 102.—LINNEUS.

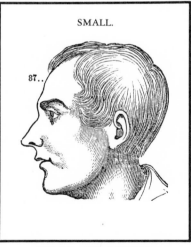

SMALL.

NO. 103.—MR. BARLOW.

181

moderate, show much mental weakness; with large Causality, have good ideas, but make wretched work in expressing them, and can not be understood; with Mirthfulness full or large, try to make jokes, but they are always ill-timed and inappropriate.

Small: Have a poor talent for drawing inferences; lack appropriateness in everything, and should cultivate this faculty.

Very Small: Have little, and show almost none, of this element.

To Cultivate: Put this and that together, and draw inferences; spell out truths and results from slighter data; observe effects, with a view to deduce conclusions therefrom; study logic and metaphysics, theology and ethics included, and draw nice discriminations; explain and illustrate your ideas clearly and copiously, and exercise it in whatever form circumstances may require.

To Restrain: Keep back redundant illustrations and amplifications, and be careful to base important deductions on data amply sufficient.

DISCERNMENT OF CHARACTER; PERCEPTION OF MOTIVES; INTUI-
TIVE PHYSIOGNOMY. ADAPTED TO MAN'S NEED OF KNOWING
HIS FELLOW-MEN. PERVERTED, IT PRODUCES SUSPICIOUSNESS.

Very Large: Form a correct judgment as to the character
of all they meet, and especially of the opposite sex, at the
first glance, and as if by intuition; may always trust first
impressions; are a natural physiognomist; and with Agreeableness large, know just when and how to take men, and
hoodwink if they choose; and with Secretiveness added,
but Conscientiousness moderate, are oily and palavering,
and flatter their victim — that, serpent-like, salivate before
they swallow; with Comparison and organic quality large
or very large, dearly love the study of human nature,
practically and theoretically, and therefore of mental
philosophy and Phrenology, etc.

Large: Read men intuitively from their looks, conversation, manners, and walk, and other kindred signs of character; with Individuality and Comparison large, notice all the
little things they do, and form a correct estimate from
them, and should follow first impressions respecting persons; with full Secretiveness and large Benevolence added,
know just how to take men, and possess much power over
mind; with Mirthfulness and Ideality large, see all the
faults of people, and make much fun over them; with
Comparison large, have a talent for metaphysics, etc.

Full: Read character quite well from the face and external signs, yet are sometimes mistaken; may generally follow first impressions safely; love to study character; with
Ideality and Adhesiveness large, appreciate the excellences
of friends; with Parental Love large, of children; with
Combativeness and Conscientiousness very large, all the
faults of people; and with only average Adhesiveness, form
few friendships, in consequence of detecting so many
blemishes in character, etc.

Average: Have fair talents for reading character, yet
not extra, and should cultivate it.

Moderate: Fail somewhat in discerning character; occasionally form wrong conclusions concerning people; should
be more suspicious, watch people closely, especially those
minor signs of character dropped when off their guard;
have ill-timed remarks and modes of addressing people,
and often say and do things which have a different effect
from that intended.

Small: Are easily imposed upon by others; with large Conscientiousness and small Secretiveness, think everybody tells the truth; are too confiding, and fail sadly in knowing where and how to take things.

Very Small: Know almost nothing about human nature.

To Cultivate: Scan closely all the actions of men, with a view to ascertain their motives and mainsprings of action; look with a sharp eye at man, woman, child, all you meet, as if you would read them through; note particularly the expression of the eye, as if you would imbibe what it signifies; say to yourself, What faculty prompted this expression or that action; drink in the general looks, attitude, natural language, and manifestation of the man, and yield yourself to the impressions naturally made on you — that is, study human nature both as a philosophy and as a sentiment, or as if being impressed thereby; especially study Phrenology, for no study of human nature at all compares with it, and be more suspicious.

To Restrain: Be less suspicious, and more confidential.

37c. AGREEABLENESS.

PERSUASIVENESS, PLEASANTNESS, BLANDNESS. ADAPTED TO PLEASE AND WIN OTHERS.

Very Large: Are peculiarly winning and fascinating in manners and conversation, and delight even opponents.

Large: Have a pleasing, persuasive, conciliatory mode of addressing people, and of saying things; with Adhesiveness and Benevolence large, are generally liked; with Comparison and Human Nature large, say unacceptable things in an acceptable manner, and sugar over expressions and actions.

Full: Are pleasing and persuasive in manner, and with Ideality large, polite and agreeable, except when the repelling faculties are strongly excited; with small Secretiveness, and strong Combativeness and activity, are generally pleasant, but when angry are sharp and blunt; with large Benevolence, Adhesiveness, and Mirthfulness, are excellent company.

Average: Have a good share of pleasantness in conversation and appearance, except when the selfish faculties are excited, but are then repulsive.

Moderate: Are rather deficient in the pleasant and persuasive, and should by all means cultivate this faculty by smoothing over all said and done.

Small: Say even pleasant things very unpleasantly, and fail sadly in winning the good graces of people.

Very Small: Are almost totally deficient in this faculty.

To Cultivate: First try to *feel* agreeably, and express those feelings in as pleasant and bland a manner as possible; study and practice politeness as both an art and a science; compliment what in others you can find worthy, and render yourself just as acceptable to those around you as lies in your power:

To Restrain is rarely necessary.

SECTION IV
RULES FOR FINDING THE ORGANS

RULES FOR FINDING THE ORGANS.

Pre-eminently is Phrenology a science of facts. Observation discovered it — observation must perfect it; observation is the grand instrumentality of its propagation. To be convinced of its truth, nine hundred and ninety-nine men out of every thousand require to see it — to be convinced by induction, founded upon experiment. Hence the importance of giving definite rules for finding its organs, by which even disbelievers may test the science, and believers be confirmed in its truth, and advanced in its study.

The best mode of investigating its truth is somewhat as follows: You know a neighbor who has extreme Firmness in character — who is as inflexible as the oak, and as obstinate as the mule. Now, learn the location of the phrenological organ of Firmness (see cuts No. 68, 69) and apply that location to his head — that is, see whether he has this organ as conspicuous as you know him to have this faculty in character, and if you find a coincidence between the two, you have arrived at a strong phrenological fact.

You know another neighbor who is exceedingly cautious, timid, safe, wise, and hesitating; who always looks at the objections and difficulties in the way of a particular measure, instead of at its advantages; who always takes abundant time to consider, and is given to procrastination. Learn the location of Cautiousness (see cuts No. 63, 64), and see whether he has this phrenological organ as conspicuous as you know this faculty to exist in his character. By pursuing this course, you can soon arrive at a sure knowledge of the truth or falsity of phrenological science; and altogether the best mode of convincing unbelievers of its truth is by means of the marked coincidence between the phrenology and character of those they know. Nor is it possible for the human mind to resist proof like this.

To promote this practical knowledge — the application of this science — we give the following rules for finding its organs, fully assured that we can fill our pages with nothing more interesting or useful. Follow these rules exactly, and you will have little difficulty in finding at least all the prominent ones.

Your first observation should be made upon temperament, or *organization* and physiology, with this principle for your basis: that when bodily texture or form is coarse,

189

or strong, or fine, or soft, or weak, or sprightly, the texture of the brain will correspond with that of body, and the mental characteristics with that of the brain. But we have already discussed the influence of various temperaments upon the direction of the faculties.

Your second observation should be to ascertain what faculties control the character, or what is the *dominant* motive, desire, object, or passion of the person examined. In phrenological language, what faculties predominate in action. And it should here be observed that the relative *size* of organs does not always determine this point. Some faculties, though very dominant in power, can not, in their very nature, constitute a motive for action, but are simply executive functions, simply carrying into effect the dominant motives. For example, Combativeness rarely ever becomes a distinct motive for action. Few men love simply to struggle, quarrel, or fight for fun, but exercise Combativeness merely as a means of obtaining the things desired by the other dominant faculties. Few men have for their motive the mere exercise of will. That is, Firmness is generally exercised to carry into effect the designs of the other faculties; and instead of subjecting the other faculties to itself, simply keeps them at their work, whatever it may be. And thus of some other faculties. But Amativeness, Friendship, Alimentiveness, Acquisitiveness, Benevolence, Veneration, Conscientiousness, Intellect, Constructiveness, Ideality, or the observing faculties, may each become dominant motives. And it requires much phrenological shrewdness to ascertain what single faculty, cluster, or combination of faculties leads off the character.

Let us take, then, for our starting-point the outer angle of the eye, and draw a line to the middle of the top of the ears, and Destructiveness (see cuts No. 55, 56) is exactly under this point, and extends upward about half an inch above the top of the ears. In proportion to its size will the head be wide between the ears. When Secretiveness is small and Destructiveness large, there will be a horizontal ridge extending forward and backward, more or less prominent, according to the size of this organ.

Secretiveness is located three quarters of an inch above the middle of the top of the ears. When this organ is large, it rarely gives a distinct projection, but simply fills and rounds out the head at this point (see cuts No. 61, 62).

190

When the head widens rapidly from the junction of the ears as you rise upward, Secretiveness is larger than Destructiveness; but when the head becomes narrower as you rise, it is smaller than Destructiveness.

To find these two organs, and their relative size, place the third finger of each hand upon the head, just at the top of the ears; let the lower side of the third finger be even with the upper part of the ear; that finger then rests upon Destructivness. Then spread the second finger about one eighth of an inch from the other, and it will rest upon Secretiveness. Let the end of your longest finger come as far forward as the fore part of the ears, and they will then rest upon these two organs.

Take, next, this same line, starting from the outer angle of the eye, to the top of the ears, and extend it straight backward an inch and a half to an inch and three quarters, and you are on Combativness (see cuts No. 53, 54). This organ starts about midway to the back part of the ears, and runs upward and backward toward the crown of the head. To ascertain its relative size, steady the head with one hand, say the left, and place the balls of your right fingers upon the point just specified, letting your elbow be somewhat below the subject's head, which will bring your fingers directly across the organ. Its size may be ascertained partly from the general fullness of the head, and partly from its sharpness, according as the organ is more or less active; yet observers sometimes mistake this organ for the mastoid process directly behind the lower part of the ears. Remember our rule, namely: a line drawn from the outer angle of the eye to the top of the ear, and continued an inch and a half or three quarters straight back. Follow that rule, and you can not mistake the position of this organ; and will soon, by comparing different heads, be able to arrive at those appearances when large or small.

To find Parental Love (see cuts No. 45, 46), extend this line straight back to the middle of the back head, and you are on the organ; and in proportion as the head projects backward behind the cars at this point, will this organ be larger or smaller.

About an inch, or a little less, directly below this point, is the organ which controls muscular motion; and in proportion as this is more or less prominent, will the muscular system be more or less active and powerful. Those who

191

have this prominence large will be restless, always moving a hand or foot when sitting, and even when sleeping; will be light-footed, easy-motioned, fond of action, and willing to work, as well as possessed of a first-rate constitution. But when that prominence is weak, they will be found proportionally inert.

Inhabitiveness is located three fourths of an inch above Parental Love (see cuts No. 47, 48). When Inhabitiveness is large, and Continuity is moderate, there will be found a prominence somewhat resembling an angle of a triangle, at the middle of the head, together with a sharp prominence at this point. But when Inhabitiveness is small, there will be a depression just about large enough to receive the end of a finger, with the bow downward.

An inch on each side of this point is Friendship. When Friendship is large, especially if Inhabitiveness and Continuity are small, there will be two swells, somewhat resembling the larger end of an egg; but if small, the head will retire at this point.

Continuity (see cuts No. 49, 50) is located directly above Inhabitiveness and Friendship. Its deficiency causes a depression resembling a new moon, with the horns turning downward, surrounding the organs of Inhabitiveness and Friendship. When Continuity is large, however, there will be no swell, but simply a filling out of the head at this point.

Amativeness (see cuts No. 43, 44) may be found thus: Take the middle of the back part of the ears as your starting-point; draw a line backward an inch and a half, and you are upon this organ. Yet the outer portion next to the ear exercises the more gross and animal function of this faculty, while the inner portion takes on a more spiritual tone.

To find Cautiousness (see cuts No. 63, 64), take the back or posterior part of the ears as your starting-point. Draw a perpendicular line, when the head is erect, from the extreme back part of the ear, straight up the side of the head, and just where the head begins to round off to form the top, Cautiousness is located. This organ is generally well developed in the American head, and those prominences, generally seen at this point, are caused by a full development of this faculty.

To find Alimentiveness (see cuts No. 57, 58), take the

upward and forward junction of the ear with the head as your starting-point; draw a line half an inch forward, inclining a little downward, and you are upon this organ. Then rise three quarters of an inch straight upward, and you are on that part of Acquisitiveness which gets property. Yet a better rule for finding it is this: Find Secretiveness in accordance with the rule already given, and Acquisitiveness is an inch forward of the point, and about an inch above the middle of the tip of the ear. Or thus: Take the middle of the top of the ear as your starting-point; draw a perpendicular line an inch upward, and you are on Secretiveness; then about an inch forward, and you are on Acquisitiveness (see cuts No. 59, 60). When the head widens rapidly as you pass from the outer angles of the eyes to the top of the ears, Acquisitiveness is large; but when the head is thin in this region, Acquisitiveness is small.

Sublimity, Ideality (see cuts No. 80, 81), and Constructiveness (see cuts No. 78, 79) can be found by the following rule: First find Cautiousness as already directed; then pass directly forward an inch, and you are on Sublimity; extend this line on another inch, and you are on Ideality; then an inch downward brings you upon Constructiveness.

It should be remembered that Cautiousness, Sublimity, and Ideality are just upon the round of the head, or between its top and sides. Usually the head is much wider at Cautiousness than at Sublimity, and at Sublimity than Ideality, When, however, the head is as wide at Ideality as at Cautiousness, the subject will possess unusual good taste, purity, refinement, elevation, and personal perfection. Half an inch forward of Ideality is the organ which appertains to dress, and secures personal neatness. In those who care but little what they wear, or how they appear, this organ will be found small.

Firmness (see cuts No. 68, 69) can best be found by the following rule: Let the subject sit or stand erect, and hold the head in a line with the spinal column. Taking the opening of the ear as your starting-point, draw a line straight upward till you reach the middle line on the top of the head, and you are on the fore part of Firmness. When this organ is large, and Veneration small, its forward termination resembles in shape the fore part of a smoothing iron, rapidly widening as it runs backward. The organ is usually about an inch and a half long.

Self-Esteem (see cuts No. 66, 67) is an inch and a half back of Firmness. Its upper part gives a lofty, aspiring air, magnanimity, and a determination to do something worthy; while half an inch farther back is that part of Self-Esteem which gives will, love of liberty, and a determination not to be ruled.

Approbativeness (see cut No. 65) is located on the two sides of Self-Esteem, about an inch outwardly. These two lobes run backward toward Friendship, and upward toward Conscientiousness.

The relative size of Approbativeness and Self-Esteem may be found thus: Place one hand, say the left, upon the forehead, to steady the head; point the finger from above directly down upon Firmness; then move it two inches directly backward, and place the balls of the second and third fingers upon the points just found. When Self-Esteem is small, these balls will fall into the hollow which indicates its deficiency, while the ends of the fingers will strike upon the swells caused by Approbativeness, when this organ is large; and the middle of the second joint of these fingers will apprehend the size of that lobe of Approbativeness which is next to it. Or thus: Stand behind the patient, and so place your fingers upon his head that the second finger shall reach upward to the back part of Firmness; then lay the first and second joints of that finger evenly with the head, and place the first and third fingers upon the head alongside of it. When Self-Esteem is larger than Approbativeness, the second finger will be pushed up farther than the others; but when the two lobes of Approbativeness are larger than Self-Esteem, the second finger will fall into a hollow running up and down, while the first and third fingers will rest upon the two lobes of Approbativeness. Or thus: In nineteen females out of every twenty, Approbativeness will be found considerably larger than Self-Esteem; and by applying this rule to their heads, a hollow will generally be found at Self-Esteem, and a swell at Approbativeness, by which you can localize these organs; and a few applications will soon enable you to form correct ideas of their appearance when large and small.

Hope and Conscientiousness (see cuts No. 72, 73) are found thus: That line already drawn to find Firmness passes over the back part of Hope, which is on each side of the fore part of Firmness, while Conscientiousness is just back of that line, on the two sides of the back part of Firmness, and joins Approbativeness behind.

As these two organs run lengthwise from Firmness down toward Cautiousness, and are near together, it is sometimes difficult to determine which is large, and which small. The upper part of Conscientiousness, next to Firmness, experiences feelings of obligation to God, or sense of duty to obey His laws; while the lower part creates a feeling of obligation to our fellow-men.

Veneration (see cuts No. 74, 75) is on the middle of the top of the head, or about an inch forward of the point already described for finding Firmness; while Benevolence (see cuts No. 76, 77) is about an inch forward of Veneration. When, therefore, the middle of the top-head rounds out and rises above Firmness and Benevolence, Veneration is *larger* than either of these organs; but when there is a swell at Benevolence, and a depression as you pass backward in the middle of the head, and another rise as you pass still farther back to Firmness, Veneration is *smaller* than Benevolence or Firmness. The back of Benevolence experiences philanthropy and a desire to do good and remove evil on a large scale, while the fore part sympathizes and bestows minor gifts in the family and neighborhood. The fore part of Veneration gives respect for our fellow-men, while the back part supplicates and depends upon the Deity. The fore part of Firmness, working with Conscientiousness, gives moral decision; while the latter, acting with Self-Esteem, gives physical decision, determination to accomplish material objects, and what we commonly call perseverance.

Spirituality is located on each side of Veneration. It may be found by the following rules: Standing behind the subject, who should be seated, so place your fingers that the first fingers of each hand shall be about an inch apart —that the ends of your second fingers shall be about three quarters of an inch forward of a line drawn across the middle of the head from side to side, and the balls of your fingers will be on Spirituality. Or, reversing your position, so as to stand in front of the subject, so place your hands that the first fingers of each hand shall be as before, about an inch apart, and the ends of your longest fingers shall just touch the fore part of Hope, and the balls of your second and third fingers will rest on Spirituality. This organ is generally low, so that it may usually be found by that *depression* which indicates its smallness. When it is large, the head is filled out in this region, instead of sloping rapidly from Veneration. Its two lobes are about an inch on each side of Veneration, and directly above Ideality.

Imitation (see cuts No. 82, 83) is upon the two sides of Benevolence, directly forward of Spirituality. The best rule for finding it is this: Standing in front of the subject, place your hands so that the first fingers of each hand shall be separated about three quarters of an inch, and the end of your longest finger shall reach a line drawn through Veneration and Spirituality — that is, through the middle of the head from side to side — and the balls of your fingers will be on Imitation. It will be found larger in children than adults; so that the ridge usually found in their heads at this point may be taken as the location of this organ. It runs from Benevolence downward toward Constructiveness. The upper part, toward Benevolence, mimics; the lower part, toward Constructiveness, makes after a pattern, copies, etc.

We are now brought to the intellectual lobe. Take the root of the nose as your starting-point; the first organ met in passing upward is Individuality (see cuts No. 88, 89). It is between the eyebrows, and when large causes them to arch downward at their inner termination, and that part of the head to project forward.

Eventuality (see cuts No. 94, 95) is three quarters of an inch upward, and slightly below the center of the forehead, which in children is usually large, and in adults frequently small. From this center of the forehead, Comparison (see cuts No. 102, 103) extends upward to where the head begins to slope backward to form the top of the head; at which point, or between Benevolence and Comparison, Human Nature is located, which is usually large in the American head, as is also Comparison. Agreeableness is located about an inch on each side of the organ of Human Nature, and is usually small, so that we can ascertain its location by observing its deficiency. When both of these organs are large, the forehead will be wide and full as it rounds backward to form the top-head, or where the hair makes its appearance. Causality (see cuts No. 100, 101) is located about an inch on each side of Comparison, and

Mirthfulness (see cuts No. 84, 85) about three quarters of an inch still farther outwardly, toward Ideality. Form (see cuts No. 90, 91) is located internally from Individuality, just above and partly between the eyes, so as to set them wider apart, in proportion as it is the larger.

Size is located just in the turn between the nose and eyebrows, or beneath the inner portion of the eyebrows; and when large, causes their inner portions to project outward over the inner portion of the eyes, like the eaves of a house, giving to the eyes a sunken appearance. Size can generally be observed by sight, yet if you would test your sight by touch, proceed as follows: Place the end of your thumb against the bridge of the nose, with the lower part of your hand turned outward, and your thumb lying nearly parallel with the eyebrows, and the ball of your thumb will be upon Size. When this organ is large, there will be a fullness in this region, as if half a bean were beneath your thumb.

To find Weight and Color, proceed as follows: Let the eyes be directed straight forward, as if looking at some object; draw an imaginary line from the middle of the eye to the eyebrow; Weight is located internally from this line beneath the eyebrows, while Color is located beneath the eyebrows, just outwardly from this line. Order is located just externally to Color, and Time partly above and between Color and Order.

Calculation (see cuts No. 92, 93) is located beneath the outer termination of the eyebrows, and in proportion as they are long and extend backward of the eye, will this organ be more or less developed. Three fourths of an inch above the outer angle of the eyebrow, Tune is located. Spurzheim's rule for finding it is this: Stand directly before the subject, and if the head widens over the outer eyebrow as you rise upward, Tune is large; but if you observe a hollow at this point, Tune is small. I have generally found this organ small in adults, so that it is difficult to find its relative size, but in children it is very easily found. Its decline is consequent on its non-exercise. Time and Tune join each other, while Time, Tune, and Mirthfulness occupy the three angles of a triangle, nearly equilateral, the shortest side being between Time and Tune.

Language (see cuts No. 96, 97) is located partly above and partly behind the eyes. When it is large, it pushes the eyes downward and outward, and of course shoves them forward, which gives them a full and swollen appearance, as if they were standing partly out of their sockets, and causes both the upper and under eyelids to be wide and broad. When the eyes are sunken, and their lids narrow, Language will be found small.

By following these rules exactly and specifically, the precise location of the organs can be ascertained, and a few observations upon heads will soon teach you the appearance of the respective organs when they are large, small, or midway in size. Some slight allowances are to be made, however, in calculating the size of the head, or the relative size of the organs. Thus, the larger Combativeness is, the longer the line from Combativeness to the ear; yet large and small Combativeness do not vary this line over from a quarter to half an inch.

Probably the most difficult point of discrimination is between Hope and Conscientiousness, and it should be distinctly borne in mind that Hope is generally placed too far forward. Between Hope, Cautiousness, and Approbativeness there probably exists an organ, the natural functions of which are discretion. It measures words and acts, and in business leads one to take receipts, draw writings, etc. There are doubtless other organs yet undiscovered, especially in the middle line of the head, between Benevolence and Parental Love, and also between Imitation and Causality. Phrenology is yet in its infancy. Though it is perfect in itself, yet our knowledge of it is not yet perfected. As every successive generation makes advances upon the preceding one in astronomy, chemistry, and other departments of science, so Gall and Spurzheim have discovered only the landmarks of this science, and have left much to be filled up by us and those who come after us.

1. TRADES AND PROFESSIONS.

Artistic. — Actor — Daguerrean — Designer — Draughts-man — Engraver — Florist — Gardening, Ornamental — Historical Painter — Landscape Painter — Portrait Painter — Modeler — Musician — Sculptor.

Mechanical. — Baker — Bookbinder — Blacksmith — Bricklayer — Butcher — Cabinet Maker — Carpenter — Carriage Maker — Carriage Ironer — Carriage Trimmer — Compositor — Cooper — Dentist — Dressmaker — Engineer — Finisher of Work — Founder — General Mechanic — Harness Maker — Inventor — Jeweler — Machinist — Manufacturer — Miller — Milliner — Molder — Penman — Picture-frame Maker — Printer — Shoemaker — Silversmith — Stone Cutter — Surgeon — Tanner — Upholsterer — Watchmaker.

Trade. — Accountant — Agent — Auctioneer — Bookseller — Cattle Dealer — Commission Business — Clerk — Dry Goods — Fancy Goods — Grocer — Lumber Dealer — Hardware — Importer — Jobber — Publisher — Salesman — Stock Jobber.

Business. — Agent, General Business, Insurance, Express, Freight — Banker — Broker — Canvasser — Cashier — Collector — Conductor — Contractor — Conveyancer — Financier — Librarian — PostMaster — President of Bank, Railroad, Insurance Co., or Deliberative Body — Real Estate Dealer — Superintendent.

Literary. — Author — Attorney — Dramatical Writer — Editor, Literary, Political — Elocutionist — Governess — Historian — Lecturer — Novelist — Orator — Poet — Preacher — Reporter — Teacher.

Scientific. — Chemist — Diplomatist — Editor — Engineer — Geographer — Jurist — Lecturer — Musical Composer — Naturalist — Navigator — Phrenologist — Physician — Surgeon — Surveyor.

Miscellaneous. — Farmer — Fisherman — Horseman — Hotel Keeper — Livery Keeper — Policeman — Politician — Seaman — Soldier — Statesman — Stock Raiser — Watchman.

Lawyers require the mental-vital temperament, to give them intensity of feeling and clearness of intellect; large Eventuality, to recall law cases and decisions; large Comparison, to compare different parts of the law and evidence — to criticise, cross-question, illustrate, and adduce similar cases; and large Language, to give freedom of speech. Phrenology will tell you how to acquire and use these powers and faculties. Try it.

Statesmen require large and well-balanced intellects, to enable them to understand and see through great public measures and choose the best course, together with high moral heads, to make them disinterested, and seek the people's good, not selfish ends.

Physicians require large Perceptive Faculties, so that they may study and apply a knowledge of Anatomy and Physiology with skill and success; full Destructiveness, lest they shrink from inflicting the pain requisite to cure; large Constructiveness, to give them skill in surgery; large Combativeness, to render them resolute and prompt; large Cautiousness, to render them judicious and safe; and a large head, to give them general power of mind. Phrenology will predict, in advance, whether or not a boy will succeed in this profession. The same is true of Dentistry.

A Clergyman requires the mental temperament, to give him a decided predominance of Mind over his animal propensities; a large frontal and coronal region, the former to give him intellectual capacity, and the latter to impart high moral worth, aims, and feelings, elevation of character, and blamelessness of conduct; large Veneration, Hope, and Spirituality, to imbue him with the spirit of faith and devotion; large Benevolence and Adhesiveness, so that he may make all who know him love him, and thus win them over to the paths of truth and righteousness. Clergymen will do well to consult Phrenology; it would enable them to account for many *seeming* mysteries, and give them power and influence to do great good. It is in harmony with the highest Christianity.

Editors also require a mental temperament, with large Individuality and Eventuality, to collect and disseminate incidents, facts, news, and give a practical cast of mind; large Comparison, to enable them to illustrate, criticise, show up errors, and the like; full or large Combativeness, to render them spirited; large Language, to render them copious, free, spicy, and racy; and large Ideality, to give taste and elevated sentiments. An Editor who understands and *applies* Phrenology possesses a power which he may use with great effect. "We can take your measure."

Merchants require Acquisitiveness, to impart a desire and tact for business; large Hope, to promote enterprise; full Cautiousness, to render them safe; large Perceptives, to give quick and correct judgment of the qualities of goods; good Calculation, to impart rapidity and correctness in casting accounts; large Approbativeness, to render them courteous and affable; and full Adhesiveness, to enable them to make friends of customers, and thus retain them. Why is *one* young man a better salesman than another? and why is one better worth a salary twice or thrice the amount than another? Phrenology answers this by pointing out the constitutional differences, and showing who is, and who is not, adapted to mercantile life. You had better consult it.

Mechanics require strong constitutions, to give them muscular power and love of labor; large Constructiveness and Imitation, to enable them to use tools with dexterity, work after a pattern, and easily learn to do what they may see others do; and large perceptive faculties, to give the required judgment of matter and the fitness of things.